Race and Racism
in
Theory and Practice

Race and Racism in Theory and Practice

edited by
Berel Lang

ROWMAN & LITTLEFIELD PUBLISHERS, INC.
Lanham • Boulder • New York • Oxford

ROWMAN & LITTLEFIELD PUBLISHERS, INC.

Published in the United States of America
by Rowman & Littlefield Publishers, Inc.
4720 Boston Way, Lanham, Maryland 20706
http://www.rowmanlittlefield.com

12 Hid's Copse Road
Cumnor Hill, Oxford OX2 9JJ, England

British Library Cataloguing in Publication Information Available

Library of Congress Cataloging-in-Publication Data

Race and racism in theory and practice / edited by Berel Lang.
    p.   cm.
    Includes bibliographical references and index.
    ISBN 0-8476-9692-8 (cloth : alk. paper)—ISBN 0-8476-9693-6
(pbk. : alk. paper)
    1. Race. 2. Racism. I. Lang, Berel.
  HT1521.R23522 1999
  305.8—dc21   99-045818

Printed in the United States of America

♾ ™The paper used in this publication meets the minimum requirements of
American National Standard for Information Sciences—Permanence of Paper for
Printed Library Materials, ANSI Z39.48-1992.

Contents

v

Part III: Race and the Literary Imagination

Part IV: Race or Class: Which Is It?

Illustrations

FIGURES

TABLES

vii

Introduction

Berel Lang

The concept of race and, all too often, its misconceptions have been central factors in twentieth-century social and political history. Fostered by a combination of the rising nationalisms of the nineteenth century and of radical innovations in the historical sciences (unexpectedly found to include biology and geology), propelled by the institution of slavery and then the battles over it, the category of race continued to make its presence felt through the first third of the twentieth century in almost every social and cultural practice. It reached a horrific crescendo in the next third of the century in the Nazi genocide against the Jews on allegedly racial grounds. The consequences of these cumulative policies and acts thus burdened the remainder of the century with not only a past but a continuing present in which racial categories figured prominently. And so too the task of articulating and analyzing the complex strands of legal theory, social policy, scientific hypotheses (in both the natural and social sciences), and the constructions of religious and artistic representation that had, willingly or not and with varied motives, become involved in that history.

Nobody observing the present social topography of Western "liberal" democracies would claim a resolution of the problems associated with what at this point—however one mistrusts its genealogy or logic—must be generally recognized and acknowledged as the "phenomenon" of race. That phenomenon is indisputably part of our social and historical reality, and it thus announces itself as a principal item on the social and moral agenda of the next century (very probably, given its extent and ramifications, of the next millennium). Whatever weakening may be detected in contemporary impulses of nationalism (a claim that is itself open to dispute), few would venture a similar prediction for the assertions of ethnic identity and distinction. And even if the category of race should be universally acknowledged as "only" a social construct (which clearly is not yet the case), the two

sources of nationalism and ethnicity—no less social constructs, after all—
which have contributed weightily to the formulation of racial distinctions
are unlikely, even if they desired it, to be able to undo that connection.
Furthermore, the scientific "foundation" of theories of race continues to
be a disputed question for biology as well as the social sciences. Just as cultural custom and practice manage to ignore scientific consensus on the rare
occasions when that is reached for less highly charged issues, it requires a
rare and naive optimism to believe that in some near future, science will
once and for all, even at the level of theory, "settle" the problem of race.
Insofar as social constructs become part of—make—social history, the ideologies and myths and varieties of bad faith that typically enter those constructs become also historically actual, with the task of revising or remaking
the social reality that includes them extending subsequently to virtually all
social institutions.

The extent of this prospect of racial theorizing and practice is daunting—
historically in both its past and its present and also spatially, as its locations
apparently continue to expand. These dimensions are actually a stronger
argument for the analysis of particular aspects of the issues of race, for attempting to concretize them and for analyzing them in their elements, than
for elaborating "grand" theories or metanarratives which, on the same
global scale, might claim the sources of racial—and/or racist—theories in,
for example, accounts of "essential" human dispositions or nature. It may
finally be impossible to avoid confronting or developing such large-scale
accounts; but even if one accepts this, what necessarily precedes those projects too would involve the study of how specific theories of race have taken
the forms they do, how and in what areas they have been applied, and,
most immediately, what their consequence are in the present. It is at any
rate this line of reasoning, working backward and outward from the present
phenomenon of race, that has shaped the essays collected here, with their
common focus on specific aspects of the theory and practice of race both
in the past and in some of their most notable (although not always most
obvious) present consequences.

The authors of the assembled essays first convened in a conference at
Trinity College in the fall of 1998 under that college's auspices. The revised
and expanded versions of the papers presented at the conference, divided
among the topics addressed at that time, comprise the present volume. The
authors of the essays represent a broad range of disciplines that extend from
evolutionary biology to medieval Spanish literature, from social psychology
to classical (Greek) history, from nineteenth-century philosophy to current
macroeconomics. It will be readily understood that the individual essays
cannot (and do not) claim to be comprehensive even for the limited topics
they address. But viewed together, the net they cast is wide, in both disciplinary terms and historically. This is itself a central motif of the volume,

which is intended to convey a clear and concrete sense of the large number of ways and occasions in which issues of race have obtruded historically (continuing into the present) on the domains of everyday (what we often too readily accept as "normal") life.

The general topic of race in theory and practice thus appears under four subtitles designed to focus on particular—in our view, central—aspects of the phenomenon of race. In part I, "Questioning the 'Science' of Race," the question raised is meant to be assertive without being tendentious. The identification of racial distinctions in terms of color has commonly been accepted as evident (if only because "visible")—with its "scientific" basis then presumably only a short theoretical step behind that. But exactly how many steps behind the "evidence" of color is the scientific foundation of race? How visible is the supposedly prima facie evidence that has at once (that is, circularly) nourished and been fed by the investigations of science—principally in biology but also from the directions of chemistry, cell biology, and physical anthropology? And what has been the course of the relationship, during the nineteenth and twentieth centuries of its flourishing, between the scientific "foundations" and the commonplace "visibility" of racial distinctions? These are questions that Daniel Blackburn confronts head-on in respect to biological analysis; that Maurice Wade and Dina Anselmi consider in terms of their philosophical and psychological histories (respectively), principally for their development in the eighteenth and nineteenth centuries; and that Dalia Ofer addresses in the context of the most openly violent claims based on the relation between science and race, as these then became the rationale for Nazi racism.

Part II considers the relation "Between Race and Slavery" as the variable of culture has shaped that relation. Viewed ahistorically, the connection between slavery and race may seem so fundamental or obvious as to go without saying; on reflection, that relationship is considerably more complex. Slavery itself has a varied history—economically, geographically, and even morally; in its origins and for much the greater part of its course, it has involved no reference to race at all. Gary Reger provides a telling example of this distinction in his essay's account of the institution of Greek slavery, and James Muldoon reinforces the point as he situates the role of race (that is, its absence) in the cultures of medieval Europe. Neither of these large historical periods was without a conception of the "Other"—but that "Other" was defined primarily in cultural and not in biological terms: an arguably modernist (or rather postmodernist) anticipation. Together, these essays pose what can now be no more than a thought experiment, namely, imagining a world from which the concept of race, with all that we know of its consequences, is absent. Setting out in quite a different historical and methodological direction, Jack Chatfield proposes to "reconstruct" the standard interpretations of the analysis of pre–Civil War American slavery by calling to witness the historian U. B. Phillips. Chatfield thus describes at this second, or "meta-historical," level how the assumption of a necessary—and racist—connection between race and slavery may blur the understanding of each of those practices independently. It might be objected, to be sure, that the character of certain institutions or practices will be evident no matter how blurred their representation, but this argument is typically made retrospectively, in historical hindsight, a point that is itself given an unusual turn by Janet Bauer's critique of certain classical anthropological analyses of culture. Where such influential figures of American anthropology as Boas, Benedict, and Mead have been repeatedly attacked (again, retrospectively) for the failure in their concepts of culture to account for race as a social rather than as a "natural" phenomenon, Bauer presents this as not so much a fault in their concepts of culture as in their refusal to view race as also culture bound, a mistake they might have avoided, she adds, had they listened to (or read) certain anthropologists who, writing from their own racial margins, had already seen—and lived—the connection.

However fundamentally the categories of race are acknowledged to be social constructs, they have also—arguably, first—to be imagined. But such "labor" of the imagination does not end at the harsh point at which social distinctions of race have been made or enforced. There is thus nothing surprising in the fact that the notable features of race as elements of cultural experience would also inspire the re-creative world of the artist—most urgently among victims of racism but also as an evocative motif for any writer concerned with significant tensions or exchanges in the social process and the shaping of social values and character. The essays in part III, "Race and the Literary Imagination," provide a diversely representative conspectus of this range of the imagination. Colbert Nepaulsingh, writing provocatively against the grain, finds in the literary constructions of the Hebrew Bible and its classical Greek counterparts at once the source and antidote for the later history of racial (and racist) distinctions. The "Continental Fallacy of Race," which Nepaulsingh ascribes only half-metaphorically to the continents of racist origins (Europe, the Americas), may thus imaginatively—and perhaps actually as well—be replaced by "island" truth, as that emerges, for example, in the culture of the Caribbean.

The evidence of literary representation in part III then continues its world tour. King-fai Tam reflects on the images of "beautiful" Americans and "ugly" Japanese as seen through the eyes of Taiwanese writer Huang Chunming—who finds the arbitrariness of racial distinctions ironically represented in the mediating view of contemporary Taiwanese culture. Margo Perkins follows the translation of race into its literary representation and its varied and significant extraliterary consequences in the work of African American writer Toni Cade Bambera. And bridging two other continents, Sonia Lee points to the "French" literature of France in francophone Africa as both expression and evidence of the priority of culture to race in that complex setting: admission to the "French School" in the cities of French Africa prefaced admission to French identity, with predictable consequences and problems for both the students who left Africa for France and those who stayed or returned. The literary representations thus addressed are not quite "worldwide," but their diversity provides specific evidence of how serious and evocative a source the concept of race has become in the contemporary literary prospect.

In social terms, the analysis of race and of the consequences associated with it has frequently been confronted by an (alleged) counteranalysis that takes as its explanatory principle the fundamental term of economic class. This displacement is most notable but by no means restricted to Marxist accounts of race. Part IV, "Race or Class: Which Is It?" attempts at once to identify the issues at the basis of the disagreement between the divided "proponents" of race, on the one hand, and class, on the other, and to assess how far that disagreement extends in fact. In confronting this dualism (as for many others), an immediate danger is that of reductionism, simply folding the alternative into one's own framework. All the writers included here, albeit by different routes, attempt both to avoid that danger and to suggest a means (conceptual or practical) for doing so. Andrew Gold, writing about the economics of housing patterns and wage differentials, argues for the defeasibility of both race and class in the determination of those patterns. This optimistic note, however, is balanced (even outweighed) by the evidence Gold provides of how patterns of racial "distancing" on a small and modest scale yet may provide sufficient impetus to turn into large-scale patterns of segregation (as in housing), which then require proportionately large efforts to be reversed. Sociologist Johnny Williams reaches back to the conceptual sources of the categories of race and class to explain how those domains came in fact to be distinguished; he then provides a number of examples of the dynamic interrelation between them, for instance, as that relation manifests itself in statistics about family incomes and in college admissions policies; he concludes that the reductionist accounts which conflate race and class (whichever direction they move in) are themselves ideologically motivated. Priscilla Kehoe's analysis of "Race and Medicine" turns to the pressing issue of health care in relation to racial categories. The evidence she finds showing that upward movement in the class status of blacks in the United States is accompanied by no comparable change in medical treatment (that is, in the perception and diagnoses of physicians who in this way, consciously or not, distinguish between black and white patients) argues strikingly against the attempt to conflate race and class. Finally, Paul Lauter turns to the common problem of future resolution that faces any priority assigned in the dualism of race and class. For him too neither the one nor the other is "It," since the structural analysis of particular social contexts consistently reveals the copresence and interrelation of those (and other) factors. If there is a hopeful note to be found here (and in part IV as a whole), it is that neither race nor class by itself is foundational, that is, unmovable. This, of course, leaves open the question of how the effects of each—or both—can be altered, but specific evidence of that possibility and against its denial seems itself a valuable step forward.

Again, the four topics addressed in the four parts, and the chapters that offer their individual perspectives on them, only touch the surface of the complexities of the concept and phenomenon of race in its appearances and consequences, past and present. But we believed it to be all the more important, just because of the constraints imposed by the single-volume format, to bring into view the broad extension of the concept of race historically, geographically, and culturally. There can be little disagreement that the array of issues contributing to (and in the end constituting) the "theory and practice" of race ought to be articulated, analyzed, judged. Although the topics considered here only begin to confront that array, they represent certain of its most significant aspects. It is our hope that they may serve as an incentive, even as a provocation, for further work along similar lines.

Part I
Questioning the "Science" of Race

1

Why Race Is Not a Biological Concept

Daniel G. Blackburn

As Europeans explored the globe during the fourteenth through sixteenth centuries, they encountered people who differed markedly from themselves in physical appearance, language, and culture. With the human penchant for classification legitimized by natural science, they categorized these people into groups that were assumed to represent stable configurations of characteristics.[1] During the eighteenth and nineteenth centuries, under the influence of biblical traditions, questions persisted over whether these groups were descended from one origin or from multiple origins. These questions were widely recognized to have theological, social, and political implications.[2] The advent of evolutionary ideas in the mid-nineteenth century gave a deeply historical dimension to racial categories, and "races" eventually became interpreted as having descended from lineages with more or less independent historical trajectories.[3] Until recent decades, "races" were commonly arranged hierarchically by Europeans and their American descendants according to putative abilities, reflecting (among many other problems) a pre-Darwinian concept of the "scale of nature."[4]

The term "race" has been used in a wide variety of ways in scientific and sociopolitical realms.[5] Even when racial equality is assumed, quasi-biological notions commonly are employed to recognize and characterize racial categories. However, powerful arguments have been adduced that biological notions of race deserve to be repudiated as typological, subjective, and based on misconceptions about genetics, human variation, and human history. For such reasons, many biologists and anthropologists rejected biological racial concepts as applied to humans decades ago.[6] Indeed, the social construction of race has been detailed in a substantial body of anthropological literature over the past decade.[7] Nevertheless, biologically based notions

3

of race continue to be used as the rationale for political agendas, empirical research, medical diagnoses, and the self-identification of individuals.[8]

How can biologists, anthropologists, and social scientists reject the concept of biological race, given the indisputable existence of physical variation among human groups that are products of evolutionary history? And if such a view is correct, how have we come to a state of affairs in which discredited notions of earlier centuries have been adopted by people on all sides of sociopolitical issues? The main goal of this chapter is to explore the concept of race from a biological standpoint and to demonstrate how and why its explanatory power is so limited. The evidence reveals that race is largely a social construct that fails to meet the criteria of a meaningful biological concept, a fact with significant implications for politics, society, and, more specifically, the practice of medicine.

THE SOCIAL CONSTRUCTION OF RACE

One variety of mankind does so sensibly pass into the other, that you cannot mark out the limits between them.

—Blumenbach, 1775

Races do not exist; classifications of mankind do.

—Dorsey, 1928[9]

To most North Americans and Europeans, the existence of objective racial categories may seem self-evident; individuals seem to fit into one of three or four groups, defined by obvious physical characteristics. Yet examination of scholarly classifications from the past three centuries reveals no consensus on how many races there are or how the boundaries between them are to be recognized.[10] For example, whereas some eighteenth-century taxonomic systems recognized three racial categories, others identified twice that number (table 1.1). These classifications often relied on such cultural features as clothing, temperament, and body adornments.[11] The ensuing century did nothing to resolve the discrepancies. As physical diversity was documented in more detail and as craniometry came into vogue,[12] the recognized "races" proliferated rapidly. In questioning the value of the concept of race, Darwin (1871) was ahead of his time, observing that the experts classified humans in as few as two and as many as sixty-three separate races.[13]

A diversity of views has persisted during the twentieth century (see table 1.1). The number of races recognized by scholarly works ranges from three to five, six, ten, thirteen, thirty-two, and thirty-four, with the same authors sometimes offering different numbers at different times.[14] In two authorita-

Table 1.1   Some Classifications of Human Races

Buffon (1749)	American, Laplander, Tartar, South Asiatic, European, Ethiopian
Blumenbach (1781)	Caucasoid, Mongoloid, American Indian, Ethiopian, Malay
Cuvier (1790)	Caucasian, Mongolian, Ethiopian
Flourens (1839)	Caucasian, Mongolian, Negro, American, Malay, Hottentot, Boschisman, Papuan, Alfourou, Zealandic
Prichard (1848)	Caucasian, Mongolian, Negro, American, Esqimaux, Hottentot + Boschisman, Papuans, Alfourous + Australian
Boyd (1950)	Early European, European, African, Asiatic, American Indian, Australoid
Boyd (1963)	Early European, Laplanders, Northwest European, Eastern European, Mediterranean, African, Asian, Indo-Dravidian, American, Indonesian, Melanesian, Polynesian, Australoid
Coon (1965)	Caucasoid, Mongoloid, Australoid, Congoid, Capoid
Garn (1971)	Northwest European, Northeast European, Alpine, Mediterranean, Iranian, East African, Sudanese, Forest Negro, Bantu, Turkic, Tibetan, North Chinese, Extreme Mongoloid, Southeast Asiatic, Hindu, Dravidian, North American, Central American, South American, Fuegian, Lapp, Pacific Negrito, African Pygmy, Eskimo, Ainu, Murrayian, Carpenterian Australian, Bushman + Hottentot, North American Colored, South African Colored, Ladino, Neo-Hawaiian

Source: E. H. Colbert and M. Morales. 1991. *Caucasoid, Mongoloid, Australian, Negroid* in *Evolution of the Vertebrates*, p. 220.
Note: The eighteen- and nineteenth-century sources are from Smith (1859)[95], Augstein (1996), and Molnar (1998).

tive works published in 1950, none of the "races" were defined in common.[15] Classifications since the 1940s contrast with those of earlier times in recognizing that the categories are tentative, subjective, and ephemeral. Thus Coon, Garn, and Birdsell (1950) indicated that their recognition of thirty races "might have been ten or 50," noting that "race is not a static thing at all, but that new races are constantly being formed."[16] Nevertheless, Coon offered voluminous evidence in support of his contention that five major racial stocks of *H. sapiens* had evolved independently from *H. erectus*,[17] a conclusion that elicited strong disagreement from anthropologists and biologists who recognized both its implausibility and its racist implications.[18] Sociocultural factors have always offered a major impetus for the construction of racial classifications. Implications of debates about the polygenic versus monogenic origins of modern humans were widely recognized outside of the sciences.[19] Moreover, historical myths constructed around race during the nineteenth and twentieth centuries were taken as justification for "Aryan" supremacy, Jewish oppression, and ultimately genocide.[20] In previous centuries, such myth making (along with miscalculations about the influence of culture) was used to justify European colonialism, slavery, and decimation of indigenous populations.[21] In the past few decades, racial classifications have continued to be adopted according to their sociocultural utility. For example, under the apartheid regime in South Africa, people were classified as "black," "white," and "colored," the last category including such diverse peoples as Khoisan Africans, East Indians, Pakistanis, and East Asians.[22] For political reasons, the Japanese were classified as honorary "whites," as was American activist Jesse Jackson during his visit to South Africa.[23] Clearly, in South Africa (as elsewhere), race has been a politically based construct to be modified or ignored according to convenience, however thin the biological evidence used as justification.

The arbitrary nature of racial categories is evident from the ways African Americans historically have been classified in the United States. Throughout the nineteenth century, "mixed" individuals were placed in categories according to their relative proportions of "black" and "white" parentage. By the 1940s, a "one-drop" custom was commonplace, in which any discernible African heritage was grounds for an individual to be considered "black."[24] This perspective has since been adopted across the political spectrum. Thus political conservatives have found common cause with minority groups who recognize the strengths in defining their group as inclusively as possible—and who are, after all, often marginalized on the basis of their assigned social category.[25] The one-drop rule has no equivalent in much of Africa and South America, where many "black" U.S. citizens would be considered "white" or "mixed."[26] But the rule retains legal standing. In 1986, for example, the U.S. Supreme Court let stand a lower court ruling that a woman who is 3/32 African American is to be considered "black."[27]

Not only is the classification of people by race an intellectually risky and culturally laden enterprise, but the very words we apply to human diversity are misleading. Over the years the term "race" has been variously applied to groups defined by appearance, language, nationality, religion, and culture. In contemporary times, "race" is often avoided in favor of "ethnic group," but the former term continues to be applied to physical types as well as to groups recognized by political or religious affinities.[28]

Specific descriptive terms are also misleading, reflecting cultural misconceptions, personal preferences, and historical accidents. After all, the fact that "Indian" has been applied for half a millennium to indigenous people of two continents reflects the geographical confusion of an Italian sailor of the late 1400s! The term "Caucasian" was adopted by Johann Friedrich

Blumenbach in part because he considered the people of the Caucasus Mountains to be physically the most beautiful of people.[29] The term "people of color" serves a sociopolitical function in the United States but is less than descriptive as applied to diverse peoples whose skin tones lie well within the range found among European Americans, the latter consisting of people who are certainly not without color themselves. Likewise, the adjectives "black" and "white" as commonly used in the United States are poor descriptors of people whose skin tones commonly intergrade between taupe, tan, and brown. These adjectives reify a spurious dichotomy, leading to preoccupation with physical distinctions that often are small to nonexistent. As applied to human beings, they are only modestly more descriptive than "yellow" and "red," words that were recently used in reference to skin color but are now deemed embarrassing, if not offensive. Terminological difficulties entangle even the most well-intentioned attempts to speak of ancestry. It is nearly meaningless to speak of a genetic background that is, for example, Italian, Asian, Jewish, Hispanic, or "black." These terms refer less to biological heritage than to political systems, continents, cultures, ethnic groups, and sociopolitical designations. One might just as well refer to a genetic background that is "Californian," "Episcopalian," or "Republican."

CRITERIA FOR A BIOLOGICAL CONCEPT OF RACE

It may be doubted whether any character can be named which is distinctive of a race and is constant.

—Darwin, 1871, *Descent of Man*, p. 217

There are no races; there are only clines.

—F. Livingstone, 1963, p. 47[30]

To recognize that race is socially constructed does not deny the existence of human physical diversity. The question is whether this diversity meets the criteria for a biological concept of race. I suggest five criteria that would allow race to be viewed as having a biological basis. First, races would have to be definable (at least in part) through readily identifiable physical features. When people mentally assign others to racial categories, they do so on the basis of observable features of face and body—not by acquired features such as clothing and language. If racial differences were confined to less apparent features such as blood proteins and genes, no one outside of a few academic disciplines would be likely to use the concept of race. Second, variation in these features should be relatively heritable, that is, their diversity would have a significant genetic component. A major valid criti-

cism advanced against classifications of previous centuries is that they include acquired, cultural attributes like temperament, attire, and personality.[31] Third, at least some characteristics used to define race arguably should
have functional significance. If we were dealing with trivial features like the
number of hair follicles on the back of the hand and not with underlying
presumptions about functional capabilities, people would not be so preoccupied with putative racial differences.[32]

Fourth, we should expect "racial" features to be useful in defining categories of people that are more or less discrete. If the categories intergrade
in such a way that many or most people are difficult to classify according
to objective criteria, then in a biological sense, the categories are artificial
constructs of little value. Some writers would disagree with this criterion.
Notably, both S. M. Garn (1971) and C. S. Coon, Garn, and Birdsell (1950)
viewed races as breeding groups that can form at any time; thus they
viewed African Americans as a new hybrid (mixed) race that is distinguish-
able from its African and European ancestors. Other writers have noted that
such an approach is of dubious utility, since extensive hybridization produces a continuum of heredities that prevent categorization of actual individuals. A more fundamental challenge is seldom noted. The very notion
of hybrid or mixed races is based on the false assumption that "African" and
"Caucasian" are pure racial types available for hybridization (see below).[33]

Fifth, we should expect the putative racial categories to reflect genealogies and evolutionary history. Although some readers might balk at the historical criterion, it follows from the combination of the criteria of heritabil-
ity and functional significance. Furthermore, genealogical factors are
implicit in almost all racial designations. Note, however, that we place arbitrary limits on this history. If accepted views about the origin of modern *H.
sapiens* are correct,[34] we are all historically African, regardless of the myriad
migratory paths our ancestors subsequently took.

Table 1.2 lists several of the physical features by which human groups
differ, including those that have been used to define human races. These
features will be considered in terms of the above criteria.

Skin Pigmentation

Skin coloration is the feature most commonly used to recognize "races" as
both social and biological categories. Skin tones vary from shades of taupe
to tan, brown, and ebony. Coloration mainly is a consequence of the
amount and distribution of the pigment melanin, which is found in the skin
of all people except for albinos.[35] Thus coloration is quantitative rather than
qualitative in nature. Several factors confound attempts to characterize individuals by skin color. Among these are ontogenetic changes in darkening
or lightening of the skin during infancy, adolescence, or adulthood, in pat-

Table 1.2   Heterogeneous Physical Features of Humans

	Identifiable	Heritable	Functional	Discrete	Genealogical
*Skin pigmentation	yes	largely	probably	no	no
*Eyelid structure	yes	yes	maybe	no	no
*Nose shape	yes	yes	maybe	no	no
*Hair form	yes	yes	in some	somewhat	in some
*Tooth form	somewhat	yes	probably	no	some aspects
*Misc. facial features	yes	yes	possibly	no	some aspects
*Height, weight	yes	somewhat	somewhat	no	no
Hair distribution	mainly	yes	unknown	no	no
Lactose tolerance	no	yes	yes	no	no
Resistance to frostbite	no	probably	yes	no	no
Adaptation to altitude	no	somewhat	yes	no	no
Lung capacity	no	somewhat	in some	no	no

Note: Items marked by an asterisk have most commonly been used to define biological races. Each characteristic is classified according to the following criteria (see text): whether its variation is readily identifiable, whether is relatively heritable, whether it has functional implications, whether it defines discrete groups, and whether the groups so defined appear on other grounds to represent genealogical lineages.

terns that differ among human populations.[36] A second complicating factor is the fact that environment plays an important role in determining skin coloration, as is obvious from the response to sun exposure in lighter-skinned people.[37] A third factor complicates the characterization of populations: the existence of sexual dimorphism that is manifested by relatively lighter skin tones in women than in men in many or most indigenous populations worldwide.[38]

Skin pigmentation shows a historical relationship to geography that is especially clear from human distributions predating the 1500s. Throughout the Old World, tropical and subtropical latitudes and other regions subject to heavy sun exposure (Australia) were inhabited by people with relatively dark skin.[39] Skin tones show a gradient toward progressively lighter coloration north of the equator in Europe and Asia. A geographical gradient is also apparent in the Americas, where it is less marked, perhaps because of the more restricted time during which natural selection could have acted. Although several functional hypotheses have been proposed for the evolution of dark skin color, much evidence points to the protection that melanin provides against ultraviolet solar radiation.[40] As for the presence of light skin in northern Europeans, one popular hypothesis notes that a certain amount of ultraviolet radiation must penetrate the skin to permit the synthesis of vitamin D. Accordingly, in northern latitudes, where solar radiation is restricted, a reduction in skin pigmentation may have been useful in allowing vitamin D synthesis. However, based on a thorough reexamination of the facts, A. H. Robins concluded that evidence for this hypothesis is extremely weak and that functional reasons (if any) for light skin color remain unknown.[41]

The common practice in particular countries of using skin color to define races founders when applied to the world's populations. As a quantitative feature, skin pigmentation shows gradients of distribution within which sharp distinctions cannot be drawn.[42] Furthermore, the distribution of skin tones cuts directly across the conventional "racial" boundaries; dark skin, for example, is found among indigenous sub-Saharan Africans, Australians, and East Indians but is by no means universal in any of those three groups. Various other reasons why skin color fails as a biological "racial" characteristic were noted above: ontogenetic variation, gender differences, questionable functions, and the significant effects of environment on its presence. Historical analysis has shown that the use of skin color by Europeans and their American descendants to define social categories was closely linked with political, social, and economic imperatives.[43] The wholesale adoption of the European categories by minority groups whose ancestors were so cruelly exploited in their name has a certain irony yet reflects persistent political realities.

Eyelid and Orbital Structure

The presence of an epicanthic fold in the upper eyelid historically was used by western Europeans from a racial perspective to distinguish eastern Asian peoples. Although the eye itself does not vary, the presence or the absence of the fold gives the impression of different eye shapes. The epicanthic fold can be associated with fat padding around the eyeball and is particularly accentuated in Siberian Asians, Inuit ("Eskimo"), and others of arctic climes. These features are postulated to be an adaptation to cold climates, with the lipid deposits providing insulation to the eyeball and sinuses, and the epicanthic fold protecting the eye against glare from the snow (snow blindness) and freezing winds.[44] The presence of a relatively flattened face (without protruding nose and cheekbones that might be subject to frostbite) is also said to be an adaptation to cold climate. The evolutionary hypotheses are plausible but difficult to test; they also have been challenged.[45] If they are correct, these features no longer serve their original function in people of Southeast Asia, among whom they may have been retained or to whom they spread through interpopulational gene flow.

Among several significant challenges to the use of eyelid form to define biological races is the fact that it varies continuously across Eurasia and thus that sharp distinctions cannot be made. First, the epicanthic fold varies widely in its degree of development; whether one or another Eurasian, native American, or Pacific Island group should be considered to have it is a matter of opinion. Second, as discussed below, even eastern Asian peoples who exhibit the feature do not represent a homogeneous group genealogically. Third, the epicanthic fold is not confined to Asians; it also occurs in Khoisan and Sudanese Africans (among others), among whom some claim that it shields against glare from the desert sun.[46] In fact, this feature commonly occurs in infants born to European couples. Clearly the epicanthic fold fails to define genealogical groups except in the most vague sense and thus is of little value in recognizing biological races in a global context.

Nose Form

Among other functions, the human nose serves to warm and humidify inspired air and recapture moisture upon exhalation. The humidification function may account for the presence of long, thin noses in peoples of arid climates, including deserts, mountains, and arctic regions. This nose shape maximizes surface area over which the air passes.[47] However, the functional explanation cannot account for the broad nose shape of indigenous Australians, who occupy some of the driest regions in the world. Some researchers have noted that nose shape is influenced by palatal width, both of which reflect the large tooth size in aboriginal Australians.[48] Thus nasal form should be viewed in the context of overall shape of the face and may not be readily accessible to selective pressures. In any event, continuous variation makes it difficult to use nasal shape in racial classifications. Even the extremes of nasal form fail to define genealogical groups. The broad nasal shape is common among aboriginal Australians and tropical Africans, whereas long, narrow noses occur in people of the eastern African highlands, as well as in Native Americans, Inuit, and Europeans. Like skin color and eyelid structure, the distribution of nose form types cuts directly across racial boundaries.

Hair Color and Type

Dark brown or black hair predominates in most people around the globe, with lighter hair (blond, red, or brown) being found among northern Europeans and their clear descendants. Yet hair color transcends contemporary racial divisions.[49] Not only is dark hair common among Europeans, but blond hair is found among Berbers of North Africa as well as aborigines of central Australia, Papua New Guinea, and Melanesia, and not through European admixture. Although dark head hair probably maximizes the absorption of solar radiation in sunny tropical climates, the functional significance (if any) of lighter hair is unknown. Because hair color bears some correlation with skin color in Europeans, skin and hair pigment may be genetically and developmentally linked.

Head hair also varies in form.[50] Dark, straight hair is common among eastern Asians and Native Americans, and it intergrades into the straight to wavy hair of people of western and southern Asia, Europe, North Africa, and Australia. Helical (loosely curled) hair is also found among Europeans, Inuit, and Ainu. Although tightly curled hair characterizes people of sub-Saharan Africa, it varies in the extent of curling and is also found in certain areas of southern Arabia, India, Malaysia, the Philippines, and New Guinea. Some have speculated that short, curly hair might provide a good insulative cushion against the sun's rays,[51] but what function other hair forms might serve is unknown. Although tightly coiled hair may be indicative of genealogy, in general the distribution of hair form shows little regard for geographical and "racial" boundaries.

Other Features

Various other identifiable physical features have also been used to characterize racial groups, including lip size, iris color, tooth size, ear shape, facial form, and body proportions. Some of these features have no known functions, and all of them vary continuously in a fashion that cuts across contemporary racial boundaries and prevents recognition of distinct categories.

Features that are routinely used to classify human races arguably have no more validity than those that are not used (see table 1.2). For one thing, developmental and intersexual differences (e.g., skin coloration, the epicanthic fold) are ignored in racial classifications, the "norm" being defined by features of adults, if not adult males. But why are other variable features, such as stature, not more commonly used? After all, average height of adult males varies by population from about 145 to 215 centimeters.[52] Groups also vary in abundance and distribution of body hair, with male Europeans, Australians, and Ainu of Japan being among the most hirsute, the tendency toward baldness in European males notwithstanding.[53] Tolerance of the milk sugar, lactose, also varies; people descended from herders of cattle, sheep, and goats (in parts of Europe, western Africa, and western Asia) are unusual in their ability to digest lactose as adults, offering a clear example of the recent effects of natural selection.[54] Likewise, populations vary in resistance to frostbite, lung capacity, and tolerance of high–altitude hypoxia.[55] Still other variable features include long-bone density, nipple shape, cerumen (earwax) form, and, possibly, skin gland abundance.[56] Perhaps most of these features are overlooked because their variability is not immediately observable, but they would probably be ignored in any case because they challenge commonly defined racial categories.

Features that vary among human populations are not concordant in their distribution.[57] Patterns of overlapping variation prevent the classification of humans into biological units, unless a very limited number of features are arbitrarily chosen. The choice itself is arbitrary and culturally determined.

As Jared Diamond observed, "Depending on whether we classified ourselves by anti-malarial genes, lactase, fingerprints, or skin color, we could place Swedes as the same race as either Xhosas, Fulani, the Ainu of Japan, or Italians."[58]

CHALLENGES FROM HISTORICAL ANALYSIS

If races are biological groups rather than sociopolitical categories, they ought to reflect patterns of evolution, migration, and mating of human populations. Three major bodies of evidence have allowed reconstruction of the prehistory of the human race—paleoanthropology, linguistics, and molecular genetics. Two contradictory scenarios are being supported, each with subvariants.[59] According to the "multiregional evolution" scenario (which some paleoanthropologists advocate), extant populations in Africa, Asia, and Europe are descended from archaic *H. erectus,* who occupied these regions about 1 million years ago. Commonality of living populations is attributed to gene flow during the transition to modern humans, which purportedly occurred simultaneously worldwide. In contrast, the "out of Africa" hypothesis (which is supported by molecular geneticists and a growing number of paleontologists) holds that all extant humans had a relatively recent origin in Africa. Thus existing human diversity would have evolved very recently, perhaps during the last 90,000 years. Questions persist, then, as to whether "racial" differences are ancient or recent in origin and whether peoples of Asia, Europe, and Australia have descended in situ from archaic *H. sapiens* or even *H. erectus,* a possibility that would lend legitimacy to the view that races evolved somewhat independently on each continent.

The multiregional model has been criticized on the basis that new species do not arise in the way posited by the model. Species arise as geographical isolates of a precursor species that only later may become widely distributed. This latter mode of speciation is consistent with the out of Africa model, and it is supported by a detailed analysis of historical biogeography.[60] In any event, all of the commonly recognized racial groupings fail to meet two crucial criteria: they are far from being discrete categories and they do not represent genealogical lineages. Geographical "races" commonly recognized by North Americans and Europeans[61] will be shown to be invalid as biological categories when each is considered in turn. The history of the Pacific Islanders, diverse peoples with complex genealogies, is not discussed here because it does not usually figure in traditionally recognized racial categories of the continental United States. Only general outlines of historical features are given here; for more detail, the reader is referred to recent reviews.[62]

People of Sub-Saharan Africa

Despite the current penchant for recognizing African people living south of the Sahara Desert as a single "black" racial category, there is more genetic diversity in Africa than in the rest of the world combined.[63] Physical diversity is also marked, with representatives of both the tallest and the smallest people in the world. Current practices notwithstanding, past biologically based classifications commonly distinguished at least two or three distinct races of sub-Saharan Africans: Khoisans of southern Africa (sometimes referred to as bush people and Hottentot), peoples of the Bantu-language group (representing the majority of indigenous Africans), and the diminutive pygmies.[64] To group these diverse peoples into a single Negroid category is to resurrect archaic eighteenth-century classifications of western Europeans (see table 1.1), classifications that cannot be supported biologically, much less culturally or politically.

In regard to Africa, additional complications stem from the historical admixture of genes from people of other continents. For example, people of eastern Africa (present-day Ethiopia) have been intermating with South Arabians from the sixth century B.C.E. onward,[65] and the two groups may have been in contact for 5,000–6,000 years.[66] Periodic contact between Ethiopia and Egypt is also evident; indeed, Kushites from the south ruled Egypt in the postdynastic period.[67] Most striking of all is the fact that Madagascans are descendants of a mixture of indigenous Africans, Southeast Asian immigrants, and possibly Arab and Persian traders. Linguistic evidence shows strong affinities to inhabitants of the Indonesian island of Borneo, some 4,000 miles away, reflecting an astonishing migration that may have occurred between 300 and 800 C.E.[68]

Asian Peoples

The vast continent of Asia also shows a pattern of diversity that defies the tradition of categorizing its people into one race distinct from all others.[69] The Indian subcontinent is home to people who are as dark skinned as many Africans and show biological and linguistic affinities with Europeans. Semitic people of southwestern Asia are not clustered genealogically or linguistically with eastern Asians. The traditional classification of these two groups as Caucasian does not resolve the problems, however. Across the expanse of Eurasia, physical features show a continuum in which no discontinuity between Asian and Caucasoid groups (however defined) is recognizable. Such is not surprising, given the scarcity of geographical barriers to gene flow, as well as the periodic, large-scale invasions of Asian peoples eastward over the past millennium.[70]

These are but a few of the difficulties with the western concept of an

Asian race. An even bigger challenge is offered by studies showing that
North Asians are genetically more similar to Europeans than to Southeast
Asians.[71] If a distinction is be made, it surely lies between Asians, as denti-
tional studies have long suggested[72]; however, even that distinction is statistical, not qualitative. Moreover, select areas exhibit striking populational
heterogeneities. For example, in northern Japan reside the distinctive Ainu
people, long thought to be a displaced Caucasian stock but now thought
by many to be largely a relictual group descended from inhabitants that
predate the subsequent migrations from the mainland.[73] Another example
is represented by isolated populations of dark-skinned people of small stature in Southeast Asia (Andaman Islands, the Malay Peninsula, the Philip-
pine island of Luzon), variously described as "Negrito" or "Australoid."
They may represent descendants of an early migration from Africa that
eventually led to Australia.[74]

"Caucasian" People

The so-called Caucasian race is commonly defined to include people of
Europe, western Asia, northern Africa (Berbers and Egyptians), and the Indian subcontinent. The term "Caucasian" reflects a putative descent from
migrants from the Caucasus region—despite evidence for habitation that
predates the putative migration. Historical scholarship has revealed that the
concept of the "white race" was a sociopolitical invention of western Europeans and their descendants that they developed during the periods of
colonialism and slavery.[75]

As noted above, people show gradual variation in physical features from
Europe through Eurasia to Asia, and thus no dichotomous distinction can
be made. Other complexities are raised by details of patterns of migration
and mating. For example, the Saame (Lapps) of northern Eurasia and Scan-
dinavia have long defied easy classification. Genetic analysis has revealed
that they share characteristics equally with adjacent Europeans and Asians.[76]
Such combinations (with less Asian influence) are also evident in Hungary
and Finland.[77] The Indian subcontinent, as yet another example, is thought
by some to have been populated through at least three successive migrations of people—from southwestern Asia, from the east, and from the
northwest.[78] These migrations may have been preceded by an earlier migration from Africa, since people anatomically similar to the southeastern
Asian "Negritos" are found as geographically isolated populations. Another
complication is that Egyptians were classified as "white" by nineteenth-
century Europeans but as "black" by individuals arguing for an Afrocentric
historical perspective.[79] This issue is more political than scientific, and it
illustrates the complexities that ensue when sociocultural categories are
confused with biological ones.

Indigenous Australians and New Guineans

Migration to New Guinea had occurred by sixty kya (thousand years ago) and to Australia by between forty and fifty-five kya. The long period of relative geographic isolation, possibly coupled with local hybridization with *H. erectus* or archaic *H. sapiens,* has been suggested by some to explain the distinctive appearance of these people.[80] Although the more recent European invaders tended to recognize indigenous Australians and New Guineans as one or two genealogical groups, the data do not support this view. Australia apparently has been invaded through multiple migrations; Negritos may have arrived first, perhaps followed by two distinct migratory waves, the last being ancestral to most pre-European inhabitants.[81] New Guinea (which was geographically united to Australia when humans arrived) also shows evidence of multiple migrations. A particular distinction can be made between peoples of the highlands and the coastal regions; Austronesians of the latter category appear to represent a more recent migration from Southeast Asia.[82]

Indigenous Americans

The indigenous peoples of the New World were classified by Europeans as a single race, based on culture, geography, and appearance. For such a classification to be justified biologically, these peoples arguably would have to have been descended from a common set of migrations. However, genetics studies and some linguistic analyses are consistent in showing indigenous Americans to represent descendants of three successive migrations from Siberian Asia.[83] The first hypothetical migration was by Paleo-Indians who were ancestral to most of the indigenous groups of North and South America. This migration had occurred by fifteen kya, although some anthropologists argue from scarce evidence for a considerably earlier date. The second migration was of people of the Na-Dene language group, whose descendants are to be found in Alaska and western Canada. Only about eight hundred years ago, some migrated south, giving rise to the Navajo and Apache, groups that have intermixed with their neighbors since their arrival. The third migration occurred about ten kya by Inuits, people adapted biologically and culturally for life in cold climates. The point to recognize is that if people migrated to the New World in three successive waves, then each of these groups was more closely related historically to an Asian stock than to each other. Consequently, Native Americans do not represent a "race" in any genealogical sense. On what historical grounds could we unite Apache with Brazilian Yanomamo and Alaskan Inuit as a single group separate from all others? Moreover, their descendants have interbred with each other and, recently, with immigrants from Europe and

Africa in combinations that show marked regional variation and that defy genealogy-based "racial" classification.

Contemporary Admixtures

A common theme throughout human history is one of pervasive genetic exchange that has prevented establishment of independent lineages. Such genetic exchange has accelerated in the past two centuries due to major diasporic movements and migrations, including those caused by European colonization and displacements of indigenous peoples.[84] As a consequence, in many areas of the globe, racial designations progressively bear less relationship to the traditional Eurocentric categories. For example, the "Cape-colored" category of South Africa includes descendants of Afrikaan-Khoisan unions, along with Malaysian, Bantu, and East Indian contributions.[85] In the United States, African American people reportedly have, on average, about 25 percent European ancestral heritage. Perhaps 90 percent of those who identify themselves as "black" on the U.S. Census could as a consequence consider themselves "mixed."[86] The number of people of diverse ancestry in Central and South America further obviates application of the traditional racial categories. Latinos can be any New World combination of Spanish, Portuguese, Indian, and African, depending on the person and region. In Brazil, this fact has led to elaborate classifications by color, in which siblings with the same parents can be categorized in separate races.[87] Clearly, in such circumstances, the concept of race serves social functions that bear little relationship to historical or biological categories.

IMPLICATIONS AND CONCLUSIONS

The idea of "race" was, in fact, a deliberate creation of an exploiting class which was seeking to maintain its privileges against what was profitably regarded as an inferior social caste.

—Montagu, 1974[88]

The foregoing discussion has shown that although some aspects of human physical diversity have functional and evolutionary implications, this diversity is not consistent with recognition of biological racial categories. Most of the features show continuous variation that transcends conventional racial categories and poorly reflects genealogical history. Further, multiple physical features cannot be used to erect racial classifications because they are not concordant in their pattern of variation. Far from clarifying the boundaries of racial groups, genetic studies have shown little justification for their recognition. In fact, genetic analysis has shown that genetic variation among individuals within a putative racial group far exceeds variation among such groups. In other words, any two inhabitants of a region chosen at random may have less in common genetically than either does with a person from another continent.[89]

Reconstruction of patterns of human migration and genetic exchange over the past 100,000 years reveals why commonly recognized races do not represent distinct groups. Among historical factors that prevent recognition of biological races, two are central: (1) diasporic migrations that led to interchange between distantly related peoples and (2) widespread genetic intermixing between adjacent populations that prevented establishment of separate human lineages. Geographic heterogeneity may well reflect periods of isolation,[90] but intergradations between regions reveal that such isolation has never been sufficient in duration to lead to distinct lineages. For centuries, Europeans attempted to make sense of human diversity, classifying people by how they differed from themselves. The resulting categories are best viewed as constructs that largely reflect Eurocentric perspectives and sociopolitical imperatives. The categories are undeniably archaic but have survived by being adapted in accord with local sociocultural practices and to suit political ends and psychosocial needs.

If physical characteristics show a continuous (rather than discrete) geographical distribution, why do racial categories seem to work in heterogeneous countries such as the United States, where people are placed in a few distinct categories? One reason is that the U.S. population simply does not represent a cross-section of the world's diversity. Until very recently, the great majority of U.S. residents could trace ancestry to three areas of the world—Europe, western Africa, and eastern Asia.[91] Little wonder that the categories "black," "white," and "Asian" (and perhaps "native American") seemed all-inclusive.[92] Another reason is that such categories tend to be social constructs, as is evident from the method of classifying people of "mixed" background. In a pattern reminiscent of the original racial definitions, people in the United States are identified by how they differ from western European standards.

The view that races are socially constructed has striking implications. Foremost among them is that biology cannot be used to justify cultural practices and political agendas, nor the inequitable distribution of wealth, power, and access to education and medical care. We can justifiably question the validity of statistical analyses in works such as Richard Herrnstein and Charles Murray's *The Bell Curve*. However, with regard to hereditarian questions, the statistical questions are moot if the groups of people being compared represent social, not biological, categories. Herrnstein and Murray recognize the principle but ignore how fundamentally it undermines their claims about racial differences. Equally problematic is the approach taken by Dinesh D'Souza in *The End of Racism*; he notes frankly that races are undefinable and that racial classifications vary widely. Nevertheless he proceeds to adopt conventional Eurocentric social categories in his attempt to attribute putative, hereditary intellectual differences to the world's population. Such attempts could be ignored as biologically illiterate and intellectually dishonest if not for their strong influence in the political realm.[93]

A final implication to be noted has to do with human medicine.[94] If race is archaic as a biological concept, then on what possible grounds can racial designations (commonly made without the patient's input or knowledge) be used in medical diagnosis and treatment? It can be argued that even a social designation can correlate with (if not confer) biological attributes, such as hypertension in African American males. Moreover, such diagnoses can retain value in a particular sociopolitical system with known patterns of immigration. A major difficulty, however, is that a high percentage of citizens of many countries (such as the United States) have a genetic heritage not determinable from their physical appearance. The real danger lies in generalizing from North America (where much medical research is done) to the world at large, for example, generalizing from African Americans to sub-Saharan Africans or from Japanese Americans to other East Asians. The confusion of social and biological categories may well have life-and-death implications.

Clearly, "race" has meaning as a concept in social, cultural, and political contexts, and this book as a whole explores these concepts in detail. But what can be concluded about the classification of human biological diversity? Have three centuries of scientific investigation rendered the question of race biologically meaningless? The abysmal level of public discourse notwithstanding, the question has been definitively answered for some time: biologically, there is one race—the human race—in its modest variety and overwhelming commonality.

NOTES

1. J. F. Blumenbach. 1775. *On the Natural Variety of Mankind*. Reprinted in *On the Natural Varieties of Mankind: De Generis Humani Varietate Nativa*. 1969. Translated and edited by T. Bendyshe. New York: Bergman. A. Pagden. 1982. *The Fall of Natural Man: The American Indian and the Origins of Comparative Ethnology*. Cambridge: Cambridge University Press, pp. 10–26. A. Smedley. 1993. *Race in North America: Origin and Evolution of a World View*. Boulder: Westview, pp. 42–71, 150–78. J. Marks. 1995. *Human Biodiversity*. New York: DeGruyter, pp. 1–12.

2. A. Montagu. 1965. *The Idea of Race*. Lincoln: University of Nebraska Press, pp. 3–41. M. D. Biddiss, ed. 1979. *Images of Race*. New York: Holmes & Meier. S. Dubow. 1995. *Scientific Racism in Modern South Africa*. Cambridge: Cambridge University Press, pp. 20–65. H. F. Augstein. 1996. *Race: The Origins of an Idea, 1760–1850*. Bristol, U.K.: Thoemmes.

3. A. R. Wallace. 1868. "The Origin of Human Races and the Antiquity of Man Deduced from the Theory of 'Natural Selection.' " *Journal of the Anthropological Society* 2: 118–20. A. Montagu 1974. *Man's Most Dangerous Myth: The Fallacy of Race.* New York: Oxford University Press. Marks, *Human Biodiversity.* M. Wolpoff and R. Caspari. 1997. *Race and Human Evolution.* New York: Simon & Schuster.

4. Smedley, *Race in North America*, pp. 169–200.

5. H. V. Vallois. 1962. "Race." In *Anthropology Today*, edited by S. Tax, pp. 46–64. Chicago: University of Chicago Press. Smedley, *Race in North America.* Marks, *Human Biodiversity*; M. P. Banton. 1998. *Racial Theories.* 2d ed. Cambridge: Cambridge University Press. As Michael Banton observed, race "is a folk concept, a word in popular use with a significance deriving from popular understanding and varying from one historical period to another" (cited by Dubow, *Scientific Racism,* p. 17).

6. A. Montagu, ed. 1964. *The Concept of Race.* New York: Macmillan. E. Shanklin. 1994. *Anthropology and Race.* Belmont, Calif.: Wadsworth; Marks, *Human Biodiversity.*

7. T. Allen. 1994. *The Invention of the White Race: Racial Oppression and Social Control.* New York: Verso. T. Allen. 1997. *The Invention of the White Race: The Origin of Racial Oppression in Anglo-America.* New York: Verso. Smedley, *Race in North America.* Dubow, *Scientific Racism.* Marks, *Human Biodiversity.* A. F. Corcos. 1997. *The Myth of Human Races.* Lansing: Michigan State University Press. Banton, *Racial Theories.* D. E. Muir. 1997. "Race: The Mythic Roots of Racism." In *The Concept of "Race" in Natural and Social Science,* edited by E. N. Gates, pp. 93–104. New York: Garland.

8. Although concepts of biological race are commonly thought to have disappeared from anthropology and biology, they continue to guide scientific studies (S. O. Y. Keita and R. A. Kittles. 1997. "The Persistence of Racial Thinking and the Myth of Racial Divergence." *American Anthropologist* 99: 534–44). Moreover, explicit formulations of biological race have been resurrected in the sociopolitical realm worldwide (M. Kohn. 1995. *The Race Gallery: The Return of Racial Science.* London: Vintage). As just one example, hereditarian claims about IQ and race are now being used openly to justify reactionary political agendas (Dinesh D'Souza. 1994. *The End of Racism.* New York: Free Press. R. J. Herrnstein and C. Murray. 1994. *The Bell Curve.* New York: Free Press. J. P. Rushton. 1997. *Race, Evolution, and Behavior.* New Brunswick, N.J.: Transaction). Shanklin (pp. 97–119) warned that anthropologists have a responsibility to continue to expose erroneous assumptions associated with the concept of race, an admonition that applies to biologists as well. As Muir (p. 93) noted, "One of the great scandals of the 20th century has been the general failure of the scientific community to publicly disavow the concept of physiological 'race.' "

9. Dorsey, G. A. 1928. "Races and Civilization." In *Whither Mankind: A Panorama of Modern Civilization,* edited by C. Beard. New York: Longman & Greens.

10. Biddiss, *Images of Race.* Dubow, *Scientific Racism.* Augstein, *Race.* Banton, *Racial Theories.* S. Molnar. 1998. *Human Variation.* 4th ed. New Jersey: Prentice Hall.

11. C. Linnaeus. 1758. *A Taxonomy of Human Varieties.* In *Biological Anthropology.* 1998. Edited by M. A. Park, pp. 157–158. Mountain View, Calif.: Mayfield.

12. S. J. Gould. 1981. *The Mismeasure of Man.* New York: Norton. P. Bowler. 1986. *Theories of Human Evolution.* Baltimore: Johns Hopkins University Press; Dubow, *Scientific Racism,* pp. 20–65.

13. C. Darwin. 1874. *The Descent of Man, and Selection in Relation to Sex.* 1st ed. New York: Appleton, p. 218.

14. E. A. Hooton. 1946. *Up from the Ape.* New York: Macmillan. W. C. Boyd. 1950. *Genetics and the Races of Man.* Boston: Little, Brown. T. Dobzhansky. 1962. *Mankind Evolving.* New Haven: Yale University Press. W. C. Boyd. 1963. "Genetics and the Human Race." *Science* 140: 1057–65. C. S. Coon. 1965. *The Living Races of Man.* New York: Knopf. S. M. Garn. 1971. *Human Races.* Springfield, Ill.: Thomas. R. A. Goldsby. 1971. *Race and Races.* New York: Macmillan.

15. Boyd, *Genetics and the Races of Man.* C. S. Coon, S. M. Garn, and J. B. Birdsell. 1950. *Races.* Springfield, Ill.: Thomas.

16. Coon, Garn, and Birdsell, *Races,* p. 140.

17. Coon, *Origin of Races; Living Races of Man.*

18. T. Dobzhansky. 1963. "Genetic Entities in Hominid Evolution." In *Classification and Human Evolution,* edited by S. L. Washburn, pp. 347–62. Chicago: Aldine. A. Montagu. 1963. "On Coon's 'The Origin of Races.' " *Current Anthropology* 4: 361–64. Montagu, *Concept of Race.* For historical accounts, see Marks, *Human Biodiversity,* and Wolpoff and Caspari, *Race and Human Evolution,* pp. 154–72. A version that is somewhat sympathetic to Coon is offered by P. Shipman. 1994. *The Evolution of Racism.* New York: Simon & Schuster, pp. 173–221.

19. Montagu, *Man's Most Dangerous Myth.* Bowler, *Theories of Human Evolution.* Marks, *Human Biodiversity.* Wolpoff and Caspari, *Race and Human Evolution.*

20. Smedley, *Race in North America;* R. Cecil. 1972. *The Myth of the Master Race.* New York: Dodd & Mead. Montagu, *Man's Most Dangerous Myth.*

21. Smedley, *Race in North America.*

22. J. Reader. 1999. *Africa: A Biography of the Continent.* New York: Knopf. See Dubow, *Scientific Racism,* for a history of South African racial concepts.

23. Wolpoff and Caspari, *Race and Human Evolution,* p. 359.

24. L. Wright. 1994. "One Drop of Blood." *New Yorker,* July 25, 1994, pp. 46–55. Kohn, *Race Gallery,* p. 269; Muir, "Race," p. 99. The one-drop rule refers to the archaic notion that features are inherited via the blood. More technically, it can be called the principle of hypodescent, in which offspring from parents of different "races" are considered to belong to the politically subordinate category (G. A. Marshall. 1973. "Racial Classifications: Popular and Scientific." In *Man in Evolutionary Perspective,* edited by L. Brace and J. Metress, p. 366. New York: Wiley).

25. "Black" Americans are said to include Lani Guinier and Frederick Douglass (each reportedly having 50 percent European American parentage) and even Tiger Woods (who counts in his background native Americans as well as ancestors from Europe, Thailand, China, and Africa); see Wright, "One Drop," p. 47; J. Marks. 1998. "Black, White, Other." In *Biological Anthropology,* edited by M. A. Park. Mountain View, Calif.: Mayfield. Wright (p. 48) discusses recent political resistance to the erection of "multiracial" categories, as does T. Morganthau. 1995. "What Color Is Black?" *Newsweek,* February 13, 1995, pp. 63–65.

26. U.S. and European classifications of race were being rejected in the 1920s in

Brazil, where their lack of utility and racist implications were readily apparent. T. E. Skidmore. 1990. "Racial Ideals and Social Policy in Brazil, 1870–1940.' " In *The Idea of Race in Latin America, 1870–1940,* edited by R. Graham, pp. 7–36. Austin: University of Texas Press. Marvin Harris documented more than forty racial categories in use in Brazil, with no consensus as to how individuals were to be assigned (Marshall, "Racial Classifications," pp. 366–67).

27. Wright, "One Drop," p. 48. Such legal contortions occur outside the United States as well. For example, in South Africa in 1966, the Race Classification Board classified an eleven-year-old girl as "colored," although her siblings and parents were classified as "white." The nation's Supreme Court denied the petition by the parents and upheld the classification. J. C. King. 1981. *The Biology of Race.* Berkeley: University of California Press, p. 112.

28. Notwithstanding the anthropologist Ashley Montagu's long battle to replace the term "race" with "ethnic group," the former word retains deep historical and sociocultural meanings not represented by the latter, meanings that resist attempts to expunge the term from our lexicon. For discussion, see Smedley, *Race in North America,* and J. Marks. 1996. "Science and Race." *American Behavioral Scientist* 40: 123–33.

29. S. J. Gould. 1994. "The Geometer of Race." *Discover* 15, no. 11: 65–69.

30. F. Livingstone. 1963. "On the Non-Existence of Human Races." In *The Concept of Race,* edited by A. Montagu, pp. 46–67. New York: Macmillan.

31. A major difficulty in applying this concept is that aspects of human form used in racial classifications can be heavily influenced by environment—including height, weight, skin color, and even head shape. Marks, *Human Biodiversity,* p. 127; Smedley, *Race in North America,* p. 298.

32. The criterion of functionality is often difficult to apply, for several reasons. For one thing, hypotheses about adaptive functions of features often are little more than speculation, being difficult or impossible to test. See, for example, Coon, Garn, and Birdsell, *Races.* R. Carrington. 1969. *A Million Years of Man.* London: Weidenfeld & Nicholson. C. S. Coon. 1982. *Racial Adaptations.* Chicago: Nelson Hall. Most of these hypotheses date to an era in which it was fashionable to view all features as well adapted to specific functions and functional hypotheses did not have to meet criteria of testability. In addition, due to widespread migrations and gene flow during human history, features can exist in different environments altogether from those in which they arose, making it difficult to infer their original functions. Further, features can be adaptive compromises between disparate functions as well as unselected correlates of functional features (e.g., the indirect relationship between tooth size and nasal form: see below). Moreover, some physical features by which human groups differ have no known functions and may be the result of random factors like genetic drift, founder effects, and neutral mutation. Darwin (1874) sought to explain some nonadaptive features in terms of sexual selection, e.g., the ability to attract mates.

33. Marks, *Human Biodiversity.* Although widespread intermixing of human groups challenges the concept behind the term "race," some anthropologists (e.g., Wolpoff and Caspari, *Race and Human Evolution*) use the term but avoid applying it to any actual categories of humans.

34. M. M. Lahr. 1996. *The Evolution of Modern Human Diversity: A Study of Cranial Variation.* Cambridge: Cambridge University Press. C. Stringer. 1997. *African Exodus.* New York: Henry Holt. R. Lewin. 1998. *The Origin of Modern Humans.* New York: Freeman.

35. A. H. Robins. 1991. *Biological Perspectives on Human Pigmentation.* Cambridge: Cambridge University Press, p. 14.

36. Robins, *Biological Perspectives,* pp. 106–7, 191–92.

37. The tanning response is not universal in people with light skins or confined to them. Many indigenous Europeans show little or no tanning response (Robins, *Biological Perspectives,* pp. 49–51, 189–90). Moreover, sun exposure is said to account in part for the dark skin color of indigenous Australians. (L. Brace. 1964. "A Non-Racial Approach towards the Understanding of Human Diversity." In *The Concept of Race,* edited by A. Montagu, pp. 103–52. New York: Macmillan.) The relative contributions of genes and environment to coloration varies among body regions and ethnic groups (Robins, *Biological Perspectives,* pp. 23–24). Thus cavalier assumptions about the relative contributions of environment and heredity in any given population or person are risky.

38. P. L. van den Berghe and P. Frost. 1986. "Skin Color Preference, Sexual Dimorphism, and Sexual Selection: A Case of Gene Culture Co-evolution?" *Ethnic and Racial Studies* 9: 87–113. Robins, *Biological Perspectives,* pp. 112–13. Anyone convinced that skin color is useful for delineating "races" might consider the following: Is a group to be characterized by its adults or its children? its men or its women? color in summer or in winter? by body parts exposed to or shielded from the sun?

39. Brace, "Non-Racial Approach," pp. 344–49. Robins, *Biological Perspectives,* pp. 187–192.

40. Brace, "Non-Racial Approach," pp. 345–346; Robins, *Biological Perspectives,* pp. 189–95.

41. Robins, *Biological Perspectives,* pp. 195–212.

42. Brace, "Non-Racial Approach," p. 344.

43. Smedley, *Race in North America.*

44. Coon, Garn, and Birdsell, *Races,* pp. 67–71. Carrington, *Million Years,* pp. 133–34.

45. S. L. Washburn. 1964. "The Study of Race." In *The Concept of Race,* edited by A. Montagu, pp. 242–60. New York: Macmillan.

46. Coon, Garn, and Birdsell, *Races,* pp. 69–71. Evidence of the epicanthic eyelid fold appears in such a notable figure as Nelson Mandela.

47. Hooton, *Up from the Ape.* J. S. Weiner. 1954. "Nose Shape and Climate." *American Journal of Physical Anthropology* 12: 1–4. M. H. Wolpoff 1968. "Climatic Influences on the Skeletal Nasal Aperture." *American Journal of Physical Anthropology* 3: 405–24. Some writers are skeptical of this functional interpretation, e.g., Corcos, *Myth,* pp. 92–93.

48. H. H. Wilder. 1926. *The Pedigree of the Human Race.* New York: Henry Holt. Brace, "Non-Racial Approach," p. 358.

49. Wilder, *Pedigree,* pp. 316–319; Coon, *Racial Adaptations,* p. 62. Robins, *Biological Perspectives,* p. 21. Molnar, *Human Variation,* pp. 246–47.

24 *Daniel G. Blackburn*

50. Coon, Garn, and Birdsell, *Races,* pp. 59–63. Brace, "Non-Racial Approach," pp. 349–51. Coon, *Racial Adaptations,* pp. 63–64, 108.

51. Carrington, *Million Years,* p. 133.

52. Wilder, *Pedigree,* pp. 324–30. L. L. Cavalli-Sforza and F. Cavalli-Sforza. 1995. *The Great Human Diasporas: The History of Diversity and Evolution.* Reading, Mass.: Addison-Wesley, p. 10. Occasional classifications have used stature as a "racial" criterion, notably to distinguish Mbuti ("pygmies") from other Africans.

53. Corcos, *Myth,* p. 94. Molnar, *Human Variation,* p. 246.

54. J. Diamond. 1994. "Race without Color." *Discover* 15, no. 11: 82–89.

55. E. F. Moran. 1982. *Human Adaptability.* Boulder: Westview. A. R. Frisancho. 1996. *Human Adaptation and Accommodation.* Ann Arbor: University of Michigan Press.

56. Garn, *Human Races.* Coon, *Racial Adaptations.* Cf. Robins, *Biological Perspectives,* pp. 66–67.

57. P. R. Ehrlich and R. W. Holm. 1964. "A Biological View of Race." In *The Concept of Race,* edited by A. Montagu, pp. 152–79. New York: Macmillan.

58. Diamond, "Race without Color," p. 88.

59. Lahr, *Evolution of Modern Human Diversity.* Wolpoff and Caspari, *Race and Human Evolution.* Stringer, *African Exodus.* Lewin, *Origin of Modern Humans.*

60. Lahr, *Evolution of Modern Human Diversity.* Stringer, *African Exodus.*

61. E. H. Colbert and M. Morales. 1991. *Evolution of the Vertebrates.* 4th ed. New York: Wiley-Liss, p. 290.

62. L. L. Cavalli-Sforza. 1991. "Genes, People, and Languages." *Scientific American,* November, pp. 104–10. L. L. Cavalli-Sforza, P. Menozzi, and A. Piazza. 1994. *The History and Geography of Human Genes.* Princeton: Princeton University Press. Cavalli-Sforza and Cavalli-Sforza, *Great Human Disaporas.* C. G. M. Mascie-Taylor and G. W. Lasker, eds. 1988. *Biological Aspects of Human Migration.* New York: Cambridge University Press. B. Fagan 1990. *The Journey from Eden.* New York: Thames & Hudson. Lahr, *Evolution of Modern Human Diversity.* J. Diamond. 1997. *Guns, Germs, and Steel.* New York: Norton.

63. Cavalli-Sforza, Menozzi, and Piazza, *History and Geography.* Diamond, *Guns, Germs, and Steel,* pp. 376–401.

64. Coon, *Living Races of Man.*

65. B.C.E. means "before the common era" and C.E. means "common era." Although equivalent to B.C. and A.D., the former are desirable as secular terms.

66. Cavalli-Sforza, Menozzi, and Piazza, *History and Geography.* Cavalli-Sforza and Cavalli-Sforza, *Great Human Diasporas,* p. 199; Reader, *Africa.*

67. Reader, *Africa.* S. Kasule. 1998. *The History Atlas of Africa.* New York: Macmillan.

68. Coon, *Living Races of Man.* Diamond, *Guns, Germs, and Steel,* p 381.

69. Cavalli-Sforza, Menozzi, and Piazza, *History and Geography.* Cavalli-Sforza and Cavalli-Sforza, *Great Human Diasporas.*

70. Diamond, *Guns, Germs, and Steel.* J. M. Roberts. 1980. *The Pelican History of the World.* Middlesex, U.K.: Penguin Books.

71. Cavalli-Sforza and Cavalli-Sforza, *Great Human Diasporas.*

72. C. G. Turner. 1989. "Teeth and Prehistory in Asia." *Scientific American* 260: 88–96.

73. I. Rouse. 1986. *Migrations in Prehistory.* New Haven: Yale University Press. Lahr, *Evolution of Modern Human Diversity.* J. Diamond. 1998. "Japanese Roots." *Discover,* June, pp. 86–95.

74. Coon, *Living Races of Man.* Lahr, *Evolution of Modern Human Diversity.* S. Venkateswar. 1999. "The Andaman Islanders." *Scientific American,* May, 82–88.

75. Smedley, *Race in North America.* Allen, *Invention of the White Race.* The history of the "Caucasian" concept has been one of growing inclusiveness. In Linnaeus's (1758) classification of man, Europeans were characterized as having blue eyes and blond or brown hair (Park, *Biological Anthropology,* p. 158). Smedley (*Race in North America*) documents how the concepts of race evolved in North America partly to facilitate and justify the slavery of Africans by the descendants of Europeans. During the nineteenth and early twentieth centuries scholars were still dividing North American "whites" into separate racial categories (Marshall, "Racial Classifications," p. 369). Ignatiev and Brodkin respectively demonstrated how the category of "whiteness" eventually was expanded to include people of Irish and Jewish extraction. N. Ignatiev. 1995. *How the Irish Became White.* New York: Routledge. K. Brodkin. 1998. *How Jews Became White Folks and What That Says about Race in America.* New Brunswick, N.J.: Rutgers University Press.

76. R. T. Anderson. 1964. "Lapp Racial Classifications as Scientific Myths." In *The Concept of Race,* edited by A. Montagu, pp. 61–85. New York: Macmillan.

77. Cavalli-Sforza, Menozzi, and Piazza, *History and Geography.* Cavalli-Sforza and Cavalli-Sforza, *Great Human Diasporas,* p. 199.

78. Cavalli-Sforza, Menozzi, and Piazza, *History and Geography.* The notion of an "Aryan" invasion of India from the north has been strongly challenged by some archaeologists (Kohn, *Race Gallery,* p. 205).

79. M. Lefkowitz. 1996a. "Whatever Happened to Historical Evidence?" In *The Flight from Science and Reason,* edited by P. R. Gross, N. Levitt, and M. W. Lewis, pp. 301–12. New York: New York Academy of Sciences. M. Lefkowitz. 1996b. *Not Out of Africa.* New York: Basic. Ortiz de Montanallo. 1996. "Afrocentric Pseudoscience: The Miseducation of African Americans." In *Flight from Science and Reason,* pp. 561–72. By modern criteria Egypt was a multiracial society (e.g., F. M. Snowden Jr. 1970. *Blacks in Antiquity.* Cambridge, Mass.: Belknap). The anthropologist Loren Brace concluded that the "attempt to force the Egyptians into either a 'black' or a 'white' category has no biological justification" (Kohn, *Race Gallery,* p. 154).

80. Wolpoff and Caspari, *Race and Human Evolution.* Lahr, *Evolution of Modern Human Diversity.*

81. W. S. Laughlin and A. B. Harper. 1988. "Peopling of the Continents: Australia and America." In *Biological Aspects of Human Migration,* edited by C. G. N. Mascie-Taylor and G. W. Lasker, pp. 14–30. New York: Cambridge University Press. Lahr, *Evolution of Modern Human Diversity.*

82. Diamond, *Guns, Germs, and Steel.*

83. J. H. Greenberg. 1987. *Language in the Americas.* Stanford, Calif.: Stanford University Press; Cavalli-Sforza, "Genes, People, and Languages." Cavalli-Sforza, Menozzi, and Piazza, *History and Geography.* Diamond, *Guns, Germs, and Steel.* Greenberg's linguistic conclusions remain highly controversial in some quarters.

84. Mascie-Taylor and Lasker, *Biological Aspects*. G. Chaliand and J.-P. Rageau. 1995. *The Penguin Atlas of Diasporas*. Translated by A. M. Berrett. New York: Viking.

85. Garn, *Human Races*. Robins, *Biological Perspectives*, p. 176. Reader, *Africa*.

86. Wright, "One Drop." Molnar, *Human Variation*, pp. 32, 287. As always, the problem with such "mixed" designations is that their recognition is based on the false assumption that there are pure races available to mix. We can all be said to be "mixed," or even more accurately, none of us are, since biological races never existed in the first place.

87. Marshall, "Racial Classifications," pp. 364–72. Corcos, *Myth*.

88. Montagu, *Man's Most Dangerous Myth*, p. 39.

89. R. C. Lewontin. [1972] 1997. "The Apportionment of Human Diversity." In *The Concept of "Race" in Natural and Social Science*, edited by E. N. Gates, pp. 7–24. New York: Garland. Marks, *Human Biodiversity*, pp. 167–176. Stringer, *African Exodus*, pp. 181–82.

90. Lahr, *Evolution of Modern Human Diversity*.

91. Marks, *Human Biodiversity*, pp. 158–60.

92. Readers who remain skeptical that racial categories recognized in the United States and Europe are of limited value might page through Tremblay's *Families of the World* and try to classify the people illustrated into the conventional categories. (H. Tremblay. 1990. *Families of the World: Family Life at the Close of the 20th Century*. 2 vols. Camden East, Ontario: Old Bridge.)

93. The reductio ad absurdum of this approach is taken by Rushton *(Race, Evolution, and Behavior)*, who divides the world's people into three categories (Europeans, "Negroids," and "Mongoloids"), which, he claims, differ in intellectual ability and reproductive characteristics. His book fails to meet even minimal standards of scholarship; the putative "races" are routinely ranked on the basis of qualitative features that reflect his own prejudices. What few quantitative data he presents are not even analyzed statistically. Nevertheless, his work has been promoted with enthusiasm by those with reactionary political agendas.

94. E. Watts. 1981. "The Biological Race Concept and Diseases of Modern Man." In *The Concept of "Race" in Natural and Social Science*, edited by E. N. Gates, pp. 147–167. New York: Garland. R. Cooper. 1986. "The Biological Concept of Race and Its Application to Public Health and Epidemiology." *Journal of Health Politics, Policy, and Law* 11: 98–116. N. G. Osborne and M. D. Feit. 1992. "The Use of Race in Medical Research." *Journal of the American Medical Association* 267, no. 2: 275–79.

95. C. H. Smith. 1859. *The Natural History of the Human Species*. Boston: Gould & Lincoln.

2

From Eighteenth- to Nineteenth-Century Racial Science: Continuity and Change

Maurice L. Wade

The central purpose of this chapter is to shed some light on important continuities and differences among the scientific accounts[1] of human diversity in the eighteenth and nineteenth centuries. Some commentators hold that the understanding of human diversity dominant among eighteenth-century scientists was nonracial in nature and therefore that, although this understanding was undeniably riddled with bigotry, it cannot be legitimately deemed an instance of scientific racism. On this view, scientific racism gained a serious foothold only with the understanding of human variation that became dominant among nineteenth-century scientists. Only after the transformations of the eighteenth-century outlook, on this account, did a genuinely racial understanding of human difference become scientific common sense.

One of the arguments I make in this chapter is that this position is fundamentally mistaken, showing that, although the eighteenth-century understanding of human variation differed profoundly from the understanding that prevailed in the nineteenth century, in both periods human difference was understood in genuinely racial terms. Thus both periods are legitimately regarded as episodes in the history of scientific racism. I propose, in other words, that the eighteenth century was not merely the precursor of the genuinely racial science of the next century but also a genuine (and interesting) form of racial science in its own right. As the reader will see, to understand this is to grasp something of fundamental importance about the theoretical bases of scientific racism and hence of importance about how best to conduct the battle against racism on the front of theory.

27

The chapter proceeds in three main sections. The first section provides an explication and analysis of the dominant perspective on human diversity among eighteenth-century scientists. The second section turns to the same task with respect to the nineteenth century. The third section then focuses on the main differences between the two periods and explains why both ought nonetheless to be regarded as genuinely racial accounts of human difference, accounts that are differently yet fundamentally racist. (In the third section I draw on the account of racism in Kwame Anthony Appiah's *In My Father's House: African in the Philosophy of Culture.*)

I

Literate Europeans were well aware of communities of human beings strikingly different from themselves, both physically and culturally, well before efforts by scientists to develop a systematic taxonomy of human diversity. Prior to the eighteenth century, however, humans were generally sorted into three broad groupings: white Europeans, brown Asians, and black Africans.[2] All were regarded as genuinely human sorts of beings descended, according to the prevailing biblical account, from the original human pair divinely placed in the Garden of Eden. These brown and black Others, while regarded by white Europeans as their kin within the human family, were nonetheless also regarded as inferiors, an attitude they manifested in referring to them as "heathen," "savage," "barbarian," "uncivilized," and the like. Yet, for the most part, inferiority was imputed to these nonwhite, non-European peoples on the basis of their sociocultural differences and not their physical differences. Their status as heathen, savages, barbarians, and uncivilized peoples resided in their non-European mode of living. They were judged inferior because their social, cultural, and political forms were assessed on the unquestioned assumption of the clear and vast superiority of Christian European social, cultural, and political institutions and conventions.[3] This imputation of inferiority to nonwhites was therefore more a matter of cultural chauvinism, of unself-conscious Eurocentrism, than of racism.

Efforts by scientists to generate systematic and rigorous taxonomies of human types began substantively only in the eighteenth century with the various racial categorizations enunciated by Carolus Linneaus, Georges Buffon, Johann Friedrich Blumenbach, and others as part of a general effort to develop systematic and rigorous classifications of all forms of terrestrial life.[4] Despite important technical disputes over the proper system of classification, the correct number of categories of classification, and the meanings of the various terms of classification,[5] one feature common to almost all these taxonomies was their linkage of particular physical characteristics with allegedly corresponding traits of intellect, character, or mentality.[6] Human diversity was thus sorted into particular categories not simply on the basis of physical differences but also on the basis of their various "inner" attributes allegedly linked to these differences. Accordingly, each distinctive physical kind of human being was regarded as a distinctive behavioral, mental, emotional, or characterological kind as well. At least implicitly, this perspective on human variation is equivalent to conceiving of the human body as a kind of readable text, the terms of which are various bodily features and the meaning of which is constituted by the "inner" attributes of the person. To locate an individual within a particular eighteenth-century taxonomic category was thereby also to attribute a particular kind of "inner" being to her by virtue of her particular gross morphology. To correctly apprehend her outer features was thus also to read her basic "inner" personhood. Insofar as such taxonomic sorting of human diversity is legitimately regarded as racial (as I argue in the final section), the notion of race, at least within science, was never founded on the supposition that physical difference is significant in its own right. Rather, physical difference was understood to be difference with meaning, difference that signified the nature of the "inner" person.

One of the most pressing issues facing eighteenth-century scientists attempting to make sense of human variation was the question of how human beings came to be so very different in both outer and inner characteristics in the first place.[7] Adherents of two schools of thought, polygenism and monogenism, debated the answer to this question throughout the eighteenth century and well into the nineteenth century—until the debate was forever put to rest by widespread acceptance of Darwin's theory of evolution. As George Stocking notes,[8] although this debate explicitly centered on the issue of human origins, it also disputed the significance of human difference, whether these differences were to be understood as differences of degree or kind, mutable or permanent differences, dynamic or static differences, and so forth.

At least in their eighteenth-century incarnations, both of these schools of thought were constrained in their accounts of the origin of human diversity by their mutual adherence to the doctrine of the fixity of species. This is the doctrine that, as Nancy Stepan puts it, "species were created, unchanging essences"[9] or as Audrey Smedley puts it, "species were distinct primordial forms dating from creation that remained essentially the same throughout all time."[10] Both polygenists and monogenists, in line with biblical orthodoxy of the day, held that all species, including human beings, were divinely created at the dawn of earthly history and that since their all-perfect Creator made them perfectly, no species, human or otherwise, had undergone any fundamental changes since original creation, had become extinct, or had been replaced by new species.

Acceptance of this doctrine meant that two main alternatives were available for conceiving the nature of human variation within the debate over its origins. Either the various types of human beings all belong to one and the same original species—or each was originally, and remains, a distinctive species in its own right. Monogenists, including Linneaus, Buffon, and Blumenbach, argued that there is, there always was, and there always will be but one human species and that therefore human variation should be understood as variation within that species. Consequently human variation, in mind and body, was seen by the monogenists as not reaching all the way down, so to speak, to the level of human nature itself. One and the same unchanging human nature, on this outlook, is common to all varieties of human beings at all times in human history. Insofar as this understanding of human variation can be legitimately regarded as racial (as I argue in the final section of this chapter), the monogenist position entails that race is a less fundamental feature of human beings than shared species membership. The diversity of racial types does not contravene the elemental unity of humankind; basic human kinship trumps racial distinctiveness.[11] Thus monogenists conceived of their task as accounting for the origins of significant diversity within the boundaries of a single human species possessed of a single human nature. How did the descendants of Adam, by way of Noah, come to be so heterogeneous? How did members of one and the same human family develop into such a diversity of types?

Polygenic thinkers avoided the burden of explaining how the descendants of Adam became so dissimilar by supposing that not all kinds of human beings are indeed Adam's descendants. On this view, the biblical narrative of the descendants of Adam through Noah was the story of but one of several original human species. Whites alone are true descendants of Adam.[12] Other kinds of human beings were referred on this view to their own unique occasions of divine creation about which the Bible was silent. Because the polygenists, no less than their monogenic counterparts, accepted the doctrine of the fixity of species, the option of holding that multiple human species had developed from an original shared ancestor species was not available. Either one had to treat human diversity as intraspecific and acquired, as did the monogenists, or one had to regard it as both interspecific and primordial. If we take this to be a genuinely racial understanding of human diversity, then in contradistinction to their monogenic opponents, the polygenists did see racial difference as penetrating to the level of human nature itself. Each race was presumed to have its own racially specific and qualitatively distinct form of human nature. In the final analysis racial difference was supposed to be more basic than human sameness.

The polygenic point of view avoided the task of needing to explain how Adam's descendants came ultimately to be so different in both mind and body by denying that all human types could lay legitimate claim to this

Noahic lineage and by regarding human diversity as primordial. But it labored under the enormous liability of contradicting the then orthodox view of the Bible, which reported only one instance of human creation. From the vantage point of the late twentieth century, when religion impinges on scientific explanation hardly at all, the severity of this liability is easy to underestimate. Virtually everyone in eighteenth-century Europe and America, scientists and nonscientists alike, regarded the authority of the Bible on this sort of matter as beyond challenge. And virtually all polygenists attempted to argue that the notion of multiple divine creations of multiple human species did not contradict the literal biblical account. They argued that, although the Bible contained hints of these other human species (where did Cain find a wife?), it simply did not narrate the separate creations of the nonwhite races. Nonetheless, the polygenic view required such a heterodox rendering of that account that the vast majority of persons inside and outside the scientific community found it unpersuasive. Polygenesis simply strained the bounds of credibility as these were set by the orthodox reading of the Book of Genesis.[13]

How, then, did the monogenic outlook account for the seemingly great, if not elemental, variability of human kinds? In an important essay[14] Stephen Asma points out that notions of organic development in the history of scientific and philosophical thought generally divide into two principal forms—those attributing development to the "'internal' properties of self-organizing matter" and those attributing development to " 'external' environmental and ultimately adaptational forces." An internalist view asserts that an organism's characteristics and capacities are determined by the intrinsic character of the organism, by its fundamental inherent makeup, whereas an externalist view asserts that an organism's properties and abilities are the product of forces external to it, the forces of its environment.

Most adherents of the monogenic camp dominant during the eighteenth century accounted for human variation in environmental terms. They maintained that the original population of (white) humans dispersed around the globe over time and, because of this, settled into different environments (different climates, different topographies, and/or different social contexts and practices).[15] Eventually these varied settings caused these populations to diverge from their original Caucasian form and to develop distinctive syndromes of bodily traits, mental abilities, and behavioral dispositions. Hence the monogenists clearly belong within Asma's externalist camp but only with regard to those human features and capacities that constitute intraspecific difference. With regard to the fundamental specific nature shared by all humans despite such difference, the monogenists just as clearly belong to Asma's internalist camp. They saw human features and capacities that cut across such difference as rooted in the intrinsic constitution of the human species as such was established by God and/or Nature. The intraspecific variations that the monogenists viewed as the substance of human diversity were the mutable and dynamic aspects of the human body and mind; those aspects that were regarded as the substance of common human nature were taken to be immutable and static.

The eighteenth-century polygenists, for the most part, belong with their far more dominant monogenic counterparts in Asma's internalist category with respect to the nature of species. But because they equated race with species, they were internalists with regard to race, unlike their monogenic counterparts. Generally, they regarded human sameness as of no real consequence and took difference to be the immutable and static substance of human existence. For them, the distinctive traits and capacities of each human type were the outcome of the distinctive intrinsic constitution of each type. Each type was divinely fitted to a particular kind of environment, but the features specific to it were not themselves products of that environment. So the polygenists regarded human variation as a permanent and irremediable aspect of the human condition.

Most eighteenth-century taxonomies of human kinds were evaluative hierarchies as well as descriptive categorizations, that is, they were also ranking systems. Remember that these taxonomies did not simply sort human beings into categories on the basis of physical differences. They also looked to the "inner" features of the person as correlated with such differences. Hence each category did not record merely a distinctive physical type of human being but also a distinctive type of "inner" person. From the belief that human beings exhibit distinctive syndromes of interrelated physical features, nothing beyond perhaps aesthetic assessment naturally follows. But from the belief that each syndrome is itself part of a larger syndrome of linked mental, psychological, and characterological attributes, from the view that each physically distinct type of human being also has a distinct sort of mind, intellect, character, set of behavioral dispositions, and so on, the conclusion that the types also constitute a rank ordering follows readily. This is especially the case given that eighteenth-century thinkers tended to view terrestrial existence through the lens of the so-called Great Chain of Being, according to which kinds of entities form an ascending chain that begins with inorganic matter and reaches its culmination in God. For these taxonomists of human variety, the hierarchy of human types was not a product of their own evaluative judgments but part of the divinely ordained order of Nature. To descriptively classify human kinds was thus to record the divine judgment of their relative status.

If this eighteenth-century conception of human variation as intrinsically hierarchical is put together with the eighteenth-century idea of the body as a readable text, the characters of which signify the main attributes of the "inner" person, reading that text clearly would be reading an evaluation as well as a description—determining where the person with a particular bodily type stood in terms of value as a person. If the eighteenth-century view of human diversity was racial (as I claim), its notion of race was not wholly or even primarily about physical difference. Physical difference was important as a racial marker not in itself but only because it signified the makeup of the "inner" person and in so doing located her status relative to other types of human beings. In other words, the external body made visible what otherwise could not be directly inspected, those "inner" aspects that constitute personhood along with the relative ranking that is supposed to be predicated upon those attributes.

An important difference between the monogenic outlook, which held sway over the understanding of human diversity of the vast majority of eighteenth-century scientists, and its largely marginal polygenic counterpart lies in their respective understandings of the notion that human variation forms a rank ordering of human kinds. Because the polygenists equated racial difference with specific difference, they tended to see the hierarchy as one of qualitatively distinct kinds of human being whose differences reflected differing levels of human nature itself. Although it by no means entailed such a conclusion, the polygenic perspective certainly could easily facilitate the idea that the difference in worth of each type of human personhood was great enough to provide each one also with a different level of moral standing. In other words, the polygenic outlook is readily usable as support for the notion that not only are some types of human beings higher than others but that the kind of moral regard owed by members of higher types to each other is weightier than would be owed by them to members of lower types. Racial supremacist conclusions could be readily drawn from such a point of view. (Indeed this is probably one important reason that polygenism gained a far greater number of adherents in the scientific community during the nineteenth century than during the eighteenth century.) None of this is entailed by polygenism. For instance, a polygenist could argue, as some did during the eighteenth century, that the enslavement of blacks was not legitimated by God and Nature's locating them at the bottom of the hierarchy of human types.[16] Being at the bottom of this rank ordering could justify extra concern and regard just as easily as it could justify the brutalities of slavery. Neither of these attitudes to one's supposed inferiors is either entailed or logically barred by polygenism. But regarding some human types as qualitatively inferior to others certainly facilitates the belief that the moral rights of some kinds of human beings are less extensive and weighty than those of other types. Indeed, the widespread belief that nonhuman animals are our inferiors is central to the view that their moral standing is substantially lower than our own.

Although monogenism was used to support white supremacist beliefs, it does not facilitate such beliefs as readily as its polygenic competitor. (At least this is true of its eighteenth-century form, which explained human variation in externalist terms. The matter changes with the form that monogenism takes in the nineteenth century, as I explain in the next section of this chapter.) Many monogenists regarded human types as falling naturally into a hierarchy of worth, but their commitment to the unity of humankind—to the notion that all types belong to a single species sharing one and the same fundamental nature—entailed that a basic human kinship cuts across human diversity, that all types of human beings were at least potentially equal in ability and worth. The degree to which that potential was realized in a given type of human being was a matter of externalist determination, a function of the environment to which it had been subjected over the course of generations.

The inferiority or superiority of a given type of human being was thus not rooted in its essential nature but was a contingent matter based in the accidental circumstances of its environmental history. Had it possessed a different environmental history, it would have come to occupy a different position in the hierarchy of human types. Were all human beings subjected to the same environment over the course of generations, racial diversity would disappear and potential equality would become a matter of fact. Thus this view implied that the superior standing of whites did not mean that their intrinsic constitution was qualitatively different from that of nonwhites; they had been able to realize their inherent human potential more fully than nonwhites because over the generations they had had the good fortune to live in environments that enabled this result. Nonwhites had lived over the generations in environments that stunted or reversed the development of the same potential they shared as members of the same species with their white counterparts. For many monogenists, the inegalitarian consequences of human diversity did not have to be permanent. All human types had the intrinsic equipment, as members of the human species, to become white (in mind and body) and thereby to return to the original human form from which their unfortunate environmental histories had caused them to diverge. Some monogenists predicted that this is precisely what would happen to the nonwhites who had been brought into such potential-enhancing environments as a consequence of the various European voyages of discovery over the previous 250 years.[17]

Thus the dominant view in eighteenth-century scientific thinking about human diversity sorted human beings into distinct types forming a hierarchy of relative worth. Even though they share one and the same intrinsic constitution, over the course of history some existed in environments that enabled fuller realization of their human potential while others existed in less felicitous environments. Accordingly, human diversity and the inequality that often accompany it are not necessary features of the human situation. All nonwhite and therefore inferior types of human beings could, in principle, become white and so realize their inherent human potential to its fullest extent.

II

The debate between monogenists and polygenists continued well into the nineteenth century, until Darwin's theory of evolution became widely accepted among scientists concerned with human variation. The nineteenth-century debate differed significantly in that polygenism moved from the radically marginal place it had occupied during the eighteenth century to center stage in the nineteenth century debates over how best to understand human difference.[18] (Indeed, in the antebellum United States, the polygenic perspective achieved near dominance within the scientific community.) Furthermore, during the nineteenth century the monogenic view of human diversity (as opposed to its origins) changed dramatically. The monogenists themselves, for the most part, while disagreeing with the polygenists over how this diversity began, did not disagree substantively with them about its character and significance.[19] What caused the monogenist–polygenist debate to change?

The answer to this question lies partly in the world beyond the debate itself. European nations had extended their reach around the globe and in the process had managed to bring much of it under their sovereign control. This typically meant the subjugation of the nonwhite peoples of these non-European lands, often against their violent resistance. An explosion of technological innovation and sophistication occurred in both the United States and Europe that played no small part in the ability of European powers to conquer and control the lands of most of the nonwhite peoples of the world with such apparent ease.[20] These factors and more coalesced to give whites a sense of unrivaled superiority among the world's peoples, a sense that the differences in capacity and ability between whites and nonwhites signified by their differences in bodily features were far greater and deeper than the monogenic understanding of human variation dominant in the eighteenth century recognized. To the majority of eighteenth-century monogenists these differences, which had once seemed to be differences of degree overlying a fundamental sameness of kind now, however, seemed to be more far-reaching. Of course, these differences continued to be understood as inequalities and as composing a hierarchy of human kinds. Yet these inequalities seemed now far too significant not to be permanent facts of Nature rather than the nonelemental outcomes of the different environmental histories of different sorts of human beings.

These and other social and political factors exerted genuine influence on nineteenth-century scientific thinking about the nature of human diversity.

But another factor is more relevant for this discussion—the loss of credibility by the externalist explanation of diversity that had previously dominated scientific thinking. The nineteenth-century rise of polygenism from its formerly marginal position in scientific thought can be legitimately attributed to the success of its proponents in attacking the notion that the sources of human diversity were located in the environmental history of the various human kinds.

Central to the polygenic attack on the externalist explanations offered by the eighteenth-century version of monogenism was the increasing use of the techniques and instrumentalities of anthropometry, the scientific measurement of human bodies. Although Buffon, Blumenbach, and others had gathered seemingly objective data on human diversity during the eighteenth century, particularly by means of cranial measurements of one kind or another, their anthropometric efforts were extremely modest in comparison to the veritable obsession with bodily measurement, with the greatest attention going to various kinds of cranial measurements, in both Europe and the United States during the nineteenth and well into the twentieth century.[21] (Anthropometry played an important role in Nazi efforts to generate "objective" proof of the superiority of the so-called Aryan race.) In the nineteenth century anthropometric data were used to argue, against monogenic externalism, that the time span of planetary history simply was not long enough for environmental production of human variation to have occurred in the way that was alleged by eighteenth-century monogenists.

Polygenists of the nineteenth century, along with their monogenic competitors, assumed, for instance, that greater cranial capacity signified higher-quality "inner" traits, that greater cranial capacity signified traits such as greater intelligence, more highly developed moral sensibilities, greater capacity for postponement of gratification, a more refined capacity for aesthetic judgment, and the like. Cranial capacity was thus believed to be an important objective basis for sorting human beings into a hierarchy of types. And, sure enough, anthropometric investigations found the largest cranial capacities among whites and the lowest among blacks, with other nonwhite races arrayed between the two extremes.[22] (Although these findings were reported in the earliest stages of nineteenth-century anthropometric investigation into human difference, later investigations were increasingly unable to replicate them or other efforts to sort human beings into objective anthropometric categories.)[23] Supposing that these bodily differences were in fact correlated with skin color and did accurately reflect intellectual ability and other significant "inner" characteristics, nineteenth-century polygenists argued that they could not have been produced environmentally, first, because anthropometric comparison of ancient skulls with contemporary ones showed these differences to have been present at the dawn of recorded human history. Thus the differentiation of human beings into distinct types had occurred some thousands of years ago and had persisted unchanged since. Accepting Archbishop James Ussher's biblically based contention that the earth itself was but a few thousand years old, they argued, second, that the span of planetary history simply was too short for differences with such antiquity to have been produced environmentally. There had not been enough time for an originally homogenous population of (white) humans to have dispersed around the globe and to have lived enough generations in their different environments for diversity of this antiquity to have originated, as the externalism of the eighteenth-century monogenists declared.[24]

Yet another polygenic argument against externalist accounts of the origins of human variation was particularly compelling to their nineteenth-century monogenic counterparts. Polygenists argued that if human difference had been environmentally produced, it ought to be environmentally reversible. If blacks, for instance, had the same human potential that whites had but had been unable to realize it as fully or had suffered some type of developmental decline because of the misfortune of generations of living in unfavorable conditions, then removal to favorable conditions ought over time to turn them white in both body and mind—as some eighteenth-century and some early nineteenth-century monogenists had predicted. Unfortunately for the proponents of externalist explanations of human variation, relevant evidence did not support these predictions. Although some blacks had lived in a European environment (in terms of topography, climate, and social context) for several generations, no exemplars of such transformation had been produced. If the reversion to original type—the metamorphosis of nonwhites into whites—did not occur after several generations of life under the appropriately felicitous environmental circumstances, then externalism was thereby falsified. Holding on to the externalist account of human diversity and the inequality that it supposedly constituted thus became untenable for nineteenth-century monogenists who took seriously the available evidence.[25]

Although the authority of the account of human origins narrated in the Book of Genesis had declined somewhat among scientists in the nineteenth century, that authority was still formidable. Many polygenists (certainly not all) continued to feel constrained to argue that their account of human origins did not conflict with the biblical account, strictly speaking. And many other scientists simply could not or would not countenance an explanation of human origins not in accord with the biblical version and so remained committed to a monogenic account of human origins.[26] (Commentators have noted that defenders of racial slavery outside the scientific community in the American South prior to the Civil War found polygenism simply too repugnant to accept even while recognizing its obvious advantages for their cause.) But those who remained within the monogenic camp for this reason could not appeal to it to refute the apparent failure of nonwhite types of human beings to become white even when living in the appropriate external conditions over the course of several generations. If the conditions that supposedly enabled human potential to be expressed to its fullest did not have this result for nonwhite types of human beings, then even if those types had originated from the same ancestors as whites, even if they too were authentic descendants of Noah and thereby true sons and daughters of Adam, then the conclusion that nonwhite humans were not equal to whites even in potential seemed irresistible even within the monogenic framework.

Although monogenic thinkers persisted in the notion that all types of human beings were types within a single species (that human diversity was intraspecific rather than interspecific), they also began to accept that this diversity was immutable, as their polygenic competitors had claimed all along. This meant that for both monogenic and polygenic thinkers in the nineteenth century, the hierarchy of human types was a permanent feature of the human situation. Inequality of human types, unchangeable differences in both body and mind, was now regarded as beyond alteration by human efforts. But ultimately the polygenic attack on the monogenic belief that human difference originated in the environmental histories of the various human kinds was itself defeated.

Two developments finally put to rest the polygenic claim that human diversity could not have been due to external forces in human history. First, developments within geology proved that Archbishop Ussher's biblically based calculation of the age of the Earth was off by many millions of years. This meant that, even if the polygenic argument that human differences had persisted unchanged over several thousand years was correct, the planet's history was sufficiently long for these differences to have originated from environmental forces. Second, Darwin's theory of evolution provided an account of organic development that undermined the doctrine of the fixity of species and made it possible to regard differences as both significant and acquired. Monogenists thus had reasons outside of religion for holding on to the belief that all types of humans had originated from the same ancestors, since Darwinism traced all life back to the same ultimate source and explained how the current diversity of life could derive from it.[27]

But polygenic thinking remained influential, even with the advent of Darwin's theory of evolution. Although the notion that human diversity was the outcome of multiple creations of multiple human species was no longer tenable, diversity was now regarded as a product of environmental forces that was beyond remediation. The account of the origin of diversity was externalist, but the diversity itself was regarded by most late nineteenth-century scientists as having become permanent, at least within the limits of a time scale that is humanly practicable. Each type of human being was a member of one and the same human species, but each type was qualitatively different within that species. The kind of difference that polygenism had understood human diversity to be was now regarded as intraspecific. The notion of qualitatively different kinds of human beings was now simply transferred within the boundaries of the human species. One way to conceptualize this notion is to think of each human sort as having the same inherent potential as every other human sort; whereas the white sort had developed that potential to its fullest, the other sorts had not and were now permanently fixed in their condition of mental and bodily retardation. Although human diversity was viewed as an acquired aspect of the human situation, it had become permanent as a result of different external forces acting on different human populations occupying different regions of the planet. Within one and the same human species there came to be a multiplicity of human types, each with a qualitatively distinct form of human nature.[28] Difference could trump sameness, even sameness of species, on this nineteenth-century version of monogenism, a position that would have been unthinkable for the externalism of its eighteenth-century precursor.

III

This is undoubtedly the most significant point of discontinuity between eighteenth- and nineteenth-century scientific thinking about human variation. Whereas the dominant perspective in the eighteenth century took such variation to be acquired but reversible, it was regarded in the nineteenth century as either primordial and therefore irreversible or as acquired and irreversible. Whereas the dominant perspective in the eighteenth century envisioned the realization of equality as humanly possible, the nineteenth century took the hierarchy of human types to be, in the final analysis, impervious to human efforts to undo it. Racial dominance came to be regarded as a permanent fact; the supposed feats of whites around the world and throughout history stood as evidence that whites were destined by nature to be superior to all nonwhite types of human beings.

Perhaps the most significant point of continuity between the two centuries is that the nineteenth century assumed the eighteenth-century view that each human type was different from every other human type in both mind and body and thus shared with it the implicit notion of the body as a readable text in which bodily features are characters whose meaning expresses the various "inner" traits linked with them. Given the discontinuity addressed above, however, from the eighteenth-century point of view this means that what was being read could be altered. From that perspective, the perfect text of whiteness was attainable for the whole species. By contrast, for the nineteenth century, each bodily type was a permanent text with its own permanently unique meaning. For the nineteenth-century scientists of human diversity, then, reading the human body was reading something of the very structure of the immutable human condition.

Small wonder, then, that such reading became a matter of far greater importance than it had been in the previous century and that nineteenth-century scientists became obsessed with objectivity and accuracy in that reading—and thus also obsessed with development and deployment of anthropometric techniques and tools. Insofar as the nature of the "inner" personhood of each type of human being could be directly, as well as objectively and accurately, inspected by anthropometric methods and instruments, the hierarchy of human types could be articulated in a more finely grained manner than with the unaided human eye. This led to the notion that even within the white type higher and lower types existed whose relative position among whites could be established by means of anthropometric inspection.[29] (Such inspections were, as is well known, used to scrutinize would-be American citizens who came from southern and eastern Europe rather than from the northern and western regions from which the original white colonizers of the continent came.)

In the introduction to this chapter I noted that a number of contemporary commentators do not regard the monogenic perspective dominant among eighteenth-century scientists as constituting a racial perspective and thereby regard it as merely a precursor to the genuinely racial science of the following century.[30] Apparently these thinkers equate the notion of race with the doctrine that Anthony Appiah refers to as "racialism" in his analysis of the nature of racism.[31] Racialism holds that the physical, psychological, and cultural characteristics of each race are linked together and are mutually determined by a distinctive set of heritable traits and tendencies constituting a racial essence. Appiah correctly notes, I think, that the doctrine of racialism is not necessarily a racist doctrine. In principle one could hold that the definitive characteristics of each race are determined by an underlying racial essence without also holding that the races thereby constitute a hierarchy of moral standing. Appiah also claims that any racist doctrine is also necessarily a racialist doctrine. In other words, he claims that the position that the races constitute a hierarchy of moral standing presupposes the claim that each race has its particular bodily, mental, and behavioral characteristics by virtue of an underlying racial essence.

For these commentators, what is missing in the monogenic rendering of human difference in the eighteenth century that is clearly present in nineteenth-century understandings of human difference appears to be a commitment to the doctrine that Appiah calls racialism. Hence (or so the reasoning of these writers seems to go) eighteenth-century monogenists simply did not have a genuine concept of race—simply did not conceptualize human variation in racial terms. It is unquestionably true that the nine-teenth-century view of human diversity was rooted in the notion of racial-ism. Their notion of race was quite explicitly essentialist. It seems equally clear that eighteenth-century monogenism was not rooted in the notion of racialism and that its notion of human diversity was clearly not essentialist. Thus to deny that the eighteenth-century monogenic understanding of human variation was not racial because it was not racialist in Appiah's sense is to hold that such an understanding is not racial because it is not essential-ist. To equate the notion of race with commitment to the doctrine of racial-ism and thereby to hold that a notion of human difference is racial only if it is also essentialist is a mistake. Why? Isn't this simply a matter of semantics, a matter of these commentators simply using one among the possible defini-tions of race?

No, it is not. And the reason lies in the continuity between the eigh-teenth-century monogenic understanding of human diversity and nine-teenth-century racial science. In both cases, at least implicitly, the human body is conceived of as a readable text. Particular clusters of bodily attri-butes are assumed to be stably linked with "inner" attributes like intelli-gence, moral character, and behavioral proclivities. These attributes can then be taken to signify those very traits, and so the features of "inner" personhood, which cannot be directly inspected, can be read off the very bodies of their possessors. Commitment to the notion that phenotype sig-nifies the type of one's personhood is the core element of the notion of race. This commitment is common to eighteenth-century monogenism and nineteenth-century understandings of human variation alike. The two periods differ in that the former did not regard the multiplicity of syn-dromes of bodily and inner traits that compose a multiplicity of bodily texts as necessarily a permanent feature of the human situation. Hence it is quite understandable that during this period these syndromes were not given the attention or degree of explanatory prominence that they would receive in the nineteenth century, when they were regarded as permanent features of the human condition. The nonessentialist conception of race thus attrib-uted to eighteenth-century monogenism is not likely to have the kind of importance for understanding human variation that an essentialist concep-tion would have.

Does it matter if the notion of race is limited to its essentialist form (which is done by the commentators who deny that eighteenth-century monogenism is a form of racial science)? It matters because to do so is to think that the battle against the theoretical underpinnings of racism (not at all equivalent to the battle against its practical manifestations outside the realm of theory) is a battle against racialism alone. Thus the commitment shared by racialism and the nonessentialist conception of race alike—the commitment to the notion that the "inner" person is displayed in type by the individual's gross morphology—would be left unopposed. This is the notion that fundamentally sustains racism within the domain of theory, irrespective of whether that notion is rendered in essentialism form as in racialism, as understood by Appiah, or in nonessentialist form as in eighteenth-century monogenism.

Furthermore, commitment to the view that the "inner" person is directly knowable through his phenotype can facilitate morally repugnant results whether or not that commitment takes an essentialist form. Remember that these inner traits are ones that have historically been regarded as relevant to the moral assessment of persons and to other types of evaluative assessments of persons. Such assessments ground views about what kind of treatment of others is morally permissible or obligatory. If the reading of personhood through gross morphology reveals a hierarchy of human kinds, as was claimed in both the eighteenth and nineteenth centuries, then at its extreme, it can be appealed to in order to justify the belief that some human beings have little or no moral standing at all and thus justify their domination or mistreatment by others.

This is not to say that there is no moral difference between essentialist and nonessentialist racism. On the essentialist view, human inequality cannot be remediated; it can be eliminated only by physical destruction of all but one of the several qualitatively distinct human types. Equality is achievable through genocide. On the nonessentialist view, human inequality is remediable but only through the transformation of nonwhites into whites. This endorses a form of genocide in its own right but one that does not have the murderous implications of physical destruction of all supposedly inferior human types.

NOTES

1. The notion of science assumed in this chapter is sociological in nature. Science is assumed to be what is practiced by persons who are recognized as and recognize each other as scientists. No particular position on what is or is not genuine scientific methodology is assumed.

2. Graham Richards, *"Race," Racism, and Psychology: Towards a Reflexive History* (London: Routledge, 1997), 1.

3. H. F. Augstein, *Introduction to Race: The Origins of an Idea, 1760–1850*, ed. H. F. Augstein (Bristol, U.K.: Thoemmes, 1996), xi; Nicholas Hudson, "From 'Nation' to 'Race': The Origin of Racial Classification in Eighteenth-Century Thought," *Eighteenth-Century Studies* 29, no. 3 (1996).

4. James Sydney Slotkin, ed., *Readings in Early Anthropology* (New York: Wenner-Gren Foundation for Anthropological Research, 1965), 175–221.

5. Jonathan Marks, *Human Biodiversity: Genes, Race, and History* (New York: Aldine de Gruyter, 1995), 6–10.

6. Audrey Smedley, *Race in North America: Origin and Evolution of a Worldview*, 2d ed. (Boulder: Westview, 1999), 158–67.

7. Augstein, *Introduction to Race*, xii.

8. George Stocking, *Race, Culture, and Evolution: Essays in the History of Anthropology* (New York: Free Press 1968), 45.

9. Nancy Stepan, *The Idea of Race in Science: Great Britain, 1800–1960* (Hamden, Conn.: Archon, 1982), 36.

10. Smedley, *Race in North America*, 160.

11. Kenan Malik, *The Meaning of Race: Race, History, and Culture in Western Society* (New York: New York University Press 1996), 48, 53.

12. Thomas Gossett, *Race: The History of an Idea in America* (New York: Schocken, 1965), 44–51.

13. Gossett, *Race*, 51.

14. Stephen Asma, "Metaphors of Race: Theoretical Perspectives behind Racism," *American Philosophical Quarterly* 32, no. 1 (January 1995): 13.

15. Richard H. Popkin, "The Philosophical Bases of Modern Racism," in *Philosophy and the Civilizing Arts: Essays Presented to Herbert W. Schneider*, ed. Craig Walton and John P. Anton (Athens: Ohio University Press, 1974), 134–39.

16. Henry Home [Lord Kames], "Preliminary Discourse, Concerning the Origin of Men and Languages," in *Race: The Origins of an Idea, 1760–1850*, ed. H. F. Augstein (Bristol, U.K.: Thoemmes, 1996), 10–23.

17. Augstein, *Introduction to Race*, xv; Popkin, "Modern Racism," 134–39.

18. Gossett, *Race*, 58.

19. Ibid., 54; George Fredrickson, *The Debate on Afro-American Character and Destiny, 1817–1914* (New York: Harper & Row, 1971), 83.

20. Richards, *Racism and Psychology*, 2.

21. John S. Haller, *Outcasts from Evolution: Scientific Attitudes of Racial Inferiority, 1859–1900*, reprint ed. (Carbondale: Southern Illinois University Press, 1995). This volume is an excellent, comprehensive account of the nineteenth-century obsession with anthropometry.

22. Gossett, *Race*, 59–78.

23. Malik, *Meaning*, 120.

24. Fredrickson, *Black Image*, 74–75.

25. Banton, *Racial Theories*, 55.

26. Haller, *Outcasts*, 78; Gossett, *Race*, 66; Fredrickson, *Black Image*, 64.

27. Richards, *Racism and Psychology*, 13.

28. Stocking, *Culture*, chap. 6; Haller, *Outcasts*, xiii; Malik, *Meaning*, 88–91; Richards, *Racism and Psychology*, 14.

29. Jacobson, *Whiteness*, 46; Gloria Marshall, "Racial Classifications: Popular and Scientific," in *The Racial Economy of Science: Toward a Democratic Future*, ed. Sandra Harding (Bloomington: Indiana University Press 1993), 122–24.

30. Michael Banton, *Racial Theories*, 2d ed. (Cambridge: Cambridge University Press, 1998), 5; Matthew Frye Jacobson, *Whiteness of a Different Color: European Immigrants and the Alchemy of Race* (Cambridge: Harvard University Press, 1998), 32; Malik, *Meaning*, 51–54; Augstein, *Introduction to Race*, xviii.

31. Anthony Appiah, *In My Father's House: Africa in the Philosophy of Culture* (Oxford: Oxford University Press, 1992), 13–14.

3

The Meaning of "Race": Psychology's Troubled History

Dina L. Anselmi

> *The Negro is a sort of seventh son, born with a veil, and gifted with second-sight in this American world,—a world which yields him no true self-consciousness, but only lets him see himself through the revelation of the other world. It is a peculiar sensation, this double-consciousness, this sense of always looking at one's self through the eyes of others, of measuring one's soul by the tape of a world that looks on in amused contempt and pity. One ever feels his two-ness—an American, a Negro; two souls, two thoughts, two unreconciled strivings; two warring ideals in one dark body, whose dogged strength alone keeps it from being torn asunder. (p. 5)*

W. E. B. DuBois wrote these words in 1903 in his elegant treatise *The Souls of Black Folks*. In it he brilliantly laid out the problem of the dual identity experienced by many black Americans as a consequence of a history of racism. In many ways, DuBois's analysis prefigured the social constructionist view of race, the idea that racial categories reflect superficial physical distinctions that are emphasized because of specific social and political power arrangements rather than underlying stable characteristics of individuals.[1] As a discipline, psychology has been slow to incorporate the social constructionist perspective in its study of phenomena related to "race." Historically, the mainstream theories in social and personality psychology have paid little attention to concepts such as dual identity, assuming instead that the structure of personality development follows a universal path (Gaines and Reed 1995).[2] The effects of social, cultural, and historical factors like prejudice and racism on an individual's sense of identity are beginning to make their way into mainstream theorizing about personality and its development. This is not to imply that psychologists have ignored questions pertaining to prejudice and racism. There is a long tradition of research on prejudice, beginning with G. Allport's (1958) influential work *The Nature of Prejudice*, in which he articulated a view of prejudice that has its etiology in the hostile or stereotyped mental categorizations of individuals. Allport's explanation of prejudice operates at the level of the individual, emphasizing an individual's faulty mental processes (Gaines and Reed 1995). Even the classic work on identity formation among African American children by K. B. Clark and M. P. Clark (1939) focused on children's internalization of a racially segregated society. Although the study of prejudice and identity formation within the individual has been influential in psychology, structural factors such as the family, education, and socioeconomic class, which influence individual variations within racial groupings, have been given much less attention.

An emerging view within psychology that is based on contemporary feminist theorizing argues that an individual's sense of identity is a dynamic entity that not only can change in different contexts but is shaped by the responses of others to the individual (Unger 1995). It can be argued that a paradigmatic shift in the discipline's approach to the study of identity formation is occurring partly as a result of the impact of this feminist scholarship, which has provided a challenge to the conceptualization of sex and gender as static and ahistorical. In the analysis of sex and gender, feminist psychologists have emphasized the difference between sex as a subject variable (seen most clearly in the study of sex differences) and sex as a stimulus variable (studying how others respond based on their perceptions of our individual characteristics) as a way of identifying the social nature of sex and gender (Unger 1979). Recognizing sex as a stimulus variable is significant in shifting the study of identity to recognize factors both within individuals (e.g., their understanding of themselves as male or female) and factors outside them (e.g., the expectations, values, and attitudes held by others toward males or females). The latter idea is similar to DuBois's claim that black Americans are forced to see themselves through the eyes of mainstream white Americans, a vantage point that in our society endows "nonwhiteness" with an inherently negative meaning. Race as a category of analysis reflects the social, cultural, and political processes (especially racial subjugation) that both create the meaning we attach to certain categories (e.g., white vs. nonwhite) and privilege certain groups (e.g., whites) whose identity may then never be brought into question.

This chapter is at once an explication and a critique of psychology's failure to appreciate the type of insight expressed in DuBois's analysis of double consciousness; it is also a call for psychology to examine the construct of race in ways that utilize the lessons of feminist scholarship. My contention is that the psychological literature still lacks a systematic analysis of exactly what "race" means, with all the corollary issues that would surround that discussion. Most significantly missing is a social constructionist framework similar to that used in feminist analyses of sex and gender issues. This framework would lead researchers to interrogate "race" as a meaningful psychological construct. This task is urgent, given the analytical naïveté traditionally employed by most psychologists and especially in light of the conclusion of many anthropologists and biologists that there is little or no biological basis for classifying individuals in terms of racial markers such as pigmentation (Montagu 1964; Cooper and David 1997; Blackburn in this volume). So too D. Hull (1998) convincingly argues that any systematic classifications of groups beyond the level of a species has no biological validity. Moreover, researchers have shown that variations within groups of individuals of similar phenotypic "racial" qualities are far greater than variations among supposed "racial" groups (Lewontin 1977).

Much of psychology's focus on race has been to use it as a subject variable in research. While this might superficially circumvent the problem of having to define race (reminiscent of psychometricans claiming that intelligence was what IQ tests measured), the use of race as a subject variable creates a host of unexamined problems. The categorization of people into racial groups represents an implicit essentialist view of race in which the search for explanations of differences among groups relies on beliefs about characteristics distinguishing one group from another, often expressed in the form of biological superficialities. For example, not only the early research on racial differences in intelligence but also the recent formulation by R. J. Herrnstein and C. Murray (1994) emphasize the search for biological differences among racial groups. These arguments are offered despite the substantial evidence that such racial groupings have no biological basis.

The act of creating categories that utilize race as a subject variable inevitably leads to such essentialist reasoning. By examining some of the questions that feminists have raised about the constructs of sex and gender, we might come to recognize the socially constructed and fluid nature of identity, as seen, for example, in the different meanings of being an African American male who is simultaneously a highly educated professional and a driver on New Jersey highways subjected to repeated "pullovers" by police using racial profiling. Although fraught with methodological and conceptual difficulties, there are ways in which research in psychology can help us understand more about what racial identity means to individuals in a complex and dynamic universe of interpersonal relationships and social and cultural institutions. Psychologists, for example, have spent significant effort trying to understand how individuals come to define themselves in many different dimensions. In these terms, "race," as well as ethnicity, cultural identity, age, or gender, contributes to explaining why individuals form or develop certain identities instead of serving as evidence of inherent characteristics that distinguish groups of individuals. The study of racial and ethnic

48 *Dina L. Anselmi*

identity formation represents a way psychologists can move beyond the practice of using race as a subject variable to studying race as a stimulus-variable by providing a comprehensive analysis of how individuals often exist in multiple spaces and varying places.

According to G. Richards (1997), certain recent critiques of the concept of race have been aware of problems inherent in the definition of race but have nonetheless continued to regard it as a scientific construct. For example, M. Zuckerman (1990) acknowledges the difficulties of definition and sampling in the use of racial groupings and raises questions about the ethical implications of such research on policy decisions. Yet he maintains that "the question of whether racial studies are racist largely depends on the quality of the research and the reasonableness of the deductions" (p. 1302). Similarly, A. Yee, H. Fairchild, F. Weizmann, and G. Wyatt (1993) review the theoretical and empirical pitfalls in the use of race in psychological work, showing that most definitions of race amount to little more than common stereotypes. Their conclusions about how to address psychology's problems with race focus on developing a scientific definition of race and providing guidelines for its use by researchers. Their solution ironically appears to seek scientific validation for a concept that their own analysis shows to be vacuous. Finally, H. Betancourt and S. Lopez (1993) illustrate how psychological studies that confuse culture with race and ethnicity render questionable many of the conclusions of such work. While recognizing the problem of generalizing from racial or ethnic grouping, especially without consideration of cultural and social variables, Betancourt and Lopez call on researchers to define, measure, and specify any racial variables under consideration. All of these researchers identify serious problems in the practice of racial groupings but assume that they will be solved by a more rigorous scientific definition of "race." None of these critiques take seriously the possibility that racial classifications are inherently unstable because race has fluid social and political meanings. Part of the reluctance to abandon "race" as a scientific construct in terms of racial classifications may be related to psychology's view of itself as an empirical science modeled on the positivism of physics. In this view, any scientific claim made must conclude in empirical observation, with specific assertions always defined quantitatively. Racial classifications seem to serve these reductionist goals, allowing for simplistic causal arguments although their conclusions are clearly not justified.

Of course, I do not mean to imply that even though racial categories have no scientific significance, they do not have important cultural significance (Dupre 1998). Like categories of gender, membership in certain racial groups will significantly affect how one is treated by others and how one's identity develops as a result of various kinds of social interaction. Although not "biologically real," these categories nonetheless have a hold on how individuals think and act, in addition to informing social and political structures. How one experiences oneself in relationships with others makes these categories experientially real. This is why race, like gender, can be meaningfully studied as a stimulus variable. Think for a moment of how traumatic it often is for liberal white parents in the United States to learn that a son or daughter is romantically involved with a black person. Reactions of this type signal the hold that racial categorizing has on us despite the evidence of its biological groundlessness.

Researchers have begun to address the dilemma of why the classification of people seems to occur so readily. D. Hull (1998), like several other theorists, claims that classification is a basic human cognitive process. He concludes from this that essentialism emerges as a key assumption of taxonomic systems. Based on his studies of children, L. Hirschfeld (1996, 1997) offers an interesting elaboration of this notion. He claims that children categorize race as if it were a natural entity. By "natural," he implies that perceptibility of race seems to appear in all individuals (children and adults alike) as one taxonomy among many (e.g., sex would be another) that helps give order to the world. Children come to naturalize and essentialize race as an immutable quality of themselves and others. Although Hirschfeld does not believe that the naturalism of race arises because it is a real or biologically valid phenomenon, he proposes a type of psychological essentialism based on the idea that things that look alike tend to share properties in common. Hirschfeld explicitly contends that children's view of race is not racist insofar as the child does not automatically acquire racial meanings that have normative evaluations but that the naturalness of race allows for the ready acquisition of social stereotypes. Such information becomes a part of the categorizing system to which children are naturally predisposed. While the social stereotypes exist as part of larger historical and cultural systems of power, the processes by which children come to impose order on the world facilitate their attachment to racial categories. His claim opposes those who have suggested that race becomes a salient factor in people's consciousness as a result of racism. For Hirschfeld, race is not a cognitive construct but is the result of one. Its resilience lies in the fact that it is "inferentially rich." According to Hirschfeld (1995), "Human beings did not construct racial categories simply because they provide a discursive reconciliation of relations of power and authority. Instead, I suggest, race was taken up as a category of power in part because of its unique characteristics as a *category of the mind*" (p. 188). This view differs from most social constructionist perspectives, which posit that political and social institutions determine and maintain racial differentiation in access to power (Omi and Winant 1994).

Insofar as Hirschfeld views the child's perception of race as a natural phenomenon, based on a quest to give order to a complex world, he may have a problem explaining why children in societies with differing constructions of race come to "naturally" adopt the prevailing racial taxonomies. For instance, in apartheid South Africa, would children have had a natural propensity to view a brown-skinned individual as colored as opposed to a white or black South African? Conversely, would children in the United States, when viewing the same brown-skinned individual identity, him as black? If Hirschfeld argues that children can only see differences between white and black, then he has simply theorized the ways that children group individuals according to skin color. But if this is what he has done, his theory is far less ambitious than he suggests (Hirschfeld 1997), and we might ask if Hirschfeld is studying "race" at all.

Moreover, Hirschfeld's theory seems not to account adequately for the many situations in which skin color simply does not reflect supposed racial differences. Racial identity in the United States was never solely defined by skin color, since racial designations are legal and social constructions. Children can easily confuse the racial designations of the light-skinned black and the darker-skinned white. At some point in their understanding of "race," children must learn that there are black Americans who look white but are not legally white. A critical question for Hirschfeld's theory is, Why do children not abandon their natural tendency to racially categorize once they become aware of this "racial" complexity? Although critics of his work offer widely diverging assessments of it,[3] his theory appears to represent a major contribution to psychology's approach to the study of "race." Since it circumvents the quagmire of essentialism, it offers one promising strategy toward an explanation of the pervasiveness and resilience of racial classification.

Psychology's present troubles with the concept of race can be partly traced to the scientific racism that appeared during the nineteenth century (Tucker 1994; Wade, this volume). Moreover, there is considerable evidence of a history of racist research in psychology both in America and in Europe (Richards 1997). Study of the linkage between race and intelligence is certainly one area in which many psychologists conducted studies with the goal of showing the inferiority of certain racial groups. Most readers are probably familiar in a general way with the contentiousness of the debate concerning the empirical data used to support such conclusions (Gould 1984). Although I am not able here to review the history of the debate about IQ and race, that debate has shown clearly that researchers do not engage in their work independently of their own cultural and historical contexts. They are therefore not immune to the effects of societal racism. How psychologists framed questions of intelligence, for example, tells us a great deal about how they conceptualized "race" as a category of study. At the most basic level, we can ask why anyone should study racial groups in relationship to intelligence to begin with. Why not focus on eye or hair color or athleticism, for example? What explicit or implicit assumptions about different groups, as marked by their skin color, were researchers in the United States carrying around with them? The study of racial differences in intelligence emerged from a segregated society that in its social organization provided abundant support for the unexamined belief that studying racial groups somehow made sense. It is interesting to note that intelligence is only one psychological phenomenon that researchers have associated with racial differences and, by inference, with racial inferiority: other phenomena include aggression, criminality, sexuality, and psychopathology (Zuckerman 1990).

The phenomena that psychologists have chosen to study in relationship to racial categories shows the extent to which psychology and all social scientists are influenced not only by political and social arguments but by the political and social arrangements in which they live. Race becomes an important area to study because race is significant in U.S. society. Moreover, to the degree that racial groups display differences in behaviors defined as problematic in the society, race becomes an obvious and easy-to-measure variable. Such reasoning, however, amounts to a tautology. For instance, if statistics show that blacks commit more street crimes than whites, some researchers immediately attribute a causal linkage between blackness and criminal activity. But this uncritical analysis of correlational evidence is not universally applied. If, for instance, evidence showed that whites engage in more embezzlement or illegal stock dealings than blacks, "whiteness" would hardly be given as the explanation for this finding.

Insofar as whiteness is defined as normative in U.S. society, it is not challenged as the source of "bad" behaviors. As a privileged category of social identity, whiteness becomes invisible (Frankenburg 1993). It is not just that blacks are more reified in a society that normalizes whiteness but that the specific character of the reification is a devalued one. In effect, whiteness is beyond negative stigmatization (except perhaps when it intersects with class, as in the stereotype of "white trash"). The pervasiveness of racist attitudes among whites has not led most researchers to conclude that whites are inherently racist. Psychological essentialism in this case is not an operative concept. In fact, studies often reverse the logic and presume that the negative attitudes of blacks led whites to think of race in certain ways—thus granting an implicit rationality to racism.

Of course, psychology's troubled history with race is not to say that it has not had troubled histories with other categories of analysis as well, for example, sex or gender (Anselmi and Law 1998). There has recently been a sustained effort to recognize problems inherent in each term, particularly the ways in which these different meanings can affect the research questions and the resulting explanations (Riger 1992). I do not mean to suggest that psychologists have resolved all of the issues that surround the use of the concepts of sex and gender in research, only that there is an awareness that these concepts are fraught with ambiguity and implicit epistemological assumptions. Many researchers have claimed that gender has no biological reality and have turned to social constructionism and postmodernism for new ways to conceptualize the meaning of gender. Researchers in this area have been made aware especially in this work that the point of view of the researcher must be examined in order to fully appreciate the meaning of their conclusions (Anselmi and Law 1998).

Psychologists predominantly study the concept of race to use it to explain variations in psychological phenomena between groups. Race is treated as an independent variable but a special type of independent variable—a subject variable. The logic of experimental research requires that independent variables be manipulated by the researcher to see if a change occurs in some outcome variable (known as dependent variables) as a result of the manipulation of the independent variable(s). For example, in studying the effects of organization on memory, researchers might manipulate organization by presenting two groups of subjects with lists of words; one list might be categorized and organized and the other, randomly chosen. Subject variables, on the other hand, are defined as characteristics of individuals that cannot be manipulated or changed. Subject variables that researchers commonly study include age, sex, education, class and religion, and race. All research that compares males to females or blacks to whites is using sex or race as a subject variable, but it is based on the traditional methodology that probes for cause and effect by manipulating a "presumed cause" to probe for an effect on some behavior.[4] This method represents a nominal approach to race, as individuals are classified into one of several mutually exclusive categories. There are several ways an individual is classified into one of these categories (Helms 1994). Sometimes assignment to a racial category is based on observable physical characteristics with cultural meanings, like skin color, facial features, and so on. In this case, researchers "assign" participants based on their perceptions of physical appearance. More often, individuals "self-designate" themselves into racial groupings. It is important to realize that such self-designation may fluctuate widely by context. According to H. Winant (1994), individuals identify themselves along a different racial continuum in South Africa and Brazil than they do in the United States. Census classifications are another form of self-identification commonly used in surveys and questionnaires. Categories employed by the census are often assumed by the public to reflect clearly defined distinctions when in reality they reflect social and political negotiations among "racial," ethnic, and sociocultural groups. The recent discussion of adding a "multiracial" classification to the next U.S. Census is one example of how the Census Bureau responds to changing cultural and political meanings (Rosenblum and Travis 1996). There are also legal definitions of "race" that are not based on phenotypic traits or self-identification (Haney Lopez 1996). A clear example of racial designation is the "one-drop rule" in the United States. This strict demarcation, based both on custom and law, explicitly denies that mixed-race individuals can be classified as "mixed" or "white" (Davis 1991). To appreciate the dilemmas inherent in the practice of categorizing by race, consider the following question: To which group does a "biracial" individual belong? If assigned by a researcher, categorization may depend on appearance; if the individual chooses the category, he or she may make a choice based on the available categories or on a personal self-designation based perhaps on one family lineage. Not only are the categories not true categories (mutually exclusive and exhaustive), but the process of assignment varies considerably by the procedure chosen as well as by the social and personal significance of the category labels. Despite the many concerns about racial categorization, researchers have continued this practice, treating each racial group as though it represented some "homogeneous" whole distinct from any other categories.

Psychologists are trained to be careful when using subject variables not to assume a causal relationship between the subject variable and the behavior they are measuring (as they would for other independent variables). Researchers recognize that subject variables are often markers for other variables not yet fully understood. For example, when researchers find that five-year-olds remember less than eight-year-olds in a memory study, they would probably not conclude that this result was simply due to the children's numerical age but rather to factor(s) associated with age that the researchers have yet to uncover. A similar approach has often been taken when racial grouping is the variable under consideration; racial categories serve as a proxy for other factors. But what factors? In the case of intelligence, researchers, both historically and in ongoing contemporary debates, have claimed that findings of differences between racial groups reflect underlying genetic differences (Jensen 1973; Herrnstein and Murray 1994). A similar tendency to attribute racial differences to genetic factors can be seen in research connected to infectious diseases. R. Cooper and R. David (1997) show that in the history of rheumatic fever in the United States, "race" (in terms of individuals labeled as Irish, blacks, and Latin American immigrants) was linked to genetic factors and then used to explain why certain groups were susceptible to the disease. What does it mean, however, to assume a genetic explanation of racial group differences for various psychological and medical phenomena, when, to begin with, the evidence suggests that there is no biological basis for the racial groupings? Racial classifications have no explanatory value for the type of questions that researchers have usually studied using the markers of racial groups. "Race" cannot serve as a proxy variable for underlying biological essences no matter how salient differences in observable physical characteristics appear to be. Similar to gender, race is a culturally defined feature that delineates power. Insofar as most psychologists who have shaped the discipline's approach to the study of "race" have been "white," we cannot overlook the ways in which their identities have become privileged in their theorizing. It is perhaps this desire to universalize the particularity of whiteness that has led many American psychologists to retain a commitment to essentialist race-based explanations although social, cultural, and economic factors are far more useful in explaining group behavior. For example, many who argue against supposed genetic IQ differences between blacks and whites suggest that factors such as family arrangements, peer groups, schools, and socioeconomic status all play a significant role in explaining any findings of differences between these two groups.[5] Similarly, Cooper and David (1997) emphasize that poverty, overcrowding, and lack of access to medical care—common conditions among new immigrant and migrant groups—led to the differential susceptibility of various "ethnic" and "racial" groups to diseases like rheumatic fever. Why have scholars of race been reluctant to relinquish the idea of race as linked to biological factors even when the evidence clearly points to the historical and social construction of the concept (Glenn 1999)? One problem with the term "race" is that it has no analog that points to the distinction between biological and social elements as in the sex/gender distinction. Pascoe (1991) suggests that in the absence of a term like "gender" to "signal a social construction distinct from biological classifications" (p. 10), researchers often confound what they mean when they use the term "race." The desire to avoid a similar conceptual conflation motivated feminists to try to tease out the epistemological distinctions between sex and gender. In an effort to clarify the meaning of race, some researchers have suggested that ethnicity should be substituted for "race" as a way to provide a term that would encourage researchers to indicate the inherent social and political fluidity of race. J. Phinney (1996) proposed that the term "race" should be avoided not only because of its imprecision but also because the psychological importance of race derives largely from how others respond to us and leads us to a specific sense of self. She contends that using the term "ethnicity" would more clearly denote the cultural aspects of race, which are often unintentionally ignored when "race" is the category of analysis. This substitution has some appeal in moving the discussion of "race" away from biological aspects to cultural values and beliefs. However, it cannot be assumed that a subjective sense of ethnic group membership and the experiences of minority group status are equitable. Not only have experiences been different for various cultural and immigrant groups, but these differences have shifted over time. The concept of ethnicity brings its own history of vagueness and lack of precision in determining what constitutes a viable ethnic category. Ethnicity is a valid proxy for "race" only if everyone of the same "race" is culturally similar. There is no homogenous "white" culture, for example. This approach to ethnicity also can assume that ethnicity, as related to identity and status, is fixed and static rather than fluid and contentious. In addition, the substitution of ethnicity for race can be a code for making unfounded generalizations about race without utilizing the term. This was clearly evident when Herrnstein and Murray (1994) in *The Bell Curve* entitled their chapter "Ethnic Differences in Cognitive Abilities" and purported to be sensitive to the issues of heterogeneity within groups (e.g., how do you classify an individual who comes from Panama but whose ancestry is African—is he black or Latino?) but consistently referred to data from studies invoking racial differences that ignored such ethnic variations. In this case, "ethnicity" was used to defuse the anticipated criticism of what were de facto racial comparisons.

Certainly the writings of feminists and others within psychology have forced many psychologists to recognize that gender and race may reflect arbitrary distinctions that stem from historical and cultural arrangements rather than represent a set of essential attributes. Many researchers, however, continue to use race as a subject variable without recognizing the inherent problems I have described. There is a continuing reluctance to admit the lack of explanatory value of "race" as a categorical variable. What accounts for this? As I have already suggested, one reason that many researchers continue to study "race" categorically is their vague belief that racial distinctions help them understand some essential differences among individuals. This approach is premised on the belief of many psychologists that the ultimate goal of psychological theory is to reduce psychological phenomena to biological explanations.

As stated earlier, whites and whiteness are usually assumed by researchers to constitute the normative group. If the behavior and beliefs of blacks differ from this white norm, then the black behavior is labeled deviant. This reflects the privilege of whiteness in a society that privileges whiteness. Yet the centrality of white people in the determination of normative behavior and beliefs has also been driven by a related but distinctly different motive. A dominant tradition in psychology has been the search for universal psychological principles that apply to all individuals. This approach has often led to silencing the significance of cultural differences between and among peoples. Given the impossibility of studying all peoples when formulating generic claims for human behavior, psychologists have historically generated universals based on the experiences of a limited number of cultures and societies. It is not surprising that many American psychologists have utilized white American or European subjects as the empirical scaffolding for their theoretical generalizations. A psychologist who studies child development among the indigenous Indians in the Brazilian rain forest will have little credibility in deriving universal explanations from that empirical sample, since his sample group would be seen as exotic, or "other." In a similar vein, a research study that utilizes only black Americans as subjects can usually sustain conclusions applicable to blacks only, whereas studies that utilize only white Americans are used to generate universal conclusions. The bias in American society that views whiteness as universal and blackness as particularistic impacts psychological studies even when the issue being studied has nothing to do with the development or assessment of racial identities. This practice is pervasive even within the scholarship of feminists who historically have ignored or marginalized women of color (Reid and Kelly 1994).

If "race" is not a useful psychological construct as a classification variable, how might psychologists approach the study of the concept of "race"? As a social construction, the idea or ideology of race certainly merits careful investigation. "Race" has significance for how individuals come to understand themselves and experience the different dimensions of their world. It has salience because it is linked to social, political, and economic forces. Insofar as racial identity is an important component of the self-definition of most Americans, psychologists have attempted to understand how racial and ethnic identity develops. J. Helms (1994), who has done extensive work on racial identity, argues that "racial-group identity is a core aspect of identity development in the United States regardless of a person's racial classification because of the country's emphasis on racial markers as preliminary credentials for access to reward or punishment" (p. 286).

"Race" is impossible to ignore in most contemporary societies. In America, however, whites, as the definers of the concept, are afforded the privilege of not having to think about their identity in terms of "race" until it is juxtaposed against nonwhites. Most research on identity has taken the experiences of whites as normative (Gaines and Reed 1995). Much of this work has assumed that identity is a fixed and stable construct, one that varies neither over the life span of the individual nor in different situations. Until recently, there has been much less emphasis on the role of the socially constructed sense of self. In studying identity, most psychologists focus on individual variables that operate at the level of the psyche and ignore interpersonal, institutional, and sociopolitical factors (Unger 1995). And even those researchers who studied the identity development of minority racial and ethnic groups in the United States have often engaged in essentializing the experiences of these individuals.

According to A. Mama, most of the researchers who studied black identity development depicted it as a progression from a less healthy form of a white-identified identity to a more healthy form of black-identified identity. Perhaps the most prominent theorist in this vein was W. E. Cross (1980), who developed a "nigrescence theory" that focused on the process of acquiring a "black identity" through a five-stage developmental process. Mama (1995), among other theorists, is highly critical of this entire enterprise. Although she credits researchers like Cross with recognizing the interplay between the individual and society, she claims that these approaches maintain an essential dualism between the internal and external worlds. Mama proposes that the study of identity must move beyond this dualism to a theory of subjectivity in which "individuals act on and use social history and experiences to invent their own identities along the interrelated dimensions of race and gender, to constitute themselves as racialized and gendered individual subjects" (p. 62). Mama's research on black British women's identity is one example of shifting the focus of the study of identity as a fixed, stable, and universal sequence to positioning the study of identity as a series of creations and recreations in response to a conflicted world. Her focus on subjectivity would require psychology to rethink its exclusive commitment to empiricism as the only way to study psychological phenomena. Other methodologies such as standpoint theory and postmodernism offer alternative ways to explore questions related to gender and race (Riger 1992). Similarly, J. Helms (1994) calls for the use of idiographic or emic methodologies when investigating racial identity. Researchers should be reluctant to assume that there is such an entity as a stable group identity. This in turn will allow psychologists to discard the idea of the individual as a fixed representation. Furthermore, since "racial" groups represent arbitrary and fluid social markers, the emphasis on group identity may need to be discarded in favor of a focus on dynamic individual histories. This approach still leaves psychology with a difficult task of making meaning from individual lives.

J. Morawski and B. Bayer (1995) suggest that when we confront categories such as race, gender, ethnicity, or class, which have long been assumed to represent some "naturalized" classes, we often create disturbance within the discipline of psychology—both in terms of methodology and theory. Resistance to change can be quite pervasive. If psychology is to move beyond its troubled history with the concept of "race," it must take seriously the challenges offered by feminists and other theorists to develop new theories and methods of inquiry about "race." These new theories and methods do not promise a trouble-free future. In fact, given the unexplored territories they face, they are likely to cause more trouble but perhaps of a different nature. It may be this kind of trouble, however, that moves psychology beyond reification of "race" and away from implicit racism. If there is one lesson to be learned from G. Richard's (1997) notion of a reflexive psychology, it is that psychology, as a discipline, needs to be more clearly informed about its own use of the concept of "race."

NOTES

Anne Law, Maurice Wade, and Berel Lang provided insightful comments on various portions of this paper, and I gratefully acknowledge their assistance. I am especially indebted to Jerry Watts, both for his *re*-readings and for continually reminding me of the social and political dimensions of "race."

1. Although I find this DuBois quotation supportive of social constructionism, his ideas concerning race that are discussed in this chapter also embraced racial essentialism.

2. There are notable exceptions to this trend. For example, Gale (1999) contends that William James's philosophy reflected multiple views of self.

3. See *Ethos* 25 (1997) for an extensive dialogue on Hirschfeld's theory.

4. Note that in the memory experiment researchers can feel confident that their two groups of subjects are equivalent except for their exposure to one of the two variations of the independent variable (organized vs. random list of words). However, when subject variables are used, researchers can never satisfy this assumption.

5. This argument does not assume that IQ is a valid measure of intelligence.

REFERENCES

Allport, G. 1958. *The Nature of Prejudice*. Garden City, N.Y.: Doubleday Anchor.
Anselmi, D., and A. Law. 1998. *Questions of Gender: Perspectives and Paradoxes*. New York: McGraw-Hill.
Betancourt, H., and S. Lopez. 1993. "The Study of Culture, Ethnicity, and Race in American Psychology." *American Psychologist* 48:629–37.
Clark, K. B., and M. P. Clark. 1939. Segregation As a Factor in the Racial Identification Of Negro Pre-School Children." *Journal of Experimental Education* 8:161–63.
Cooper, R., and R. David. 1997. "The Biological Concept Of Race and Its Application to Public Health and Epidemiology." In *The Concept of "Race" in Natural and Social Sciences,* edited by N. Gates, pp. 127–46. New York: Garland.
Cross, W. E. 1980. "Models of Psychological Nigrescence." In *Black Psychology,* edited by R. L. Jones. New York: Harper & Row.
Davis, F. J. 1991. *Who Is Black?* College Park: Pennsylvania State University Press.
DuBois, W. E. B. [1903] 1989. *The Souls of Black Folk*. Reprint, New York: Viking Penguin.
Dupre, J. 1998. "Normal People." *Social Research* 65:221–47.
Frankenburg, R. 1993. *White Women, Race Matters: The Social Construction of Whiteness*. Minneapolis: University of Minnesota Press.
Gaines, S., and E. Reed. 1995. "Prejudice: From Allport to DuBois." *American Psychologist* 50:96–103.
Gale, R. M. 1999. *The Divided Self of William James*. Cambridge: Cambridge University Press.
Glenn, E. N. 1999. "The Social Construction and Institutionalization of Gender and Race." In *Revisioning Gender,* edited by M. Ferree, J. Lorber, and B. Hess, 3–43. Thousand Oaks, Calif.: Sage.
Gould, S. J. 1984. *The Mismeasure of Man*. New York: Norton.
Haney Lopez, I. 1996. *White by Law: The Legal Construction of Race*. New York: New York University Press.

Helms, J. 1994. "The Conceptualization of Racial Identity and Other 'Racial' Constructs." In *Human Diversity: Perspectives on People in Context*, edited by E. Tricket, R. Watts, and D. Birman, pp. 285–311. San Francisco: Jossey-Bass.

Herrnstein, R. J., and C. Murray. 1994. *The Bell Curve: Intelligence and Class Structure in American Life*. New York: Free Press.

Hirschfeld, L. 1996. *Race in the Making: Cognition, Culture, and the Child's Construction Of Human Kinds*. Cambridge: MIT Press.

Hirschfeld, L. 1997. "The Conceptual Politics of Race: Lessons from Our Children." *Ethos* 25:63–92.

Hull, D. 1998. "Species, Subspecies, and Races." *Social Research* 65:351–67.

Jensen, A. R. 1973. *Genetics, Educability, and Subpopulation*. London: Methuen.

Lewontin, R. C. 1977. "Race and Intelligence." In *The IQ Controversy: Critical Readings*, edited by N. Block and G. Dworkin, pp. 78–92. New York: Pantheon.

Mama, A. 1995. *Beyond the Masks: Race, Gender, and Subjectivity*. London: Routledge.

Montagu, M. F. A., ed. 1954. *The Concept of Race*. New York: Free Press.

Morawski, J., and B. Bayer. 1995. "Stirring Trouble and Making Theory." In *Bringing Cultural Diversity to Feminist Psychology: Theory, Research, and Practice*, edited by H. Landrine, pp. 113–37. Washington, D.C.: American Psychological Association.

Omi, M., and H. Winant. 1994. *Racial Formation in the United States*. New York: Routledge.

Pascoe, P. 1991. "Race, Gender, and Intercultural Relations: The Case of Interracial Marriage." *Frontiers* 12, no. 1:5–18.

Phinney, J. 1996. "When We Talk about American Ethnic Groups, What Do We Mean?" *American Psychologist* 51:918–927.

Reid, P. T., and E. Kelly. 1994. "Research on Women of Color: From Ignorance to Awareness." *Psychology of Women Quarterly* 18:477–86.

Richards, G. 1997. *"Race," Racism, and Psychology: Towards a Reflexive History*. London: Routledge.

Riger, S. 1992. "Epistemological Debates, Feminist Voices: Science, Social Values, and the Study of Women." *American Psychologist* 47:730–38.

Rosenblum, K., and T. Travis. 1996. *The Meaning of Differences: American Constructions of Race, Sex, and Gender, Social Class, and Sexual Orientation*. New York: McGraw-Hill.

Tucker, W. 1994. *The Science and Politics of Racial Research*. Urbana: University of Illinois Press.

Unger, R. 1979. "Towards a Redefinition of Sex and Gender." *American Psychologist* 24:1085–94.

Unger, R. 1995. "Conclusion: Cultural Diversity and the Future of Feminist Psychology." In *Bringing Cultural Diversity to Feminist Psychology: Theory, Research, and Practice*, edited by H. Landrine, pp. 413–32. Washington, D.C.: American Psychological Association.

Winant, H. 1994. *Racial Conditions: Politics, Theory, Comparisons*. Minneapolis: University of Minnesota Press.

Yee, A., H. Fairchild, F. Weizmann, and G. Wyatt. 1993. "Addressing Psychology's Problems with Race." *American Psychologist* 48:1132–40.

Zuckerman, M. 1990. "Some Dubious Premises in Research and Theory on Racial Differences: Scientific, Social, and Ethical Issues." *American Psychologist* 45:1297–1303.

4

Nazi Anti-Semitism and the "Science of Race"

Dalia Ofer

The horrors of Nazi racial policies during World War II make one reluctant to speak of the "science of race." Today no reasonable person accepts the idea that race is a biological determinant of an individual's character, normative views, or ability to function in society. Biologists no longer believe that distinct racial boundaries separate human beings from one another. Rather, human differences are located within a continuum of historical, geographical, political, and cultural factors. Intermarriage among people of different races and cultures and huge migratory movements in the modern era have demonstrated the fundamental unity of humankind.[1]

But the evidence and moral lessons of the war did not discourage the use of racist terminology and its development into a social and political system of discrimination and domination. The apartheid political system of South Africa, for example, was implemented after World War II, when the results of Nazi racial policy were already well known.

The "scientific" theories of race were developed in the second half of the nineteenth century, when big migrations were already underway and when European rulers of nonwhite colonial populations had reached a peak of imperialist rivalry. Animosity between Jews and Gentiles was an even older tradition. However, the racial ideology of the nineteenth century contributed to a radicalization of existing anti-Semitic ideas and toward a new definition of "rational" ways of dealing with the Jews. Together with a radical political movement that recruited the masses followed by a regime that carried a revolutionary message for all of Europe and in its own understanding an apocalyptic mission, this ideology culminated in the annihilation of most European Jews.

Although anti-Semitism reached its climax when the Nazis came to

61

power, the racist ideology of the late nineteenth century was clearly the precursor of post–World War I developments. The "science of race" and the racist ideology supplied modern anti-Semitism with a new energy in the first decades of the twentieth century that enabled it to overcome the essentially pessimistic vision of earlier anti-Semites, who envisaged no solution, certainly no "final solution," to the "Jewish question." I do not claim that the Nazi path was predetermined but that the persistent issue of German identity, which so concerned the Second Reich, was reinforced in Weimar Germany and in particular among right-wing parties that viewed Weimar as a degenerate regime. Thus long-standing racial anti-Semitism nurtured and invigorated the German search for self-definition.

CULTURE, FOLKLORE, AND RACE

From the late 1700s through the 1800s, scholars in a number of disciplines in the humanities and the social sciences were preoccupied with the classification of human beings according to their physical and cultural similarities and differences—in body features, skin color, language, religion, and other factors. Philologists, folklorists, and anthropologists were involved in these efforts. The results of their intellectual endeavors were manifested in political life through the assertion of nationalism.

In the late 1700s Johann Fichte assembled folktales and German-language idioms and Johann Gottfried von Herder presented the idea of the German *Volkgeist*. During the early 1800s the Grimm brothers collected tales that became a symbol of authentic German culture and a national legacy. A particular form of national expression embodied in German language and mythology was defined as a collective characteristic that grew out of the tradition of the *Volk*. The formulation of German national identity also embodied resentment of the legacy of liberalism and the French Revolution, criticism of modernity, and nostalgia for the German *Urvolk,* the "original" Volk. This romantic perspective competed with a liberal understanding of Germany and became an important tool in the hands of nationalist politicians. Intellectuals, artists, and writers identified with this trend and shared its political goals. Prominent among these personalities were Richard Wagner and his Bayreuth circle and Heinrich von Treitschke, the leading nationalist historian. They and many others saw themselves as leaders of a new social and cultural direction and contributed their academic and artistic efforts to encourage the political agenda they favored.[2]

Although these phenomena were explicit in some other European countries as well, they were most apparent in Germany because of its specific political and religious conditions. The competition among political powers (Prussia, Austria, and the states of southern Germany) over Germany's unification, together with the rapid and agonizing industrialization process, made the question of nationalism—who is a German and who belongs to the German state—very complex.

In such fields as philosophy, history, and social research, the works of German scholars made a great impact on intellectuals all over the world. In such an intellectual environment the social sciences progressed toward a definition of a methodology and an understanding of human societies.

France was the cradle for social science research on the characteristics of races. Count Joseph Arthur de Gobineau, who was battling on behalf of the declining aristocracy, was one of the first to suggest a hierarchy of human races, with the Indo-European people at the apex. Philologist Ernst Renan devoted much academic effort to understanding the relation between the linguistic structure of Hebrew and the contribution of the Jews to world religion and culture by "converting the world to monotheism." He was preoccupied with a paradox: the people whose fanaticism and exclusivity had made them, since antiquity, the least fit of all groups to make great contributions had in fact made the greatest contribution.[3]

In his study of Renan, Shmuel Almog finds a link between the more "innocent" classification of human races and the normative approach, which proposed a human racial hierarchy. Renan did not start from a rigid definition of race as unaffected by social and historical events. On the contrary, he defined the Jews of antiquity as a race on the basis of their language and geographical position; history, however, moved them away from their original location and race, and in modern times they became Europeans. (This position did not prevent Renan from later identifying the different races normatively.)

To Renan the Indo-European Aryan race was superior. It had produced "all the great movements in the history of the world—military, political, and intellectual."[4] The Semitic race lacked a sense of discipline and was incapable of effective political organization. Subjectivity was at the root of Semitic morality, which was different in essence from conventional morality. Renan was very ambivalent about the Jews; as noted above, he had to reconcile what he considered the Jews' negative traits, past and present, with their contributions to humanity, which did not cease even after Christ. Renan thought that in modern times Jews acted as the leaven among the nations in order to advance society. Almog offers a dialectic to explain how Renan was able to accept the contributions of the inferior Jews to the superior Aryan people: thesis—the Semites were limited; antithesis—their limitation prepared them for monotheism; synthesis—only when the monotheism of the Semites had permeated Aryan civilization did it achieve its true meaning.[5]

Renan thus drew a complex and contradictory image of the contemporary Jew, whom he described as "a man who has overthrown the world by his faith in the kingdom of God, who now believes in nothing but wealth." This, of course, is very similar to the conventional depiction of Jews in anti-Semitic writing as worshipers of mammon. In the same spirit, Renan wrote that "the Synagogues corresponded with one another and exchanged letters of recommendation. They formed a vast secret society, a sort of free-masonry." Here again he was approaching a central anti-Semitic accusation of a worldwide Jewish conspiracy. On the other hand, he opposed the "zoological division of races" and feared the implications of the racial school of thought for future society. Nevertheless, Renan's work established an important foundation for racist interpretations of human societies and the role of Jews and Judaism. Renan even questioned the Jewish origins of Jesus, claiming that the region of the Galilee, where Jesus was born, accommodated a mixed community of converts.[6]

SOCIAL DARWINISM AND ITS IMPLICATIONS

Darwinism challenged social scientists to offer a new way of thinking. The turn toward a racist school of thought occurred only when Darwinian theory was applied to human societies. The so-called social Darwinism originated in Britain in the work of Sir Charles Galton, Darwin's nephew, who claimed in a book published in 1869, *Hereditary Genius*, that both mental and physical abilities were inborn. In a later work, *Inquiries into Human Faculty and Its Development* (1883), he introduced the term "eugenics" to describe a program for improving the human race.[7] Eugenics became the discipline in which the social and life sciences such as biology and medicine "offered general models for construction of an ordered and developing society."[8]

Social Darwinism represented the effort of the social sciences at the end of the nineteenth century to reveal the laws of human societies and to crown these laws with scientific sanction. Extrapolating laws from the natural sciences into social analysis provided scholars (or so they thought) with an accurate understanding of human biological and mental nature. It enabled them to predict the future development of human societies and to suggest alternative social policies to improve humanity. Their aim was to reform society and design human beings and thus to ensure the well-being of all. The collective, not the individual, was the target of these social planners. The pursuit of happiness by the individual and his entitlement to natural rights, according to the vision of the Enlightenment, were not the subject of their efforts; they were interested, rather, in the contribution of the "reformed individual" to the collective—the nation or race.

The application of Darwinism to social policy meant that the weaker members of society, including the physically infirm, the mentally retarded, the deaf and blind, were to be ignored—or worse. The attenuation of traditional religious beliefs and the emergence of neopagan approaches reinforced this radical approach to human life. "Scientific findings" contributed the ultimate support for such ideas in the eyes of a generation that greatly appreciated knowledge and higher education. To many, these justified society's intervention in the lives of certain categories of human beings. To the social Darwinists, the categorization of some individuals as worthy of support and others as disposable was not arbitrary but a consequence of natural laws.

In view of the broad acceptance of social Darwinism in academic circles, the new field of eugenics flourished. From the late nineteenth century to the end of World War II, eugenics had a strong impact on social and public health policies in Europe and the United States. Eugenics, it was said, could reform humankind through direct intervention and restrictions on those individuals who carried undesirable genes. A new profession, eugenics, was created in which individual scholars, whole fields of knowledge, and prestigious research institutions had a stake. In the social and cultural environment of the early twentieth century, these professional groups became a center of influence that also attempted to implement eugenists' findings with specific governmental and social policies.[9]

The ideas and proposals of the eugenists appealed to different social classes. Members of the upper middle class opposed taxation for the care of the weak. The declining aristocracy, which had lost much of its influence as a consequence of democratization and the rise of new social classes, hoped that the application of eugenics would somehow halt this process. There were also social workers frustrated by their inability to deal successfully with the problems of the impoverished classes in the big cities. Lacking funds and overwhelmed by the rapid growth of prostitution, alcoholism, and violence in families, mostly among the poor, they were looking desperately for new solutions. The forced abortion or sterilization of young girls forsaken in the streets of big cities sounded like a rational suggestion. In view of the repeated failure of attempts to change social behavior and the recurrence of criminality among members of the same families, some social workers concluded that criminality was a hereditary disease rather than an outcome of substandard living and economic conditions. Thus they were willing to listen to the physicians and biologists who preached the doctrine of eugenics.

This unusual combination of conservatives and socialists supported eugenics under the umbrella of the well-being of the society. The disregard for individual rights and freedom of choice seemed irrelevant in the context of such strong arguments based on the social sciences.[10] In this atmosphere, the declarations of the eugenics activists, which were echoed three or four decades later by Nazi leaders, did not sound strange or outrageous despite their direct assault on Christian tenets regarding the sanctity of human life.

"Our starting point," said Himmler at a rally in 1938, "is not the individual and we do not subscribe to the view that one should feed the hungry, give drink to the thirsty or clothe the naked—those are not our objectives. Our objectives are entirely different. They can be put most crisply in the sentence: we must have a healthy people in order to prevail in the world."[11]

Without delving further into the origins of eugenics and its relation to the racist thought of Nazi Germany, I find it interesting to note that the German government in 1914 initiated a law that would prohibit abortion unless there was an immediate threat to the life of the mother. The government was alarmed by proposals from the *Deutsche Gesellschaft für Rassenhygiene* (German Society of Race Eugenics) that the law incorporate provisions for sterilization when such a procedure appears to be "medically desirable." The government proposal stressed that neither social nor eugenic grounds were sufficient for abortion. The proposal did not clear the legislative process because of the beginning of World War I.[12]

The crucial issue that concerns me here is the nature of the connection, if any, between these racial theories and popular attitudes toward the Jews. Could eugenicists make the Jews central to their social vision? These questions have become important for historiography because of the involvement of so many people of the "euthanasia project" in the death camps of Poland administering the Final Solution.[13] Almog writes: "Since Eugen Düring and Houston Stewart Chamberlain (the notorious German and English scholars in the second half of the 19th century and the beginning of the 20s, who developed racial anti-Semitism and the ideology of Aryan superiority), the concepts of racism and anti-Semitism have become to some extent synonymous. The merger of anti-Semitism and racial ideology has been so striking that one hardly remembers now that these were originally two independent factors,"[14] each with its own history.

Neither racial theory nor eugenics was the initial motivation for the anti-Semites, but both positions greatly supported and reinforced their ideology and activities. With the rise of racism and eugenics, theories, concepts, images, and beliefs that were already deeply internalized gained "scientific substance" and produced more rigorous anti-Jewish (and also anti-Gypsy and other non-German) convictions. Racism and eugenics were crucial in establishing a milieu that legitimized radical steps against the Jews, and both helped lower the long-standing religious and moral barriers that might have prevented the excesses of a regime that disregarded individual well-being and centered on the superiority of the Aryan race. The result was that anti-Semitism and racism formed two sides of one coin.

MODERN ANTI-SEMITISM

Modern anti-Semitism not only had racial elements but also "generally appeared as one component of an entire set of factors—social, ideological, cultural, and political—and was organically combined with other elements. There are examples of Right Wing, Left Wing, radical and conservative anti-Semitism, and in each case the anti-Semitic element is integrated into the broader context. That is to say, anti-Semitism is not an alien element attached to any given constellation but an essential element. At times, it even functions as the cement that binds all parts into one."[15]

The term "anti-Semitism" was coined in 1879 by Wilhelm Marr, a radical German nationalist. In his book *The Victory of Judaism over Germanism* he argued that the Jews had already won their inevitable struggle with Germany. They had weakened the German spirit through their involvement in Germany's life and had gained a decisive influence over the mind of the German *Volk*. The Jews had established their Jerusalem in the heart of Germany, and the Germans did not even understand that they were facing a real battle. During the political upheaval of 1848, Marr fought to establish a new social and political order in Germany. At that time he favored full emancipation of all classes and minorities, including the Jews. But in 1862, he was asked by a friend to further support Jewish emancipation. He refused in a sharply worded letter, charging that the Jews did not deserve emancipation because they always deserted the revolutionary cause once they had achieved their own ends. Marr claimed that the particularism, egoistic spirit, and tribal behavior of the Jews led to their nonloyal conduct and kept them from being interested in universal human causes. Marr related to the Jews as a *Stamm* (tribe, clan), not as a race, but he rationalized his position by suggesting an ethnic explanation for group behavior, not by referring to an actual conflict with any individual Jew in his own experience.[16]

In the late 1870s, Marr adopted a racist discourse stimulated by the growing popularity of the anti-Semitic movement. Many anti-Semites were quick to adopt racial interpretations of Germany's ills based on concepts suggested by social Darwinism. Thus a variety of negative Jewish images filled the arsenal of anti-Semitism, which combined traditional Christian anti-Jewish stereotypes with antiliberal, antimodern, and racist sentiments. Expressions such as "the Jews are our misfortune" *(die Juden sind unser Unglück)*, coined by the prestigious historian Heinrich von Treitschke, added to the popularity of anti-Jewish slogans. The Jews and their purported financial manipulations and greed were blamed for causing the economic crisis of 1873–1879 and were construed as the source of Germany's social troubles and human sufferings.

Jacob Katz, in his work on anti-Semitism, reflected on the centrality of the popular press, particularly a few renowned journalists, in promoting the anti-Jewish motifs. The attacks on the Jews were not always direct. The press sometimes hinted, in a language that became a code, that the Jews were the dominant factor in the swindles and frauds that had brought about the crisis of the stock exchange. This approach not only singled out the Jews as the cause of the trouble but also implied its solution. The popular press and pamphlets, cards, and leaflets spread the anti-Semitic message all over Germany. The same insulting language was used in oral representations, such as public speeches and sermons, especially as democratization and the coming elections forced politicians to address social issues. Those who wished to attack the Jews and those who were bewildered by the situation were inclined to understand the message.[17]

Saul Friedländer describes the impact of the representation of Jews in Wagner's operas in shaping the image of the Jew and the vision of Germany without the Jews. The Jew represented the erotic, materialistic creature devoured by worldly cravings—the direct antithesis of the German, the idealist who was ready to sacrifice himself for the cause of justice and extended his help to those in need with no limits or egoistic considerations. The noble, brave, and pure Siegfried and the ugly, evil dwarf Mime confronted each other in a war to the death. The musical language of instruments and voices carried the spirit of the end of days, symbolizing "the ultimate fate of the Jew."[18]

In the discourse of political conservatives, the role of the Jew in politics and the economy was strongly attacked. Jewish bankers, stockbrokers, and merchants alike were construed as parasites on the healthy body of the nation, unable to produce real goods or be truly creative. The conservative parties in Germany leaned heavily on religious and Christian values and by and large did not follow a racial ideology. However, even devoted Christians commonly used the racial terminology of purity of *Volk* and the contamination of the *Volksgemeinschaft* (national community).[19] Thus the role of the Jews in the culture was identified as contaminating the spirit of the German people.

The "Jewish problem" was a single factor that explained all the evils and ills of society—and it was the key to society's salvation. Ruth Kluger writes in reference to Austrian anti-Semitism, "To the gentile world it simply was not a problem of Anti-Semitism, it was the 'Jewish problem' " (emphasis added).[20] Jacob Katz summed up the immanent danger of modern anti-Semitism: "If Jews are inferior, alien, and neither worthy nor equipped to assimilate, then they are an irredeemable vexation. The question has become; what is to be done with this group, which society must not tolerate? The unique seriousness of modern anti-Semitism lies in the very fact that this question could even be asked."[21]

WEIMAR AND NAZISM

Nazism did not contribute new concepts to anti-Semitism, racial theories, and eugenics; Nazi ideas on these issues were derived from late-nineteenth-century notions. But a change in style and in language created a different, more radical substance that eventually developed into a state policy. Nazis and proto-Nazis such as Dietrich Eckart used a discourse designed to produce a feeling of exaltation. Repetition of words and phrases created a rhythm and built up an expectation in the listener or reader. This and other devices were intended to liberate the listener, to raise new options in his mind, and to instill the desired understanding of the reality.[22]

A great deal of Nazi anti-Semitic propaganda was delivered orally in town squares during election campaigns. Much of it addressed crucial political or economic issues such as the Locarno Accord and the agreement on Germany's reparation. The Nazis vehemently rejected the Weimar government's stand on these issues, presenting it as the embodiment of the betrayal of the German *Volk*. The vague alternatives they suggested emphasized the need for "racial purity" to enable Germany to regain its power and status in the world.[23]

Conditions in Germany after World War I provided a fertile field for the growth of disappointment and ill feeling toward the enemy within. The outcome of the war was shocking to most Germans. The political changes and economic hardships that followed destroyed any conventional order. The invisible hand of destruction could be concretized through the revolutionary attempts of the Communists in Germany and were demonized in the shadow of the Bolshevik revolution. In anti-Semitic allegations, the Jews embodied all these evils—they were said to be behind the Bolshevik revolution, the shattering event that destroyed Russia and was aimed at all Europe, particularly Germany. The notorious *Protocols of the Elders of Zion*, a forgery that spread throughout Europe following the escape of the White Russians to the West, was regarded as the ultimate proof of the Jewish plan to dominate the world. These events enabled anti-Semites to identify what they said were enduring traits of the Jews: their tendency to conspire and their plans to dominate the world. Thus the invisible betrayer of Germany was made visible, and his purposes and means were known. On this ground solutions could be proposed.[24]

The issue of German identity became even more painful after World War I. The country's human losses were immense and affected many families; vast territories in which Germans were residing were handed over to foreign powers, making Germans a minority in what they considered their own land. This was especially painful in East Prussia, where the despised Polish minority became sovereign.[25] The disappearance of the kaiser, the focus of identification and admiration in the united Germany, left many perplexed and in a search of a national symbol. The new republic, which the majority supported when it was established, lost many supporters because of the economic and political crisis. National identity, which was unresolved and highly debated in the Second Reich, continued to be a source of confusion in the Weimar Republic.

The vigorous attacks on the new regime by the right-wing aristocracy and the more radical *völkisch* right suggested simple explanations and uncomplicated solutions for Germany's crisis. Three major elements were at the center of their proposals: anti-Semitism and the rejection of world revolution, the reestablishment of the German *Volksgemeinde* (the term for the nation that is bound by ethnicity in the discourse of the radical conservative right), and a strongly antimodernist philosophy. Anti-Semitism was implicit or explicit in all three elements. Kluger's conclusion is pertinent: "With the defeat of liberalism, anti-Semitism became more than dislike for Jews. It was a dislike of the world that the Jews represented, the world of tolerance and equality and freedom and democracy."[26]

What Nazism contributed to this analysis was not only a definition of the "Jewish problem" as a racial problem and the promotion of anti-Semitism as the sole solution, but a declaration of a permanent war against the Jews. Unlike the pessimism of such anti-Semites as Marr and others in the fin de siècle who prophesied victory for the Jews in the struggle with Germans,[27] Hitler and his followers had a vision and offered the means to fulfill it. Their mission was to rescue Germany and purge it of Jewish blood. They thus paved the way toward a new German identity that had nevertheless been mentioned in the past.

The simplistic and unsophisticated racial argumentation that Hitler displayed in his writings and talks fell on ground well prepared by preexisting beliefs to absorb such familiar rhetoric. Anti-Jewish prejudice was a common social and cultural code for most Germans. One did not have to believe in racial ideology to accept the anti-Semitic propaganda that the *Ostjuden* were poisoning German society; respected bourgeois values endorsed this charge, as well as those who opposed assimilated German Jews.[28] It was not difficult to identify the Jewish threat as revealed in the *Protocols of the Elders of Zion* and by recent political events.

A German receptive to the notion of racial or *völkish* German identity was also disposed to accept the rhetoric of purity and fear of the contamination of German blood and the argument that the ultimate qualification for participation in affairs of state must be the individual's belonging to the German race. The demand that Germans clear their minds of the deceiving influence of the Jews as a precondition for understanding the political situation sounded reasonable. That Jews should be banned from the press, the publishing houses, the educational system, and other cultural institutions was for many almost a natural conclusion.[29]

Nazi anti-Semitism presented a comprehensive Weltanschauung that drew on anti-Semitic images and concepts from all traditions, including religious anti-Jewish discourse, *völkish* antimodern, back-to-nature slogans, and of course the racist social Darwinist notion. The intensive and aggressive anti-Semitic propaganda was appealing even to some who refused to vote for the Nazis. The very excessiveness of the anti-Jewish hate propaganda disseminated by the Nazi leaders and press made people in some respects deaf to this discourse and thus inattentive to its real meaning and dangers. Some believed it was only propaganda rhetoric that the Nazis hoped would win some votes and thus disregarded it without paying much attention. Many others were eager to adopt the racist concepts and to view the *Volksgemeinschaft* through the lens of the radical right.

In the 1920s and 1930s, eugenics and the radical solution to the "problem" of disabled persons became even more respectable in most European countries. In Germany the centralization of medicine, public health clinics, and the health insurance system placed great authority and responsibility in the hands of medical staff. A growing tendency to encourage families and guardians of the mentally ill and physically disabled persons to send them to institutions made many families dependent on the decisions of government and physicians.

In Germany, as in other countries, medicine was highly respected. In a culture that viewed the healthy as the "good" people, national policy endeavored to enlarge their numbers. Healthy reproduction was an issue of concern as the losses of human life in the Great War and the declining birth rate added to German anxiety about the future of their nation. All these factors, of course, had many positive effects on the general health of the population. Preventive medicine and specifically inoculation were among the achievements of medical treatment in Germany. But there was also hostility toward the chronically ill and those suffering from hereditary diseases. Thus the overlap between medical science and racial theory created an even greater risk to respect for human life and dignity than had existed in the late nineteenth century.[30]

Could Jews as Jews become a category in the eugenics programs? They were not less healthy than the general population, and they did not have a higher retardation rate or more hereditary diseases; many eugenicists were not anti-Semitic at all. However, the notion of legitimizing the exclusion of people because of health problems and the many "academic" talks about the advantages of racial purity reinforced the racial myth. In anti-Semitic allegations, Jews were conspiring to destroy the German *Volk* through birth control devices. Jewish doctors and family-planning clinics that encouraged abortions for young single women were presented as part of a Jewish plot to decrease the German population. Hitler attacked inoculations as a Jewish invention intended to weaken the German *Volk*. All this of course seems contradictory to the thrust of eugenics, which also encouraged abortion and even suggested the sterilization of prostitutes and other antisocials.

Clearly, anti-Semitism could easily tolerate many contradictions and conflicting images of the Jews.[31]

CONCLUSION

All this may sound like a resurgence of late-nineteenth-century eugenics and racial discourse. In many respects it was, but in a different historical situation that endowed this discourse with revolutionary impact. The traumatic experience of the Great War, the economic crisis of the early 1920s, and the growing resentment against democracy and liberalism among Germans intellectuals from both the right and the Communist left created a new political, social, and cultural environment. In the generation after the beginning of the Great War, one crisis followed another, culminating in the depression of 1929. The post–World War I racial, anti-Semitic, and eugenics discourse sounded different and transmitted different messages.

The major change of course occurred when Nazism became the ruling power of Germany. I will not here provide a detailed description of the Nazi legislation that expanded the idea of eugenics into an extensive euthanasia program. These actions received the support of respected scientists who adopted the Nazi ideology and joined the movement, among them the well-known Eugen Fischer of the Kaiser Wilhelm Institute for Anthropology, Human Heredity, and Eugenics. It is worth mentioning that, despite the legal facade, whenever the most radical decisions in the euthanasia program were taken, the decision making ignored the issue of legality. In 1934, for example, Hitler issued an order to terminate the pregnancies of women who had a hereditary illness or whose partners had such an illness. The consent of the victims was not sought, nor were other legal provisions respected; ad hoc committees would make the decisions and the doctors would implement them. Some 350,000 men and women were sterilized because they were defined as feeble-minded or schizophrenic according to medical criteria that would not withstand any serious medical test today. In the euthanasia centers established during 1940–1944, another 100,000 were murdered.[32]

Hitler stated in 1929 that "if Germany was to get a million children a year and was to remove 700,000–800,000 of the weakest people, then the final result might even be an increase in strength."[33] He was sharing with his listeners a concept that he was ready to follow if circumstances allowed. Some of the major eugenics scientists praised his willingness to implement such daring policy.

The "Jewish question" did not come under the standard categories of eugenics but was embodied in the encompassing racial theory. Jews were not feeble-minded or chronically ill human beings; they were regarded as subhuman *(Untermenschen)* and also as anti-Aryan (in the meaning of anti-Christ), seriously threatening the very existence of the German *Volk* and the thousand-year Reich. Clearly their existence in the midst of the German population seemed dangerous.[34]

Until the decision was made to murder the Jews en masse—the so-called Final Solution—the Jewish policy had a theoretical ideological frame of reference, though not a systematic plan or a clear direction. Legal actions usually followed everyday practice. When the Nuremberg Laws for the protection of German blood and German honor were enacted, the barriers against the intermarriage of Aryans and Jews were already in practice and mixed couples were virtually unable to get married. Extreme actions had an inner logic in Nazi ideology; considerations such as the need for economic recovery, the desire to have the Olympic Games in Berlin, or the fluctuations of foreign policy might have slowed down these actions but could not have prevented them. On January 30, 1939, Hitler spoke in the Reichstag in a celebration of his six years in power. "In the course of my life," he said,

> I have very often been a prophet, and have usually been ridiculed for it. During the time of my struggle for power it was in the first instance the Jewish race alone that received my prophecies with laughter when I said that I would one day take over the leadership of the State, and with it that of the whole nation, and that I would then among many other things settle the Jewish problem. Their laughter was uproarious, but I think that for some time now they have been laughing on the other side of their face. Today I will once more be a prophet: If the international Jewish financiers in and outside Europe should succeed in plunging the nations once more into a world war, then the result will not be the bolshevization of the earth, and thus the victory of Jewry, but the annihilation of the Jewish race in Europe![35]

In his last hours, when Germany was in ruins, Hitler dictated his last testament. By then he thought that the Germans did not deserve a dignified future because of their failure to sustain National Socialism. He described the destruction of European Jewry as a consequence of the Jewish responsibility for dragging the world into war. He ended his testimony with a final request: "I call upon the leadership of the nation and those who follow it to observe the racial laws most carefully, to fight mercilessly against the poisoners of all the peoples of the world, international Jewry."[36]

NOTES

1. For an interesting presentation of this issue, see Gavin I. Langmuir, *Toward a Definition of Anti-Semitism* (Berkeley: University of California Press, 1990), pp. 311–52.

74 *Dalia Ofer*

2. George L. Mosse, *The Crisis of German Ideology: Intellectual Origins of the Third Reich* (New York: Grosset & Dunlap, 1964); Saul Friedländer, *Nazi Germany and the Jews: The Years of Persecution, 1933–1939* (New York: HarperCollins, 1997), pp. 73–90; Hans Rosenberg, "Anti-Semitism and the 'Great Depression,' 1873–1896," in *Hostages of Modernization: Studies in Modern Anti-Semitism, 1870–1933/39,* ed. Herbert A. Strauss (Berlin: Walter de Gruyter, 1993), 1: 19–29; Werner Jochmann, "Structure and Function of German Anti-Semitism, 1878–1896," in *Hostages of Modernization,* pp. 41–61.

3. Shmuel Almog, "The Racial Motif in Renan's Attitude to Jews and Judaism," in *Anti-Semitism through the Ages,* ed. Shmuel Almog (Oxford: Pergamon, 1988), p. 255; see also Robert S. Wistrich, *Anti-Semitism: The Longest Hatred* (London: Thames Methuen, 1991), pp. 46–47.

4. Quoted in Almog, "Racial Motif," p. 270.

5. Ibid.

6. Ibid., p. 272. See Langmuir's definition of the transition from anti-Jewish to anti-Semitic allegations; Langmuir, *Towards a Definition of Anti-Semitism,* pp. 282–97, 301–10.

7. Jeremy Noakes, "Nazism and Eugenics: The Background to the Nazi Sterilization Law of 14 July 1933," in *Idea into Politics: Aspects of European History 1880–1950,* ed. R. J. Bullen, H. Pogge von Strandmann, and A. B. Polonsky (London: Croom Helm, 1984), p. 76.

8. Paul Weindling, *Health, Race, and German Politics between National Unification and Nazism, 1870–1945* (Cambridge: Cambridge University Press, 1989), p. 1.

9. For an analysis that compares the different social policies in the United States and other European countries, see Henry Friedlander, *The Origins of Nazi Genocide from Euthanasia to the Final Solution* (Chapel Hill: University of North Carolina Press, 1995), pp. 1–22.

10. In this discussion I lean heavily on the following sources: Noakes, "Nazism and Eugenics," pp. 75–94; Weindling, *Health, Race, and German Politics,* pp. 1–10, 48–141, 305–68. See also Henry Friedlander, *Origins of Nazi Genocide,* pp. 1–22; George L. Mosse, *Towards the Final Solution: A History of European Racism* (New York: Howard Fertig, 1978), pp. 65–150; and George L. Mosse, *Nationalism and Sexuality: Respectability and Abnormal Sexuality in Modern Europe* (New York: Howard Fertig, 1985), pp. 133–94.

11. Quoted in Michael Burleigh and Wolfgang Wippermann, *The Racial State: Germany 1933–1945* (Cambridge: Cambridge University Press, 1991), p. 69.

12. Noakes, "Nazism and Eugenics," p. 81.

13. Henry Friedlander, "Euthanasia and the Final Solution," in *The Final Solution: Origins and Implementation,* ed. David Cesarani (London: Routledge, 1994), pp. 51–61; and also Henry Friedlander, *Origins of Nazi Genocide,* pp. 21–22, 295–302.

14. Almog, "Racial Motif," p. 255.

15. "Modernization, Modernism, and Anti-Semitism" (paper presented at workshop entitled "Radical Political Movements and Anti-Semitism" in the Vidal Sassoon International Center for the Study of Anti-Semitism, the Hebrew University of Jerusalem, January 1997). Quoted in SICSA, *Annual Report 1997,* p. 3.

16. Moshe Zimmermann, *Wilhelm Marr: The Patriarch of Anti-Semitism* (New

York: Oxford University Press, 1986); Moshe Zimmermann, "From Radicalism to Anti-Semitism," *Jerusalem Quarterly* 23 (Spring 1982), pp. 114–28.

17. Jacob Katz, "The Preparatory Stage of the Modern Anti-Semitic Movement (1873–79)," in *Anti-Semitism through the Ages*, pp. 279–89.

18. Saul Friedländer, *Nazi Germany and the Jews: The Years of Persecution, 1933–1939* (New York: HarperCollins, 1997), pp. 87–90.

19. Katz, "Preparatory Stage," pp. 285–86; Wistrich, *Anti-Semitism*, pp. 57–58.

20. Ruth Kluger, "The Theme of Anti-Semitism in the Work of Austrian Jews," in *Anti-Semitism in Times of Crisis*, ed. Sander L. Gilman and Steven T. Katz (New York: New York University Press, 1991), p. 176.

21. Katz, "Preparatory Stage," p. 288.

22. For an interesting analysis of Eckart's text, see *Bolshewismus von Moses bis Lenin: Ein Zweigespräche zwischen Adolf Hitler und mir* (Bolshevism from Moses to Lenin: A dialogue between Hitler and myself), (Munich: Franz Nachf., 1925); Yale Raz, "Eckart's Dialogue" (M.A. thesis [in Hebrew], Hebrew University of Jerusalem, 1995); see also Saul Friedländer, *Nazi Germany*, pp. 97–100.

23. Shulamit Volkov, "The Written Matter and the Spoken Word, on the Gap between Pre–1914 and Nazi Anti-Semitism," in *Unanswered Questions: Nazi Germany and the Genocide of the Jews*, ed. Francois Furet (New York: Schocken, 1989), pp. 33–53. Although I disagree with Volkov's distinction between the written and spoken anti-Semitic propaganda in the Second Reich and the Weimar Republic, I find her analysis very interesting.

24. For a full description of the invention of the *Protocols of the Elders of Zion*, see Norman Cohn, *Warrant for Genocide: The Myth of the Jewish World Conspiracy and the Protocols of the Elders of Zion* (New York: Harper & Row, 1967). For an interesting discussion of the *Protocols* and their relation to "the myth of the Jewish conspiracy" and racism, see Mosse, "Towards the Final Solution," pp. 120–22, and Saul Friedländer, *Nazi Germany and the Jews*, pp. 94–95.

25. On the issue of the Polish minority in East Prussia and legal steps taken against them, see Hans-Ulrich Wehler, "Anti-Semitism and the Minority Policy," in *Hostages Of Modernization*, pp. 29–40.

26. Kluger, "Theme of Anti-Semitism," p. 176.

27. See, for example, Herman Ahlwart, *Der Verzweiflungskampf der arischen Völker mit dem Judentum* (The desperate struggle between Aryans and Jew) (Berlin: F. Grobhäuser, 1890).

28. See, for example, "Do a Proper Job on the Jews," *Völkischer Beobachter*, March 10, 1920, quoted in *Documents on the Holocaust*, ed. Yizhak Arad, Yisrael Gutman, and Abraham Margaliot (Jerusalem: Yad Vashem, 1981), p. 19; Shulamit Volkov, "Anti-Semitism as a Cultural Code: Reflections on the History and Historiography of Anti-Semitism in Imperial Germany," *Leo Baeck Year Book* 23 (1978): 25–46.

29. These points appear in "The Program of the National-Socialist German Workers' Party," February 24, 1920, quoted in Arad, Gutman, and Margaliot, *Documents on the Holocaust*, pp. 15–18.

30. On the rather complex relationship between the eugenics scientists and National Socialism, particularly the differences between the anti-Semites among the

scholars and the physicians, see Weindling, *Health, Race, and German Politics,* pp. 488–564.

31. For a fascinating discussion on the issue of health and bourgeois values and nationalism see Mosse, *Nationalism and Sexuality.*

32. Burleigh and Wippermann, *Racial State,* pp. 136–150; Friedlander, *Origins of Nazi Genocide,* pp. 97–100.

33. Ibid., p. 142.

34. Adolf Hitler, *Mein Kampf,* trans. Ralph Manheim (Boston: Houghton Mifflin, 1943), pp. 300–327.

35. Arad, Gutman, and Margaliot, *Documents on the Holocaust,* p. 134.

36. Ibid., p. 162.

Part II

Between Race and Slavery: The Variations of Culture

5

Race or Culture: Medieval Notions of Difference

James Muldoon

Since the eighteenth century, race has been one of the most important factors in defining "the Other," those who are not us. Contemporary racial theory has identified skin color as the key marker in determining racial identity, although certain other physical standards have been used, for example, head shape. So important has the issue of race and color become that there is an inclination to see it as a fundamental and long-standing part of the human psyche.[1] Furthermore, in the United States the issues of race and color are inextricably entwined with slavery. Yet as Frank Snowden has pointed out, these linkages have not always existed: "The ancients did not fall into the error of biological racism; black skin was not a sign of inferiority." Snowden added that there is "a tendency to read modern racial concepts into ancient documents and to see color prejudice where none existed."[2] What Snowden has said about the ancient world also applies to the medieval world, that is, racism as we understand the term did not exist and skin color was not a mark of inferiority or of slavery. This is not to say that medievals did not discriminate in judging the Other or that they did not judge others as inferiors or that there was no slavery in medieval Europe. It only means that race as we understand it was not employed as a standard of judgment in these matters.[3]

What relevance could medieval notions of race and culture possibly have for a late-twentieth-century audience? Such knowledge might be of intellectual interest but would be of no value to understanding our current situation, since the medieval world is far removed from the modern world.[4] In fact, however, this is not the case. The modern world, generally considered to have begun in the sixteenth century, is constructed upon a medieval foundation. Medieval institutions, values, and beliefs continued to define

79

European society and culture into the eighteenth century. Perceptions of the Others whom Europeans encountered following Columbus's first voyage were rooted in medieval conceptions about the Others whom medievals met as they pushed out from the heartland of medieval Europe, that is, the old Carolingian empire.[5] It is well known that Columbus initially identified various plants in the Americas as the Asian spices he sought because, based on contemporary geographical knowledge, he was convinced that he had reached Asia and so the plants he saw must be the spices he sought.[6] The same is true of the peoples he and subsequent explorers encountered, whom Columbus perceived in terms of the Europeans' experience with the people they had encountered in the course of five hundred years of expansion.[7] Europeans applied this experience to the peoples they encountered in the sixteenth, seventeenth, and eighteenth centuries, seeing them in terms of those who had formed the medieval Other.[8] The English, for example, often compared the native Americans they encountered in North America with the Irish or the Scots, the "barbarous" peoples who populated the frontier of English expansion.[9]

It was not until the eighteenth century that Europeans had accumulated enough knowledge of the peoples beyond Europe to see at least some of these people as biologically different from Europeans, perhaps not descended from Adam and Eve at all.[10] Consequently, it became possible to argue that certain creatures who seemed human were not human at all or that there were some humanoids who lacked the capacity for the level of intellectual and moral development to which Europeans had risen. This could also mean that they formed the class of natural slaves that Aristotle had suggested might exist.[11] In other words, three centuries of experience in Africa, Asia, and the Americas gradually forced Europeans to reconsider the nature of the Other. As Columbus finally discovered that what he believed to be the fabled spices of Asia were not spices at all, so other Europeans gradually came to realize that the peoples of the several new worlds they had encountered were not like the peoples of the medieval European frontiers after all. Thus the lessons learned along the medieval frontiers would not be applicable in the Americas or elsewhere. It is out of this gradually developing awareness, I suggest, that modern notions of humanity emerged, including the belief that there are several biologically distinct races of mankind and that they possess varied intellectual and moral capacities. This experience, supported by modern scientific notions, created the notion of racism and the consequences that flowed from it.

Racism as a means of defining the Other did not exist in the Middle Ages. According to the dictionary, racism "is a belief that race is the primary determinant of human traits and capacities and that racial differences produce an inherent superiority of a particular race." Race is defined as follows: (1) "a breeding stock of animals," (2) "a family, tribe, people, or nation belonging to the same stock," (3) "a division of mankind possessing traits that are transmissible by descent and sufficient to characterize it as a distinct human type."[12] In the Middle Ages, there could be only one race because there was only one stock, creatures who were descended from Adam and Eve by way of Noah and his children as described in the opening chapters of the Book of Genesis. As long as this story lay at the foundation of biological theory, it was not possible for a Christian to argue that there were fundamental biological differences among human beings because that would mean that several races had sprung from different first parents.[13] The logical result of this perspective was that all differences among peoples were culturally constructed, that is, humanly made.

Any argument that there were several Adams and Eves, the sources of several human races, would also raise serious theological problems for three of the fundamental teachings of Christianity: original sin, Christ's redemptive sacrifice, and the universal mission of the Church. According to the doctrine of original sin, Adam and Eve's sin affected all of their descendants, making them flawed from birth. The doctrine of Christ's redemptive sacrifice explained that His death on the cross repaired the damage done by Adam's fall. If all human beings were not descended from Adam and Eve, Christianity would not be a universal religion—one that had a mission to all mankind—because not all humans would have been affected by Adam's sin, only those descended from him.

The biblical view of the oneness of humanity received support from the revival of Aristotelian philosophy in the twelfth century. Aristotle had pointed out that "man is by nature a political animal."[14] Elsewhere he observed that "a social instinct is implanted in all men by nature."[15] In other words, nature intended for people to live together in organized communities, communicating with and aiding one another in order to achieve a good life through the use of speech. Specifically, this meant the life of the city-state. "When several villages are united in a single complete community, large enough to be nearly or quite self-sufficing, the state comes into existence, originating in the bare needs of life, and continuing in existence for the sake of the good life." For Aristotle the proper way of life for humans was a settled, agricultural society in which people lived together in order to achieve a good life, that is, a moral life. Furthermore, the state "is a creation of nature [so that] he who by nature and not by mere accident is without a state, is either a bad man or above humanity."[16] Like his fellow Greeks, Aristotle took for granted that the barbarian was not a biologically different creature but someone whose language had the sound of childish babbling to the Greek ear and whose way of life was not the settled world of the city-state.[17] The barbarians included those who did not live in city-states but traveled with their flocks on a regular basis. Aristotle took it for for granted, however, that all human beings could create the kind of urban, settled life that he had identified as the norm for fully developed human existence. In effect, according to Aristotle, what differentiated one body of people from another was not racial difference but differences in political structure.[18] There is no indication that Aristotle believed other peoples to be incapable of rising to the level of life in the city-state, only that thus far they had not.[19]

Almost two millennia later, Thomas Aquinas (d. 1274), writing on politics, expressed the Aristotelian formula as "man is by nature a political and social animal."[20] He reemphasized the importance of language and communication as the vehicles by means of which men express their thoughts and ideas to others as they contribute their individual skills and insights to the formation and direction of the community as a whole.[21]

The important aspect of the Aristotelian and Thomistic discussion of politics is what is missing. The discussion has nothing to do with what we would call race nor does it include any discussion of the physical characteristics of people. Those whom Aristotle designated barbarians differed from the Greeks not in appearance but in actions. They did not live at the level of organized society that Aristotle argued was the natural basis of the good life. Neither Aristotle nor Aquinas claimed that barbarians were not capable of living at the natural level of existence, only that they did not. As all humans possessed reason and speech, so they possessed the capacity to create states.

The one exception to the rule that any group of humans could create a state in Aristotle's terms would be a society composed of those he identified as natural slaves. The natural slave would be the individual who "participates in rational principle enough to apprehend, but not to have, such a principle." Aristotle did not refer to any specific people as being natural slaves; such people, if they did exist, could not be identified on the basis of their physical appearance.[22] In other words, even if natural slaves actually existed, their condition had nothing to do with racial or physical characteristics. The Aristotelian–Thomistic view of humankind thus rested not on physical characteristics but on behavioral and structural standards—the form of social life that a group of people possessed. The difference among societies is best illustrated by a term that emerged in English around 1600— "civilize."[23] Literally, to be civilized is to live in a civitas, that is, to live in the Latin equivalent of the Greek polis, a city-state. The uncivilized were those who roamed about the world, following their flocks and not having a permanent place of their own. The epitomal barbarians, a stereotype reaching back to the ancient Greeks, were the Scythians, who "had become by 650 B.C. the masters of northwest Iran and eastern Turkey."[24] The Scythians were warrior nomads, the opposite of the settled people of the city-state.[25]

Although the distinction that the Greeks made between civilized and barbarian was not racial in the modern sense, biological and climatological elements could be involved. Ancient, medieval, and early modern thinkers saw the differences among societies in terms of the body's response to the environment within which it lived and in terms of the structure of government within which a people lived.[26] When barbarians created the institutions essential to the formation of a city-state, they too would become civilized. If the ancients and the medievals were not racists in the modern sense, they were, to use another modern term, behaviorists—they were inclined to believe that circumstances shaped the ways in which people lived. They were not, however, determinists—they did not believe that circumstances absolutely determined the ways in which people lived because, as Aristotle noted, they possessed skills, above all communication and reason, that enabled them to rise above the circumstances of their physical environment in order to create a state that would enable them to live a full moral life.

As we have seen, for medieval observers the key determinant of humanity was not physical appearance but language and the capacity for communication. Christians understood the multiplicity of human languages to reflect the dispersion of humankind after the collapse of the Tower of Babel and the end of a "culturally homogeneous mankind."[27] On the other hand, the ability of people to learn new languages or to communicate through translators was a reminder that humankind originally formed a single community and could do so again.[28]

What then of physical markers of difference? What role did they play in the medieval perception of the Other? The extreme case of people with significant physical differences from Europeans were the various creatures described by Herodotus and subsequently incorporated into the European conception of otherness. These creatures included those whose facial elements were in their chests, those who hopped along on one great foot, and those who had other kinds of bizarre bodies.[29] Augustine provided medieval thinkers with the answer to the question about the humanity of such creatures: As long as communication with such creatures was possible, then they were human. Their deformities were only temporary because in the afterlife God would restore them to proper human form. Such creatures were descendants of Adam and Eve and therefore beneficiaries of Christ's redemptive sacrifice.[30]

Europeans also considered cultural factors when determining difference. The first of these was religion. The fundamental distinction was between Christian and non-Christian, or, to look at it in a slightly different way, between Christians and those who were potentially Christians.[31] The most detailed statement of this distinction appeared in the canon law of the Church. Although this law was applicable to all baptized Christians, it recognized the existence of non-Church members with whom Christians would have to deal. Within the realm of the baptized there were those who had separated themselves from orthodoxy through schism or heresy and were thus deserving of punishment.[32] The Fourth Lateran Council (1215) threatened excommunication for Christian rulers who refused "to exterminate in the territories subject to their jurisdiction all heretics pointed out by the Church."[33] Over the next two centuries, secular rulers, beginning with Emperor Frederick II (1220–1250), followed with legislation ordering the burning of condemned heretics.[34]

Churchmen also had to deal with the unhappy reality of non-Christians living within Christian Europe. There were small Jewish communities in many parts of Europe and a large Muslim population in Spain, the result of the need for a labor supply in the lands reconquered from the Muslims. As a result, canon law recognized the existence of Jews and Muslims living within Christian society and laid out rules for Christian contacts with them.[35] Some efforts were made to convert these people to Christianity, but their presence within Christian society had to be tolerated because their services were useful and baptizing nonbelievers forcibly was not legitimate. Should they decide to convert, they would be the equals of all other Christians in theory, although in practice this was not always the case.[36]

In addition to differentiating among people on the basis of language and religion, medieval writers also saw law as providing a basis for distinguishing Them from Us. Each distinct society had its laws and, especially in the early Middle Ages, an individual could expect to be tried by the law proper to him and the society to which he belonged.[37] As Robert Bartlett put it, "Distinctive legal status was one way of recognizing or constituting separate ethnicity."[38] Throughout Europe, Jews, for example, lived by Jewish law, and in Spain the subject Muslim population lived according to its own laws. On the other hand, one way of indicating the assimilation of a conquered people was to impose the legal system of the conqueror.

Another basis for determining difference was way of life. This might mean the way in which people dressed, arranged their hair, rode their horses, and prepared their food. It could also mean their marriage practices, child rearing methods, and attitudes toward work. Robert Bartlett has pointed out that these characteristics created ethnic groups, not racial ones. That is, differences in religion, law, and language were the products of social life, not biological constants, and were malleable—they could be changed by human action.[39] Although human nature is singular, people have developed a variety of ways of life based on their particular circumstances. Individuals or groups can change their religion, their language, their law, or their style of dress, and in so doing change the nature of their society. A conquered people, for example, might be coerced into making some or all of these changes by a conqueror bent on the complete assimilation of the vanquished. Or, faced with the power—military, economic, or cultural—of a stronger society, individuals or an entire society might voluntarily adopt one, several, or all aspects of another culture in order to ensure their own survival or to obtain some advantages.[40]

That the medieval determination of Otherness rested on a cultural and not on a biological basis is exemplified in the interaction between the English and the Irish that took place from the twelfth to the early seventeenth centuries. This experience is interesting for two reasons. First, it demonstrates that the interaction between Europeans and Others was not a one-way street. Although the English anticipated transforming the Irish and leading them to a civilized level of existence, many of the English residing in Ireland eventually adopted the Irish way of life, moving from a civilized existence to an uncivilized one, as the English defined it. Second, experience with the Irish provided the English with an image of the Other and a model for dealing with the Other that was to shape the initial English response to the inhabitants of North America.

In the twelfth century, the English entered Ireland for a variety of reasons. The stated basis was set out in a papal bull of 1155 that Pope Adrian IV (1154–1159) issued at the request of King Henry II (1154–1189). The bull, known as "Laudabiliter," declared that in order to "enlarge the boundaries of the Church, to proclaim the truths of the Christian religion to a rude and ignorant people, and to root out the growths of vice from the field of the Lord" the English were authorized to rule over the Irish.[41] The Irish had of course been converted to Christianity centuries earlier, but the Irish church had for the most part, or so it was claimed, been untouched by the great ecclesiastical reform movement of the eleventh and twelfth centuries.[42] Henry II promised to reform the Irish church in return for the papal award of rule over the Irish. The underlying assumption was that the Irish were human but living at a less-than-human level of Christian life. For the next several centuries, papal letters authorizing Christian rulers to take control of other societies always asserted the papacy's responsibility for ensuring that members of a Christian society lived up to Christian standards of civility and that non-Christian societies lived according to the standard of civility implied in the natural law known to all rational creatures.[43]

From the perspective of this discussion, the interesting aspect of the English occupation of Ireland is not what happened to the Irish, but what happened to the English when they entered a new social and cultural environment and what this experience tells us about medieval notions of race and culture. A century after Henry II landed in Ireland to reform the state of religion and society in Ireland, Englishmen who lived there had begun a process that would inevitably lead to their being termed "more Irish than the Irish."[44] That is, to employ a much later term, many of the English in Ireland "went native" so that instead of transforming the Irish they themselves were transformed.

The basic reason for this unexpected turn of events was that the English hold on Ireland was weak and that problems at home and with possessions on the continent occupied the attention of English kings from the thirteenth century to the sixteenth century. Faced with having to choose between further expansion in Ireland and war in France, the English kings and their nobles found the effort to place the English monarch on the throne of France a much more profitable proposition than campaigning in Ireland.[45] Those noble families that chose to cast their lot with the conquest of Ireland found themselves in a very weak position.

As early as 1297, a parliament held in Ireland outlined what many of the English residing in Ireland had already done to protect their interests. They had "become degenerate in recent times, dress themselves in Irish garments and having their heads half shaven grow the hair from the back of the head, conforming themselves to the Irish as well in garb as in countenance." One consequence of this conforming to the Irish mode of dress was that on some occasions "Englishmen reputed as Irishmen are slain" because the killer could not differentiate between Englishmen and Irishmen. From a legal point of view this presented a problem because "the killing of Englishmen and Irishmen requires different modes of punishment."[46] The English and the Irish were thus differentiated not only by dress but by the laws to which they were subject as well.

The word "degenerate" became the common designation of Englishmen who adopted Irish garb and way of life. They had descended from the civilized standard of existence maintained in England and had sunk to the level of the "wild and barbarous Irish" whom they had been expected to raise to the civilized standard of life. The tension between degeneracy and uplift became an overriding theme of English–Irish relations over the next several centuries.

From very early on, then, the English recognized that the differences between themselves and the Irish were not racial but cultural, so that changing the structures within which the Irish lived would transform the Irish. As early as 1277, for example, there was a proposal to place the native Irish under English law. The existing Irish laws were "detestable to God and contrary to all law so much so that they ought not to be deemed law" at all.[47] This proposal was not enacted and the English and the Irish continued to exist in parallel universes, both living according to their own legal system and therefore within their own social and political culture which, as we have seen, was a common medieval practice.

In addition to the English and the Irish, by the early fourteenth century, there emerged what came to be termed a "middle nation" composed of English families that had remained in Ireland, intermarrying with leading Irish families and going native, in effect, creating new Irish tribes. Whereas the English authorities often saw such people as having degenerated to the Irish level of existence, the Irish saw them as a "mixed race" that was called by the pope "to rule our nation with justice and moderation" but had "set themselves wickedly to destroy it instead."[48]

Until the sixteenth century English monarchs were not in a position to impose their power over all of Ireland and the three peoples (often termed "nations") who now dwelled there. But they did explain what they would like to do. The Statutes of Kilkenny (1366) outlined a policy of ruling Ireland that recognized the emergence of a middle or mixed nation in Ireland that posed a fundamental threat to English control of the island. The statutes opened with a description of the effects of English degeneracy in Ireland:

> But now many of the said land, forsaking the English language, fashion, mode of riding, laws, and usages, live and govern themselves according to the manners, fashion, and language of the Irish enemies.
>
> Furthermore, these Englishmen have also married Irishwomen and allied themselves with "the Irish enemies aforesaid" with the result that "the English language, the allegiance due to our lord the King, and the English laws there are put in subjection and decayed and the Irish enemies exalted and raised up contrary to right."[49]

The Statutes of Kilkenny went on to ban marriage, "concubinage or amour" between the English and the Irish. Furthermore, the statutes required "that every Englishman shall use the English language and be named by an English name, use the English custom, fashion, mode of riding and apparel according to his estate," and forbade the use of the Irish language by Englishmen or Irishman "living amongst the English."[50] The English in Ireland were to stop going native and creating what were in effect new Irish tribes. The statutes were thus directed at families such as the FitzGeralds, the Earls of Kildare, who had entered Ireland with the earliest Norman invaders and had determined to establish themselves permanently there, even at the cost of adopting the Irish way of life.[51] In the late Middle Ages, the FitzGeralds and related families became the greatest threat to English control of Ireland. One historian has described them at the end of the Middle Ages as possessing "the all-but-kingship" of Ireland.[52] In 1541, after putting down a FitzGerald-led rebellion that threatened to end English power in Ireland, Henry VIII adopted the title king of Ireland in addition to his other titles in order to demonstrate that Ireland was again an important focus of English royal concern.[53]

Although some critics have described the Statutes of Kilkenny as racist and as a form of apartheid, it is clear that at this point the English did not see the Irish as biologically different from themselves or lacking some qualities, moral and intellectual capacities for example, that the English possessed.[54] The primary goal of the statutes was to protect the royal interest in Ireland by forcing the English in Ireland to retain their distinctive culture and to maintain their separation from the Irish by retaining the external manners of Englishmen. In addition, those Irishmen who wished to live among the English and to be treated as equals would have to adopt the English language and way of life. There was no suggestion that the Irish were incapable of living in English fashion, only that the native Irish way of life was not conducive to civilized existence.

By the end of the sixteenth century, as a new English effort to colonize Ireland was beginning, several English officials and other observers commented on the problem of dealing with the Irish and discussed the reasons for the failure of the English to perform the tasks that Laudabiliter had imposed on them as the price for being granted control of the island. One of the most important of these writers was Sir John Davies, the attorney general for Ireland, who bluntly titled his book on Ireland *A Discovery of the True Causes why Ireland was never entirely Subdued* (1612). In his opinion, the fundamental reason for the English failure in Ireland was "the Irish custom, or Brehon law," which failed to provide suitable punishment for major crimes such as "murder, manslaughter, rape, robbery and theft," only fining the perpetrators instead of putting them to death as required by "the just and honourable law of England."[55] Davies doubtlessly realized that the Anglo-Saxon kingdoms of England had also employed fines to punish what would become capital crimes.[56] He saw the transition from defining murder as a tort that could be punished by money compensation to a crime that the king's court could punish by hanging as a social and cultural advance.

Davies went on to indicate other elements of Irish law that prevented the Irish from becoming civilized in the English understanding of the term. In the first place, Irish law did not guarantee possession of property by an individual and his heirs. A man had only a life interest at best in his land, and his eldest son did not succeed to it at his death. Even tribal chiefs were not automatically succeeded by their sons with the result that "all their possessions [were] uncertain being shuffled, and changed, and removed so often from one to another, which uncertainty of estates hath been the true cause of such desolation and barbarism in this land." He went on to list other evils that afflicted the Irish—evils that stemmed from the Brehon law, not from some inherent flaw in the Irish themselves. Indeed, he professed being puzzled by the condition of the Irish, given the fact that "though the Irishry be a nation of great antiquity, and wanted neither wit nor valour, and though they have received the Christian faith and were lovers of music, poetry, and all kinds of learning," they built no buildings and did not improve the land in which they dwelled. Sir John attributed these failures "to those unreasonable customs which made their estates so uncertain and transitory in their possessions."[57] By imposing the Common Law on the Irish, the English king would be providing them with the legal structure necessary to live as civilized men.

The Statutes of Kilkenny and Sir John Davies's discussion of Irish law illustrate the medieval English conception of Otherness. The Irish were biologically identical with the English but culturally different, and, presumably, the Irish would have developed socially and culturally as the English had if only they had adopted the kind of laws that the English had. At the same time, English observers were aware that even civilized people, if placed in circumstances such as existed in Ireland, could degenerate to the Irish level of existence if allowed to do so. Clearly, civilized society as the English defined it was not simply the natural and inevitable result of human development. It required conscious effort to achieve and constant vigilance to maintain. Furthermore, as these and other documents demonstrate, the English government had good reason to fear the attraction of the Irish way of life on the English settled in Ireland. It was after all the degenerate English who posed the greatest threat to English domination of Ireland in the late Middle Ages and the beginning of the modern era. A middle race that could join the tribal alliances typical of Irish society with sophisticated English knowledge of military and diplomatic matters posed the greatest threat of all to the English in Ireland. Degeneracy led to the formation of a middle people and then led to rebellion against the Crown. That was one of the most important lessons that the English learned from their centuries of experience in Ireland. This lesson was to have important long-term consequences for English colonial policy in North America.[58]

When the English encountered the native peoples of North America in the seventeenth century and established American colonies, they initially perceived them in terms derived from their experience in Ireland: They saw native Americans existing at a level of primitive life that they associated with the Wild Irish. Early English observers saw similarities to Irish dress and practices in the native Americans' long, flowing hair, deerskin robes, and game of lacrosse. From the perspective of these English observers, they were at a stage of social development roughly similar to that of the Irish. Presumably, both the Irish and the native Americans would rise to the civilized, truly Christian stage of human development under English guidance.[59] In fact, of course, this did not happen. By the middle of the seventeenth century, English settlers in Ireland and in North America appeared to have given up all hope of converting and civilizing the Irish and the natives.[60] These peoples seemed impervious to all instruction in religion and manner of life. By the end of the seventeenth century, the native Irish leadership class had died or was living in exile in Spain and France. The plantation of Ireland with Protestant settlers followed the exiling of surviving Catholic landowners from the fertile lands of Ulster to the rocky soil of Connaught, paralleling the subsequent removal of native Americans from the eastern shores of North America. The first trail of tears was not from Georgia to Oklahoma but from Ulster to Connaught.[61]

It might be concluded at this point that by the seventeenth century the English were employing racist policies in dealing with the Irish and the native Americans. It would be easy to assume that racism had undergirded English thought all along, emerging when the English had to face people unlike themselves. Seen from this perspective, the Statutes of Kilkenny and similar legal texts become signposts along the route to full-fledged racism. To think in this way, however, is wrong because it reads back into the medieval and early modern eras a concept, racism, that emerged at a much later date.

Racism is the theory that people exist as biologically distinct groups and not as a single biological humanity. The differences among these biologically distinct groups are not simply external differences in size, color, and so forth. Rather, the external characteristics of each group signify fundamental differences in intellect and moral capacity. Racism began to emerge when the medieval world was breaking up. The Protestant Reformation generated a number of theological theories, including the possibility that there had been more than one set of first parents—the theory of polygenesis instead of monogenesis.[62] The subsequent development of modern biology reinforced the notion of polygenesis, providing a secular basis to explain it in place of the biblical arguments.[63] If a common humanity did not exist, then native Americans or Africans or Irish could be argued to fit Aristotle's category of natural slaves, that is, people who lacked the capacity for the full development of the moral virtues necessary for truly human existence. It was even possible to define some humanoid creatures as nonhuman because they lacked souls.[64]

This is not to say that all non-European peoples were regarded as natural slaves. It was well known that China, India, and, later, Japan, were as socially and culturally developed as European Christian society. The Jesuit Joseph Acosta (d. 1600) even developed a threefold hierarchy of societies, demonstrating that the only significant difference between these advanced Asian societies and European society was that they were not yet Christian. Below these Asian states were societies such as the ones created by the Aztecs and Incas in the Americas, which were well along the path to fully civilized status. At the bottom of the hierarchy were primitive peoples who moved constantly from place to place, having no fixed habitation. Even these people were fully human in Acosta's opinion, since they had been civilized at some earlier time but had degenerated from civilized ways of living in the course of moving from Asia to the Americas. They could, however, be "reduced to civility," that is, brought back to a civilized level of existence, under European Christian guidance.[65]

There are aspects of medieval thought that some scholars have identified

as at least protoracist. Medieval writers employed words that form the vocabulary of modern racism, but we must be careful to appreciate the meaning they attached to these words and the contexts within which they employed them. As Robert Bartlett has pointed out, along the medieval
European frontiers there was a "language of race—*gens, natio,* 'blood,'
'stock' " that is biological in form, "but its medieval reality was almost entirely cultural."[66] Examining the same medieval vocabulary, Richard Hoffmann has taken a different stand, arguing that "when medieval writers and
men of action chose words and images like 'birth,' 'blood,' 'inheritance,'
and 'lineage' to refer to large social groups, they exhibited a fundamentally
biological explanation of how the groups came into being."[67] Hoffmann,
however, underestimates the role of cultural transformation in the course
of interaction between Christian Europeans and others along the frontiers
of Europe. In his opinion, medieval observers could conceive of "non-ge-
netic explanations of large-scale cultural phenomena," cultural transformation for example, only in terms of "conversion to Christianity," a process
that required direct divine intervention.[68] As indicated previously, however, medieval observers recognized that changing the legal system within
which a people lived would cause significant cultural change as well.

It is important to realize, nevertheless, that medieval notions of difference
operated within the context of kinship-based societies, societies that
stressed common descent and blood relationships. Furthermore, in addition
to pre-Christian roots of kinship-based societies, which would encourage a
precise understanding of an individual's origins and relationship to others,
Christian marriage law also encouraged the need to understand one's genealogy in order to avoid marrying within the forbidden degrees of kinship.[69]

It is also clear that converting to Christianity did not automatically mean
that the members of a newly converted group were fully acceptable to
other Christians. As the status of Jews in medieval society indicates, Jewish
converts were not fully accepted and, as in Spain, remained identifiable as
New Christians. It was possible for a group that conformed externally to
European Christian standards of existence to be considered a "middle people" demonstrating characteristics of two groups, the one they left and the
one they joined, but remaining quite distinct from each and not accepted
as equals in social and cultural terms.

One possible solution to the problem of cultural differentiation was intermarriage with the goal of raising the uncivilized Other to the European
level of civility. As the English experience in Ireland suggested, however,
intermarriage might be taken to lead to the degeneracy of the civilized partner. Thus, in spite of the belief held by some leading Virginians that intermarriage with and assimilation of the native American population should
be the goal of British colonial policy and in spite of the famous marriage of
Pocahontas and John Rolfe in 1614, this was not to be the case. The massa-

cre of 1622 spelled the end of any policy of peaceful assimilation, which was replaced by a policy designed "to exterminate and to dispossess" native Americans.[70] Subsequently, intermarriage was "nearly nonexistent, due largely to racial prejudice and early balanced sex ratios."[71] Even in Massachusetts, where the Praying Towns created (or at least attempted to create) a Christian Native American population, separate development, not intermarriage, was the goal.[72] What the work of Bartlett, Hoffmann, and other medievalists demonstrates is that the emergence of biological theories of human difference has some links to the medieval experience, if not medieval theory. Although medieval observers assumed that all humankind was descended from one set of parents, they were puzzled by the fact of significant differentiation among peoples. This differentiation was, for the most part, seen in cultural terms—the way of life that a people followed. The puzzlement arose from the fact that even after conversion to Christianity and full adoption of the European manner of living, some peoples, such as Jews, were still identifiable as Others. Retained cultural characteristics such as food preferences, manner of dress, and other cultural markers, as well as real or perceived physical markers such as the shape of the head or nose, color or length of the hair, served to create the feeling that the differences were more than cultural, that in some way the differences were innate. After all, the consequence of the medieval notion of a common humanity was the conclusion that all human societies would evolve in roughly the same way, yet clearly they did not. What could explain the failure of other societies to become like European society, especially after the gospels of Christianity and Aristotelian civility had been preached to them? One answer was that some people did not possess the intellectual and moral capacities to do so. They were, in a word, inferior to Europeans morally and intellectually, perhaps because of some innate flaw. From this conclusion sprang, among other evils, the argument that it was better for Africans to be enslaved in the American South than to live in their own society. While such an existence was assumed to be an improvement over the slaves' original way of life, there was no like assumption that after a few generations of servitude the slaves would advance to the social and cultural level of their masters. The relationship between slave and master was fixed by a biological imperative. It was a law of nature that could not be repealed. The medieval notion that humanity was one and that all humankind had the same capacity for transformation was replaced by a pseudoscientific view people existed as biologically different races, the mental and moral capacities of which were fixed for all time.

NOTES

I wish to thank Professor Roxann Wheeler, Indiana University of Pennsylvania, for reading the earlier version of this paper and suggesting revisions.

1. "We assume that the racial and ethnic diversity we see around us has always existed as a historical, social, and biological fact that needs no further interrogation." Ivan Hannaford, *Race: The History of an Idea in the West* (Baltimore: Johns Hopkins University Press, 1996), 3.

2. Frank M. Snowden Jr., *Before Color Prejudice: The Ancient View of Blacks* (1983; reprint, Cambridge: Harvard University Press, 1991), 63–64.

3. For a different perspective, see James H. Sweet, "The Iberian Roots of American Racist Thought," *William and Mary Quarterly*, 3d series, 54 (1997): 143–66.

4. The question of the significance of the medieval experience for Americans was recently raised by two medievalists; see Paul Freedman and Gabrielle M. Spiegel, "Medievalisms Old and New: The Rediscovery of Alterity in North American Medieval Studies," *American Historical Review* 103 (1998): 677–704.

5. Christopher Dawson, *The Making of Europe* (New York: Sheel & Ward, 1932; reprint, Cleveland: World, 1956), 240–41; concerning the medieval expansion of Europe and its implications for post-Columbus European expansion, see James Muldoon, *The Expansion of Europe: The First Phase* (Philadelphia: University of Pennsylvania Press, 1977); and J. R. S. Phillips, *The Medieval Expansion of Europe,* 2d ed. (Oxford: Oxford University Press, 1998).

6. *The Log of Christopher Columbus,* trans. Robert H. Fuson (Camden, Me.: International Marine Publishing, 1987), 129. To understand how Columbus perceived the world, see Valerie I. J. Flint, *The Imaginative Landscape of Christopher Columbus* (Princeton: Princeton University Press, 1992).

7. For example, he compared the inhabitants of the Caribbean Islands to the inhabitants of the Canary Islands; see *The Log,* 76.

8. As Anthony Grafton has pointed out, recent historical revisionism argues "that the actual pace of change was slower and the power of inherited authority more durable and more complex than many historians have acknowledged." *New Worlds, Ancient Texts: The Power of Tradition and the Shock of Discovery* (Cambridge: Harvard University Press, 1992), 7.

9. James Muldoon, "The Indian as Irishman," *Essex Institute Historical Collections* 111 (1975): 267–89; Arthur H. Williamson, "Scots, Indians and Empire," *Past and Present* 150 (February 1996): 46–83, esp. 54. It has been argued that the Indian–Celtic analogy has been overemphasized; see Alden T. Vaughan, "Early English Paradigms for New World Natives," *Proceedings of the American Antiquarian Society* 102 (1992): 33–67, esp. 46–50.

10. In addition to the works of Flint and Grafton on the ways in which the past controlled the European understanding of the New World, see John H. Elliott, *The Old World and the New, 1492–1650* (Cambridge: Cambridge University Press, 1970).

11. Hannaford, *History of an Idea,* 44–45.

12. *Webster's Ninth New Collegiate Dictionary* (Springfield, Mass.: Merriam-Webster, 1990), 969.

13. The story of Noah and the curse placed on his son Ham (Genesis 9:22–27) is often cited as the basis for the justification of African slavery and therefore of racism. One important difficulty in linking this story with racism is that the biblical

story does not mention the color of Ham and his son Canaan, only that the son will be the "servant of servants unto his brethren." Thus slavery or subordination was a consequence of Ham's actions, but this was not linked to skin color. It is sometimes argued that the rabbinic tradition of commentary on the Bible eventually made the connection between skin color and slavery and passed from this tradition to the larger society. For a careful analysis of this debate, see David M. Goldenberg, "The Curse of Ham: A Case of Rabbinic Racism," in *Struggles in the Promised Land*, ed. Jack Salzman and Cornel West (New York: Oxford University Press, 1997), 21–51. I wish to thank William Jordan for this reference.

14. Aristotle *Politics* 1.2. The translation cited here is that of Benjamin Jowett as excerpted in *Thomas Aquinas: On Politics and Ethics*, trans. and ed. Paul E. Sigmund (New York: Norton, 1988), 96.

15. Ibid., 97.

16. Ibid., 96.

17. The Greek term *barbaroi* initially meant people who did not speak Greek. Eventually it came to include the implication that "those who were (linguistically) unintelligible were well on their way to being seen as unintelligent." J. K. Davies, "Greece after the Persian Wars," in *The Cambridge Ancient History*, vol. 5, *The Fifth Century B.C.*, 2d ed. (Cambridge: Cambridge University Press, 1992), 15–33, esp. 16.

18. Hannaford, *History of an Idea*, 57.

19. He pointed out that the Greeks had not always lived at this level of existence but had evolved from rule by kings to rule by citizens; Sigmund, *Thomas Aquinas*, 96.

20. Ibid., 14.

21. Ibid., 15.

22. Ibid., 98–99. Aristotle's ideas about slavery have often been identified as a source of racist thought. For a survey of this issue and a critique, see Hannaford, *History of an Idea*, 43–57.

23. *Webster's Ninth New Collegiate Dictionary*, 244.

24. Hannaford, *History of an Idea*, p. 29.

25. On the Scythians, see T. Sulimirski and T. Taylor, "The Scythians," in *Cambridge Ancient History*, vol. 8, pt. 2, *The Assyrian and Babylonian Empires and Other States of the Near East, from the Eighth to the Sixth Centuries B.C.* (Cambridge: Cambridge University Press, 1991), 547–90. On the use of this image as a synonym for barbarism in the sixteenth century, see Muldoon, "Indian as Irishman," 275.

26. Hannaford, *History of an Idea*, 25–30, 47.

27. Margaret T. Hodgen, *Early Anthropology in the Sixteenth and Seventeenth Centuries* (Philadelphia: University of Pennsylvania Press, 1964), 56; see also Robert Bartlett, *The Making of Europe* (Princeton: Princeton University Press, 1993), 198.

28. The role of interpreters in European expansion has been little studied. Concerning their role on the medieval European frontier, see Bartlett, *Making of Europe*, 198–99. In the fifteenth century, as the Portuguese moved down the western coast of Africa, they developed the practice of obtaining local residents, purchased, kidnapped, or "delegated by the local political authority," to train as interpreters; see Ivana Elbl, "Cross-cultural Trade and Diplomacy: Portuguese Relations with West Africa, 1441–1521," *Journal of World History* 3 (1992): 165–204, esp. 171.

29. Hodgen, *Early Anthropology,* 53, 57.
30. Augustine *City of God* (trans. John Healey) 16.8. Roxann Wheeler pointed out to me that William Blake echoed Augustine's point in "The Little Black Boy" (*The Oxford Book of English Verse 1250–1918,* new ed. [Oxford: Oxford University Press, 1939], 575–76).
31. This paralleled the Islamic distinction between "the House of Islam (Dar al-Islam) and the House of War (Dar al-Harb)." See Bernard Lewis, *The Muslim Discovery of Europe* (New York: W. W. Norton, 1982), 60.
32. *Corpus Iuris Canonici, Decretales* 5.7; *De Haeretics* 5.8; *De Frigidis* 5.9; *De Apostatis.*
33. Decree of the Fourth Lateran Council (1215), in *The Middle Ages,* vol. 1, *Sources of Medieval History,* 5th ed., ed. Brian Tierney (New York: McGraw-Hill, 1992), 267.
34. David Abulafia, *Frederick II: A Medieval Emperor* (1988; reprint, Oxford: Oxford University Press, 1992), 211–13.
35. Joseph F. O'Callaghan, *A History of Medieval Spain* (Ithaca: Cornell University Press, 1975), 459–66.
36. Jewish converts, of whom there was a large number, remained clearly identifiable as New Christians, or conversos. They formed a middle people between Christians and Jews, indicating that their conversion did not automatically incorporate them fully into Spanish Christian society; see Edward Peters, "Jewish History and Gentile Memory: The Expulsion of 1492," *Jewish History* 9 (1995): 9–34. For a specific case of a converted Jew who remained identified as a Jew, see Jonathan Elukin, "From Jew to Christian: Conversion and Immutability in Medieval Europe," in *Varieties of Religious Conversion in the Middle Ages* (Gainesville, Fla.: University Press of Florida, 1997), 171–89.
37. "This is the principle of the 'personality' of law: whatever his place of residence and whoever the sovereign of the place, an individual remains subject to the law of his own people of origin." R.C. van Caenegem, *An Historical Introduction to Private Law,* trans. D. E. L. Johnston (Cambridge: Cambridge University Press, 1992), 19.
38. Bartlett, *Making of Europe,* 204.
39. Ibid., 197.
40. Bede gives the example of the pagan high priest Coifi who became a Christian because he received little material benefit when he served his god, although he served him faithfully; Bede, *A History of the English Church and People,* trans. Leo Sherley-Price (Harmondsworth, 1955), 124–26.
41. Laudabiliter, *Irish Historical Documents 1172–1922,* ed. Edmund Curtis and R. B. McDowell (1943; reprint, New York, 1968), 17–18, esp. 17. For the use of this papal letter in connection with the conquest of the Americas, see James Muldoon, "Spiritual Conquest Compared: Laudabiliter and the Conquest of the Americas," in *Iure Veritas: Studies in Canon Law in Memory of Schafer Williams,* ed. Steven B. Bowman and Blanche E. Cody (Cincinnati: University of Cincinnati College of Law, 1991), 174–86.
42. Concerning the condition of the Church in Ireland on the eve of the English invasion, see J. A. Watt, *The Church and the Two Nations in Ireland* (Cambridge: Cambridge University Press, 1970), 1–34.

43. The most extensive examination of these papal bulls is Luis Weckmann, *Las Bulas Alejandrinas de 1493 y la Teoriá del Papado Medieval* (Mexico City: Instituto de Historia, 1949); see also Weckmann, *The Medieval Heritage of Mexico,* trans. Frances M. Lopez-Morillas (New York: Fordham University Press, 1992).

44. Some recent scholarship has suggested that "the older nationalist view that they [the Norman invaders] became 'more Irish than the Irish themselves'" should not be taken at face value; see F. X. Martin, "Introduction: Medieval Ireland," in *A New History of Ireland,* vol. 2, *Medieval Ireland, 1169–1534,* ed. Art Cosgrove (Oxford: Clarendon Press, 1993), xlix–lxii, esp. lxi. Another scholar has argued that "the extent to which English habits had been abandoned by the Anglicized population in favour of Gaelic ones was greatly exaggerated by contemporaries." Nicholas Canny, "Early Modern Ireland, c. 1500–1700," in *The Oxford History of Ireland,* ed. R. F. Foster (Oxford: Oxford University Press, 1992), 90.

45. For a survey of the situation in late medieval Ireland, see Art Cosgrove, "The Emergence of the Pale, 1399–1447," in *New History of Ireland,* 2:533–56.

46. Parliament of Ireland, 1297 (25 Edward I); Curtis and McDowell, *Irish Historical Documents,* 32–38, esp. 37.

47. Ibid., 32.

48. The Remonstrance of the Irish Princes to Pope John XXII, 1317, in Curtis and McDowell, *Irish Historical Documents,* 38–46, esp. 45.

49. The Statutes of Kilkenny, 1366; in ibid., 52–61, esp. 52.

50. Ibid., 53.

51. On the FitzGeralds, see Brian Fitzgerald, *The Geraldines: An Experiment in Irish Government, 1169–1601* (London: Staples, 1951).

52. Edmund Curtis, *A History of Ireland,* 6th ed. (1950; reprint, London: Methuen, 1966), 146.

53. An Act that the King of England and His Successors be Kings of Ireland, in Curtis and McDowell, *Irish Historical Documents,* 77–78.

54. "Undoubtedly these amounted to a policy of racial exclusiveness on the part of the English in Ireland." Seán Duffy, *Ireland in the Middle Ages* (New York: St. Martin's, 1997), 154. On the other hand, Watt has pointed out that the term "racial" should not be applied because an Irishman could obtain "the same legal status as any Englishman" by adopting the English way of life; see Watt, *The Church,* 200 n. 4.

55. Sir John Davis, *A Discovery of the True Causes Why Ireland Was Never Entirely Subdued, in Irish History from Contemporary Sources (1509–1610),* ed. Constantia Maxwell (London: Allen & Unwin, 1923), 351–54, esp. 352.

56. See, for example, the list of compensations in the "Dooms [Laws] of Alfred (871–901)," in *Sources of English Constitutional History,* ed. Carl Stephenson and F. G. Marcham (New York: Harper, 1937), 10–12.

57. Davies, *Discovery,* 352–53. For a brief survey of Irish land tenure practices, see Kenneth Nicholls, "Gaelic Society and Economy in the High Middle Ages," in *New History of Ireland,* 2:397–438, esp. 430–33.

58. Michael Zuckerman, "Identity in British America: Unease in Eden," in *Colonial Identity in the Atlantic World, 1500–1800* (Princeton: Princeton University Press, 1987), 115–57, esp. 137–38, 150.

59. Muldoon, "Indian as Irishman," 287–89.

60. During the Cromwellian era "many plans were proposed for their [the Irish] conversion, and a number of ministers deputed to preach in Irish, though converts were few and their motives nearly always suspect. The assembly of ministers in 1658 discussed this topic, though by this time it seems to have been accepted that in fact there would not be large-scale conversions." Patrick J. Corish, "The Cromwellian Conquest, 1649–53," *New History of Ireland* 3:336–86, esp. 380. Missionary efforts among native Americans in the Massachusetts Bay colony declined after the death of John Eliot in 1690; see Jean M. O'Brien, *Dispossessing by Degrees: Indian Land and Identity in Natick, Massachusetts, 1650–1790* (Cambridge: Cambridge University Press, 1997), 87–88.

61. For a survey of this period of Irish history, see Nicholas Canny, "Early Modern Ireland, c. 1500–1700," in *The Oxford History of Ireland,* ed. R. F. Foster (Oxford: Oxford University Press, 1992), 88–133. Perhaps recognizing the similarity of their situations, the Choctaw tribe (who had been forced to move from Georgia to Oklahoma in 1831) collected $170 to send the Irish for famine relief during the 1840s famine; Christine Kinealy, *A Death-Dealing Famine: The Great Hunger in Ireland* (London: Pluto Press, 1997), 111.

62. For a survey of the development of theories of polygensis, see Hodgen, *Early Anthropology,* 223–38.

63. Hannaford, *History of an Idea,* 147–49; Stephen Jay Gould, *The Flamingo's Smile* (New York: Norton, 1985), 185–98. The discovery of the Americas and its inhabitants set off a great debate about their origins. Their existence raised the possibility that they had been created separately from all of the previously known peoples: see Lee Eldridge Huddleston, *Origins of the American Indians: European Concepts, 1492–1729* (Austin: University of Texas Press, 1967).

64. According to one scholar, "sixteenth-century Europeans had no compunction about killing Indians because the Indians had no souls." Henry Steele Commager, "Should the Historian Make Moral Judgments?" *American Heritage* 17, no. 2 (1966): 27, 87–93, esp. 91.

65. James Muldoon, *The Americas in the Spanish World Order* (Philadelphia: University of Pennsylvania Press, 1994), 67–71. The Latin root of "to reduce," *reduco,* means "to lead back." To reduce to civility, therefore, means to bring back the uncivilized to the cultural level of social existence from which they had slipped or degenerated.

66. Bartlett, *Making of Europe,* 196.

67. Richard Hoffmann, "Outsiders by Birth and Blood: Racist Ideologies and Realities around the Periphery of Medieval European Culture," *Studies in Medieval and Renaissance History* 6 (1983): 1–36, esp. 3.

68. Ibid., 23.

69. James Brundage, *Law, Sex, and Christian Society in Medieval Europe* (Chicago: University of Chicago Press, 1987), 355–56.

70. Frances Mossiker, *Pocahontas: The Life and the Legend* (1976; reprint, New York: Da Capo, 1996), 188, 307; Alden Vaughan, *New England Frontier: Puritans and Indians, 1620–1675,* 3d ed. (Norman: University of Oklahoma Press, 1995), 209.

71. James Axtell, *The Invasion Within* (New York: Oxford University Press, 1985), 304; see also Zuckerman, "Identity in British America," 145–47.

72. Zuckerman, 145.

6

Enslavement and Manumission in Ancient Greece

Gary Reger

The concept of "race" has no place in the study of slavery in the ancient Greek world. In this regard, historians of Greek antiquity enjoy a liberty not shared by our colleagues specializing in the modern world, who must deal daily with the burden imposed by an idea that was developed in Europe in the eighteenth and nineteenth centuries out of then current thinking in biology and anthropology. In contrast, "Kushites, Ethiopians, and Nubians, the blackest, most woolly-haired people known to the Greeks and Romans, unlike blacks in later societies, were not subjected to economic, political, and social discrimination on the basis of their color. . . . Ancient slavery was color-blind. Both whites and blacks were slaves, and the ancient world never developed a concept of the equivalence of slave and black; nor did it create theories to prove that blacks were more suited to slavery than others."[1]

This conclusion, the most recent comment on the matter of race in antiquity by its most learned student, has been widely accepted by historians of the ancient Greek world. This is not to say, of course, that the Greeks were blind to physical differences in human beings or to the fact that those differences correlated with place of origin; indeed, they exploited those phyiscal differences in their depictions of people on vases and in other plastic media, and they sought philosophical explanations for them in theories about climate or other factors.[2] Nor did this mean that the Greeks were entirely without prejudice—quite the contrary. The Greeks harbored strong prejudices against people who were not Greek, and even had their suspicions about certain "marginal" Greeks (like the Boiotians or the Aitolians, not to mention the Macedonians).These prejudices could and did issue in notions about suitability for enslavement that may look, at first glance, not unlike the notions about the suitability of Africans for enslavement that underlie justifications of New World slavery in more modern times. But there are important differences too, as we shall see. A "taint" that may have been attached to a group did not necessarily infect every individual in that group, and, perhaps even more interesting, persons of the same "ethnicity" could be slaves and free men in the same place at the same time.

There are passages in Greek literature that may seem to develop, at least in embryo, a notion that certain populations, certain "ethnic groups,"[3] or certain persons were indeed more suited for enslavement than others. Perhaps the most explicit statement appears in the locus classicus justifying Greek slavery, a lengthy discussion near the beginning of Aristotle's *Politics*. In essence, Aristotle asserted that some men are naturally suited to lead, others to obey, just as the body is naturally inferior to and subject to the soul; and so those who are by nature inferior (he classified women in this group too) are slaves by nature, for whom it is advantageous to be ruled by others. Aristotle recognized a problem here, however: some people end up as slaves because they are captured in war; clearly this is an accident (or so the critics Aristotle cited claim), and their enslavement was thus neither just nor natural. Aristotle's answer to this objection was convoluted; he toyed with the notion that "might makes right," but the nub of the problem for him was that Greeks cannot be slaves by nature,[4] whereas "barbarians" can, indeed are, and that assertion seems to be Aristotle's final word on the matter. If Aristotle had a "racial" theory of slavery, this was it. I shall return below to the question of just what he was trying to say after exploring some other types of evidence about the relationship between ethnic origin and enslavement in ancient Greece.

The only method of acquiring slaves that Aristotle mentioned was capture in warfare. For Aristotle, eager to justify his view of the "natural" superiority of Greeks to all other peoples, the "unenslavability" of Greeks formed a crucial element of this identity. This notion recurs elsewhere. In the *Republic*, Plato explicitly argued that Greeks should not enslave Greeks, and in his *Menexenos* he added that warfare between Greek *poleis* should proceed no further than "victory," that is, the defeated should suffer no further humiliation, which, among other things, could include enslavement. A common alternative fate for war captives was to be ransomed by relatives, friends, or their home *poleis*. Despite the claims of the philosophers and a considerable amount of ancient distaste, Greeks might indeed enslave Greeks owing to warfare. In the Archaic period the town of Methymna on the island of Lesbos completely enslaved its neighbor Arsiba after a military victory. During the later phases of the Peloponnesian War the Athenians captured the town of Iasos in Asia Minor and sold all its inhabitants, "slave and free," to the local Persian governor for the same price each. In 223 B.C. Aratos and his Achaians completely enslaved the Peloponnesian city of Mantineia, an action that Aratos' much later biographer Plutarch regarded as un-Greek. These are only three out of many possible examples.[5] In practice, the body of slaves in Greece always included Greeks, and it would have been impossible, except in a completely theoretical way, to maintain a distinction between persons enslavable by ethnicity and those not.

There were other methods of procuring slaves as well.[6] Piracy and brigandage were practiced throughout antiquity and, of course, children born to slaves were slaves themselves.[7] There was also a "legitimate" trade in slaves imported by specialists or generalized traders from regions more or less far away from the Greek *poleis*. Herodotus claims that the Thracians, who inhabited the part of the Balkan peninsula now roughly occupied by Bulgaria, actively sold their own children to slave dealers.[8] Also to Herodotus is owed the story of the specialist in eunuch slaves, Panionios of Chios, who came to a bitter end. According to Aristophanes (and a scholiast), the Thessalians, who lived north of Athens between Boiotia and Macedon, specialized in trading in slaves by buying them from former owners for resale.[9] Another important point of exchange for slaves was located in the northern Black Sea area. As for piracy, Pausanias, the Greek travel writer of the second century A.D., offers a vivid description of the methods of Illyrian pirates, who originated in what is now roughly Albania. Some Illyrians put in at the city of Mothone, pretending to be interested in trading. Once local suspicions were lulled, "women as well as men came down to the ships to sell wine and obtain things from the visitors in exchange. At this point the Illyrians violently seized many of the men and an even greater number of the women; they put them on board their ships and sailed back to the Adriatic, leaving the city of Mothone depopulated."[10] Evidence that such actions were common enough can be seen in Herodotus, who attributes the first instance of Greco-Persian conflict to the same kind of kidnapping.[11] For our purposes, it is important to bear in mind that these mechanisms did not yield slaves of one particular origin only. Piracy and brigandage were especially suited to harvesting an indiscriminate crop, but more focused processes, like slave trading, might bring in slaves from various regions and of various backgrounds. Warfare directed against political enemies enslaved whoever happened to be the enemy of the moment. But it is also important to remember that we have no figures, no "statistics," that would enable us to gauge the relative importance of these processes, which must in any case have varied over time and space.

To illustrate some of these processes, I would like to focus on a set of documents from Classical Athens. One morning in May 415 B.C., Athenians awoke to a scandal. During the night, person or persons unknown had rampaged through Athens, mutilating dozens of small statues called *hermai* ("hermes") that were used as boundary markers. The act was sacrilegious and sparked a witch-hunt for the perpetrators; ultimately, many aristocrats, members of prominent families, were tried and convicted of the crime. In Athens the state typically confiscated people's property as part of their punishment. Such confiscated property was put in the charge of a board of public officials whose duty it was to sell the property at auction. In order to account for the money so realized and to create a permanent record of the action taken in punishment for the crime, these officials arranged for complete lists of the property, by owner, with the prices fetched, to be inscribed on marble tablets and erected in a public place in Athens. American excavators have rediscovered many fragments of these documents, which offer a gold mine of information about the household goods of wealthy Athenians in the Classical period.[12] The texts include information on thirty-six slaves identified by place of origin. The patterns here are very interesting. Eleven of these thirty-six are from Thrace, the single largest ethnic group in the texts. The next largest group consists of seven Carians (from the southwestern corner of Asia Minor). All other ethnicities, which include Illyrian, Syrian, Scythian (south Russia), Lydian (west-central Asia Minor), Macedonian (northern Greece), Phrygian (central Asia Minor), and Cappadocian (southeast Asia Minor), are represented by only one, two, or three slaves. Only two slaves, one from Messenia and the other from Crete, were Greek. Three are identified as "house born" (oikogenes).

We do not know how these people became slaves, but one avenue at least seems unlikely.[13] Since Athenian operations during the Peloponnesian War in the northern Aegean were confined to the coastal regions, it is unlikely that the many Thracian slaves sold by the state here originated as war booty. Instead, they were probably victims of the peacetime trade in slaves undertaken by the Thracians themselves, probably with Greek intermediaries, as Herodotus describes. The same is probably true for the Carians. There were two Athenian operations in Caria in the early stages of the Peloponnesian War. The first, in 430–429 B.C., ended in disaster when the Athenian general was killed in neighboring Lycia and part of his army was destoyed. The second in the following year was even less successful: the Athenian general and his forces were utterly defeated before they had even entered Caria proper.[14] It is perfectly possible, perhaps even likely, that some of these slaves may have fallen into slavery as a result of Athenian operations. Nevertheless, the military history of Athens in the fifteen years prior to their appearance in the historical record strongly suggests that many of them are more likely to have been enslaved as a result of peacetime trade in slaves.

The variety of non-Greeks who were enslaved is striking; slaves from north and east of Greece, belonging to at least nine different identifiable ethnic groups, are attested. Moreover, and more importantly, these groups did not mark out peoples who were regarded as exclusively, or predominantly, fit to be slaves. Let's consider just the two groups that contributed the most slaves to our lists, the Thracians and the Carians. It is easy to find persons from these regions in Athens in honored positions. The Athenians struck treaties with Thracian kings, and Thracians show up as paid mercenaries at Athens in a list that includes men from most of the Greek world. Miltiades, father of the great mid-fifth-century Athenian general Cimon, married a Thracian princess, and the mother of Themistocles, the Athenian hero of the second war against the Persians, was either a Thracian or a Carian.[15] A Carian named Tymnes son of Skylax died and was buried in Athens toward the end of the sixth century B.C.; the epitaph makes it clear that he was an important person. Many Carian cities paid tribute to the Athenians during the years of the empire, and the Carian dynasts Tymnes and Pigres were loyal allies of the Athenians (at least for a few years). Carians appear also in the list of mercenaries mentioned above.[16] Despite their numbers—and this is the crucial point—there was no presumption that either the Thracians or the Carians as a group "deserved" to be enslaved or were especially "fit" for slavery. Contingent historical circumstances determined that some Carians and Thracians happened to end up as slaves while others lived in Athens as free men or enjoyed close political and military ties with the Athenian government.

A very different set of evidence comes to us from the temple of Apollo at Delphi. Work there has revealed roughly a thousand inscriptions that record the manumission of slaves from the late fourth century B.C. into the Roman imperial period, with the preponderance of texts dating from the second and first centuries B.C. Here is an example, slightly abridged: "In the archonship of Tharres [144 B.C.] . . . Telon and Cleto, with the approval of their son Straton, sold to Pythian Apollo a male slave whose name is Sosus, of Cappadocian origin, for the price of three minas of silver. Accordingly Sosus entrusted the sale to the god, on condition of his being free and not to be claimed as a slave by anyone for all time."[17] Sometimes the sale was conditional, requiring continued service on the part of the slave to the former masters: in 167 B.C. "Critodamus son of Damocles . . . sold to Pythian Apollo a male slave whose name is Maiphatas, of Galatian origin, and a female (slave) whose name is Ammia, of Illyrian origin, for the price of seven minas of silver. Maiphatas and Ammia shall remain with Critodamus for as long as Critodamus lives, doing for Critodamus what they are told to do; if they do not remain and do what they are told to, the sale shall be null and void. When Critodamus dies, Maiphatas and Ammia shall be free and the sale shall remain with the god on the condition that they are free and not to be claimed as slaves by anyone for their whole life, doing whatever they wish and going wherever they wish."[18] Slavish conditions might be inflicted on supposedly manumitted persons. For example, the unfortunate

Bion was manumitted but, like Maiphatas and Ammia, was required to stay
with his former masters and was obligated to "do everything possible that
he was ordered; but if he should not do it, they (his masters) have the authority to punish Bion and whip him in whatever way they like."[19]

To explore the legal complexities of these sales, however interesting,
would take us far from the limited purposes of this chapter, as indeed would
discussion of their rich contribution to our understanding of the social and
economic history of the Hellenistic period, and so I leave these questions
aside.[20] For our purposes their most important feature is their inclusion of
a place of origin for slaves who are manumitted. A sample of 197 slaves
(which is itself only part of the total numbers preserved) whose origins are
given yields interesting patterns.[21] The ultimate origins of the vast majority
(152 of the total) are obscured by the fact that they are listed as "house
born" (endogenes). It is clear, however, that all of these must have traced
their ancestry back to a parent (very rarely a more distant ancestor) who
was enslaved, like the four house-born children of Sostrata, herself a Syrian
by origin.[22] Of the forty-five slaves in the sample who were not house
born, ten came from Syria and two from nearby Sarmata. Cappadocia and
Thrace each produced five. There are individual slaves from other areas
outside the Greek world, including Illyria, and from Galatia,[23] Phrygia, Pis-
idia, and Bithynia, all in Asia Minor. But the Greek slaves show the most
surprising origin, without exception originating in towns close to Delphi.
Thus there are five slaves called Boiotians, one from Phokis, one from Kor-
oneia, and one from Delphi itself. If any more proof is needed that origin
did not matter in questions of enslavement, we may consider two cases in
which, on the one hand, a master manumitted a slave from Aitolia (a region
near Delphi; the Aitolians controlled the sanctuary for much of the Hellenistic period) and, on the other, the manumittor was himself an Aitolian.[24]

In all this evidence we have reviewed (which is of course only a small
sample of the total available), there is no indication of a tie between "race,"
however construed, and slavery. But, it may be objected, Aristotle makes
just such a connection in the passage from the *Politics* with which I started.
There Aristotle draws a clear distinction between Greeks, who are "by nature" not fit for slavery, and "barbarians," who are. Doesn't this at least
show one strain of thinking in Greek antiquity that equated race and enslavement?

I think not. It would be a mistake to equate Aristotle's barbarians with a
race. Barbarians were defined for Aristotle, as for most Greeks, entirely by
a negative: they were any people who were not Greek. Greek means, most
specifically, not just speaking the Greek language and sharing Greek culture
(a prominent part of which was the Olympic Games, which were open
only to Greeks) but enjoying citizenship in a Greek *polis*. People who
lacked this most defining feature were simply, ipso facto, not Greek, and so

barbarian. But ethnically, they could claim any identity: Phoenician, Egyptian, Nubian, Roman, Carian, Phrygian, Scythian, or what have you. These ethnicities, though themselves highly labile and exceedingly difficult to define,[25] were mutually exclusive, and that exclusivity was recognized by the Greeks themselves; I need only point to Herodotus' careful characterization of all the peoples of the world known to him. Barbarian, then, cannot be construed, even loosely, as a racial identification.

But Aristotle's comments require further historical context. He wrote *Politics* between 336 and 322 B.C., years that saw the extraordinary achievements of Alexander the Great.[26] Carrying out his father's plans, Alexander invaded Asia and conquered the Persian empire. In the preceding century the Persians had frequently intervened in local Greek politics. It was Persian money that helped secure victory for the Spartans over the Athenians in the final acts of the Peloponnesian War, and in the following decades the Persians on several occasions had imposed a common, or king's, peace on warring Greek city-states when it suited their purposes.[27] Moreover, Greek armies had been defeated or stymied on Persian soil. All this was a far cry from the triumphs of the Persian wars of the start of the fifth century B.C., when a handful of Greek warriors defeated the might of the Persian army (as the legend went). The climate of opinion in the fourth century reflected Greek frustration with a de facto Persian overlordship. As Pierre Ducrey has clearly documented,[28] the notion of "barbarian" as equivalent to "slave" arose in exactly this context, with explicit claims of Greek superiority in texts like Euripides' *Iphigeneia at Aulis,* the passages from Plato cited above, and Isocrates' call for a war of vengeance against the Persians in his *Panegyrikos.* It was this war that Philip planned and Alexander executed. These claims reached a crescendo with Alexander's war. Alexander was urged by many to divide the world into two groups, Greeks, who were to be treated as friends, and barbarians, who were to be treated as enemies. Plutarch tells us explicitly that this advice came from Aristotle.[29]

Claims that the Persians were naturally inferior, then, formed part of the propaganda fueling and justifying the drive for war. There may, however, have been another factor in Aristotle's mind. Alexander did not treat the Persians he defeated as "natural slaves." Quite the contrary: he confirmed several Persian satraps (provincial governors) in office, accepted Persian advisers, and, in his most controversial move, trained Persian youth to fight in Macedonian style and forced his Greek and Macedonian officers to marry Persian women. The precise nature of Alexander's plans remains obscure, but there can be no doubt that he recognized, and intended to exploit, the Persians' vast experience at running a huge land empire; he seems to have envisioned a joint Macedonian–Persian ruling aristocracy, to which even the Greek *poleis* of his domain would have been subject.[30] Such a vision clashed with the fantasies of revenge and Greek superiority that had

fueled the desire for the war. Aristotle, who had served for a while as Alexander's tutor, may well have had some of his former student's activities in
mind when he asserted unequivocally the natural inferiority of the "barbarians," a term that was often code in Greek for Persians. Thus Aristotle was
not offering a racial theory of slavery here but a warning against equating
barbarians and Greeks as natural leaders—a warning that Alexander and
many of his successors completely ignored.

There are many issues that I have left unexplored in this chapter. For
example, I have not tried to disentangle the elements in notions of "race"
and notions of "ethnicity," whether in ancient Greece or today. Nor have
I entered the debate—which animated many Greek philosophers who
thought about the meaning of "natural slavery"—on the role played by
nature *(physis)* and convention *(nomos)* in making people the way they are
and thus creating some groups who were regarded as fit for leadership and
others who were fit to be slaves. (Aristotle adumbrated these debates in
his brief allusion to people who thought that slavery is entirely a matter of
convention; one would dearly love to know who these thinkers were, to
say nothing of having some of their writings!) But there is one matter about
which I must say something, since it may have influenced Greek attitudes
toward the people they enslaved. The Delphic manumission inscriptions
discussed above hint at the extraordinary role that manumission, or at least
the possibility of manumission, may have played in Greek slavery (much
more can be said about this with respect to Roman slavery). This fact, along
with the presence of large numbers of slaves both in skilled crafts like smi-
thing or cobbling and as servants in Greek cities, sometimes quite well educated and granted broad, important responsibilities in wealthy households,
must have given slavery a very different texture from the unskilled and
largely rural character it had in the southern United States. Greeks in cities
like Delphi and Athens met slaves on a daily basis, buying and selling from
those set up by their masters in small businesses, served by others at elite
dinner parties, sung to or read to (or otherwise serviced) by still others at
those same parties. Athens has preserved for us many texts attesting to the
manumission of slaves, mostly in skilled occupations, from the later fourth
century B.C.[31] Along with these slaves, Athenians also met ex-slaves on a
daily basis.

In this situation, combined with the fact that Greeks themselves might
be enslaved—as we have seen above—no Greek (except of course Aristotle) could luxuriate in smug self-confidence that he was innately superior
to those enslaved around him. There was a strong factor of contingency in
the likelihood that one would be enslaved—and that one would be manumitted after enslavement—which surely moderated attitudes to the extent
that it forbade absolute certainty about the permanence of one's status.
(This contingency drives the plots of many plays of Greek New Comedy

that are preserved in Plautus's Latin adaptations.) By this of course I do not mean to excuse or ameliorate the institution of slavery in ancient Greece. The Greeks were fully capable of barbarity toward their slaves individually and, as M. I. Finley argued many years ago with great precision and moral depth, Greek society was structured in a way that supported and perpetuated enslavement: it was a "slave society," no matter how great or small the actual numbers of slaves.[32] But I do think it fair to argue that the particular historical character of Greek slavery made it difficult for ethnic markers of slave versus free to arise the way such markers arose around race in modern Western society. The clumsiness in Aristotle's attempt to do something like that in the *Politics*, and the transparency of his political motives, flow in part from the particular complexities and ambiguities of Greek slavery.

NOTES

1. F. M. Snowden, "Bernal's 'Blacks' and the Afrocentrists," in *Black Athena Revisited*, ed. Mary Lefkowitz and Guy MacLean Rogers (Chapel Hill: University of North Carolina Press, 1996), 121, 123. The most recent general book on Greek slavery known to me is N. R. E. Fisher, *Slavery in Classical Greece* (Bristol: Bristol Classical Press, 1993). I am very grateful to Berel Lang for organizing the conference at which an earlier version of this chapter was read and for his careful editorial comments, which have greatly improved the version of that paper which is printed here. The lively discussion that followed, moderated by Adrienne Fulco, raised many interesting points that I have not been able to enter into here, more for want of expertise than space. It would be invidious to single out individuals, but I must thank by name at least Helen Lang, who directed my attention toward some philosophical issues I had not considered. Remaining errors—and there are surely some—must be credited to my account.

2. See generally still Frank M. Snowden Jr., *Before Color Prejudice: The Ancient View of Blacks* (Cambridge: Harvard University Press, 1983) with plenty of illustrations and references to learned studies and primary literature.

3. See now Jonathan Hall, *Ethnic Identity in Greek Antiquity* (Cambridge: Cambridge University Press, 1997).

4. Aristotle *Politics* 1.2.2–23 (1253b15–1255b40); for the "nub of the problem," see 1.2.18–19 (1255a23–b3). Another use of the same metaphor of the household occurs at *Metaphysics* 12.10 (1075a19–22); I owe this reference to Helen Lang, who offers her interpretation of this chapter of the *Metaphysics* in "The Structure and Substance of Metaphysics L," *Phronesis* 38 (1993): 257–280. One might compare the medieval Islamic prohibition on enslaving fellow Muslims, which explains in part why Islamic regimes sought their slaves among non-Muslims, including the Mamluks and the Christian victims of the Ottoman *devsirme*.

5. Plato *Republic* 469b–d; *Menexenos* 242d; Herodotus 1.151.2; Thucydides 8.28.4; Polybius 2.62.11–12; Plutarch *Aratus* 45.6. The subject has been studied in detail by Hans Volkmann, *Die Massenversklavungen der Einwohner eroberter Städte in*

der hellenistisch–römischen Zeit, 2nd ed., ed. Gerhard Horsmann, Forschungen zur antiken Sklaverei 22 (Stuttgart: Franz Steiner, 1990), with abundant bibliography. (All
Greek texts cited are Loeb Classical Library editions.)

6. For a good summary of the mechanisms (which I basically follow), see Yvon
Garlan, Slavery in Ancient Greece, 2d ed., trans. Janet Lloyd (Ithaca, N.Y.: Cornell
University Press, 1988), 45–55.

7. There is now a comprehensive study of this phenomenon for the Roman
imperial period: Elisabeth Herrmann–Otto, Ex ancilla natus: Untersuchungen zu den
"Hausgeborenen" Sklaven und Sklavinnen des römischen Kaiserreich, Forschungen zur
antiken Sklaverei 24 (Stuttgart: Franz Steiner, 1994).

8. Herodotus 5.6.1. See M. I. Finley, "The Slave Trade in Antiquity: The Black
Sea and Danubian Regions," in Economy and Society in Ancient Greece, ed. Brent D.
Shaw and Richard P. Saller (London: Penguin, 1981), 167–75.

9. Herodotus 8.105.1–2; Aristophanes Ploutos 520–21 with scholiast.

10. Strabo 11.2.3. Pausanios 4.35.6, translation by Thomas Wiedemann, Greek
and Roman Slavery (Baltimore: Johns Hopkins University Press, 1981), 111 n. 107.

11. Herodotus 1.1–2.

12. The locus classicus is Thucydides 6.27–29, 53, 60; the texts are Inscriptiones
Graecae I³, 421–30 (column I only of 421 as R. Meiggs and D. M. Lewis, A Selection
of Greek Historical Inscriptions² [Oxford: Oxford University Press, 1988], 240–47 no.
79). The editio princeps is W. K. Pritchett, "The Attic Stelai: Part I," Hesperia 22
(1953): 225–99. Commentary appeared in subsequent issues of the same journal;
for discussion of the slaves, see W. K. Pritchett, "The Attic Stelai: Part II," Hesperia
25 (1956): 276–81. His numbers differ from mine, which are taken from inspection
of the latest edition.

13. Pritchett, Hesperia 25 (1956): 280 assumes that "the majority of slaves came
from war."

14. Thucydides 2.69, 3.19; cf. also Pausanias 1.29.7. See Antony G. Keen,
"Athenian Campaigns in Karia and Lykia during the Peloponnesian War," Journal
of Hellenic Studies 113 (1993): 152–57; on the identity of Sandios lophos, see Louis
Robert, "Philologie et géographie II. Sur Pline l'Ancien livre II: 1. Le lac Sannaus.
2. Hybanda. 3. Le courrier Philonides," Anatolia 4 (1959): 19–22 (Opera Minora
Selecta 3 [Amsterdam: Habbert, 1969] 1441–44).

15. IG II² 126 (M. N. Tod, Greek Historical Inscriptions 2 [Oxford 1948]: 151–54
n. 151), 127; IG II² 1956.184–86. Plutarch, Cimon 4.1; Plutarch, Themistocles 1.1–2.

16. Cf. Supplementum Epigraphicum Graecum 13 (1956): 36. Benjamin Dean Mer-
itt, H. T. Wade–Gery, and Malcolm Francis McGregor, The Athenian Tribute Lists,
vol. 1 (Cambridge: Harvard University Press, 1939), 495 (Tymnes), 551–52 (Pigres). IG II² 1956.94–95, 97–103.

17. SGDI II 2143, trans. M. M. Austin, The Hellenistic World from Alexander to the
Roman Conquest: A Selection of Ancient Sources in Translation (Cambridge: Cambridge
University Press, 1981), 221 n. 127a.

18. SGDI II 1854, ibid., 221 n. 127b.

19. P. Thémélis and D. Mulliez, "Un acte d'affranchissement delphique inédit
du Trésor de Cnide," Bulletin de correspondance hellénique 113 (1989): 343–46, lines
8–10 (my translation). A few more of these texts are translated by Wiedemann,

Greek and Roman Slavery, 46–48 n. 23–24, 48–49 n. 26. For a full catalogue of these and similar texts, see Linda Collins Reilly, *Slaves in Ancient Greece: Slaves from Greek Manumission Inscriptions* (Chicago: Ares, 1978), passim. Similar procedures for freeing slaves can be seen at nearby Chaironeia in Boiotia, Paul Roesch and John M. Fossey, "Neuf actes d'affranchissement de Chéroneé," *Zeitschrift für Popyrologie und Epigraphik* 29 (1978): 123–37; on the island of Kalymnos off the western coast of Asia Minor, Mario Segre, "Tituli Calymni," *Annuario,* n.s., 5–6 (1944–1945) n. 152–208a, on which see A. Babakos, *Shesis oikogeneiakou diaiou eis ten neson kalymon ton A'm. Ch.aiona* (Athens, 1963), though this dating requires reconsideration; and in Thessalia, Antoine M. Babacos, *Actes d'aliénation en commun et autres phénomenes apparentés d'après le droit de la Thessalie antique* (Thessalonike: University of Thessaloniki, 1966), 29–46 (analysis), 98–230 (inscriptions).

20. Some of the issues can be explored through Babacos, *Actes d'aliénation*; Keith Hopkins with P. J. Roscoe, *Conquerors and Slaves* (Cambridge: Cambridge University Press, 1978), 99–115; Richard P. Duncan-Jones, "Problems of the Delphic Manumission Payments 200–1 B.C.," *ZPE* 57 (1984): 203–9.

21. The texts can be found at *Fouilles de Delphes* III 1.293, 297, 302, 305, 310, 311, 320, 336, 565–68; 2.121–85 (not continuous); 3.1–439 (not continuous); 4.70, 78, 479, 480A–B, 482–503 (not continuous); 6.5–137 (not continuous).

22. *Fouilles de Delphes* III 1.566.

23. *Fouilles de Delphes* III 3.208, 6.118.

24. Georges Nachtergael, *Les Galates en Grece et les Sôtéria de Delphes: Recherches d'histoire et d'épigraphie hellénistiques* (Brussels: Palais des académies, 1977); R. Flacerlie. re, *Les Aitoliens à Delphes: Contribution à l'histoire de la Grèce centrale au IIIe siècle avant J.–C.* (Paris: E. de Boccard, 1937); Georges Daux, *Delphes au IIe et au Ier siècle, depuis l'abaissement de lÉtolie jusqu'à la paix romaine (191–31 av. J.–C.)* (Paris: E. de Boccard, 1936); and see Joseph Scholten, *The Politics of Plunder: The Aitolians and Their Koinon in the Early Hellenistic Era, 279–217 BC* (Berkeley: University of California Press, 1999), *Fouilles de Delphes* III 3.9, 6.13.

25. Hall, *Ethnic Identity in Greek Antiquity.*

26. The latest event mentioned is the death of Philip II of Macedon, which occurred in 336 (5.8.10.1311b2–4); Aristotle died in 322.

27. T. T. B. Rider, *Koine Eirene: General Peace and Local Independence in Ancient Greece* (Oxford: Oxford University Press, 1965); Martin Jehne, *Koine Eirene: Untersuchungen zu den Befriedung– und Stabilisierungsbemühungen in der griechischen Poliswelt des 4. Jahrhundert v. Chr., Hermes Einzelschrift* 63 (Stuttgart: Franz Steiner, 1994).

28. Pierre Ducrey, *Le traitement des prisonniers de guerre dans la Grèce antique des origines à la conquête romaine,* Travaux et memoires 17 (Paris: E. de Boccard, 1968), 271–74; note his remark at pp. 273–74: "La thèse est pousée à son extrême par Aristote, pour qui, par essence, Barbare et esclave sont synonymes."

29. Strabo 1.4.9 [C66]; Plutarch *Moralia* 329B.

30. See A. B. Bosworth, *Conquest and Empire: The Reign of Alexander the Great* (Cambridge: Cambridge University Press, 1988), 158–62 (Persians and Macedonians at Babylon), 229–41 (appointment of Persian administrators and administrative policy), 271–73 (use of Persian and other eastern troops). An interesting reflection of this attitude recurs in the pseudo-Aristotelan tract preserved only in Arabic

and called "The Letter of Aristotle to Alexander on the Policy toward the Cities";
see *Lettre d'Aristote à Alexandre sur la politique envers les cités*, ed. Józef Bielawski and
Marian Plezia (Warsaw: Polskiej Academii Nouk., 1970).
    31. *IG* II² 1553–78. Several new texts have appeared since this collection was
made.
    32. M. I. Finley, "Was Greek Civilization Based on Slave Labour?" in *Economy
and Society in Ancient Greece,* 97–115. See also Finley's *Ancient Slavery and Modern
Ideology* (New York: Chatto & Windus, 1980), esp. 67–92.

7

American Negro Slavery: A Reconsideration

Jack Chatfield

The year 1918 saw the publication of a landmark in American historical writing. The book was *American Negro Slavery: A Survey of the Supply, Employment, and Control of Negro Labor as Determined by the Plantation Regime*. Written by Ulrich B. Phillips, a Georgia-born historian who had already gained distinction as a prolific and pioneering scholar of the antebellum South, the work was greeted by a chorus of accolades from academic and lay circles alike. The *Baltimore Sun* praised the book as a "fair and impartial account" of slavery. A rural Georgia paper, apparently mistaking the University of Michigan professor for a Yankee, said the book was written from "a Northern perspective" but commended Phillips for abandoning prejudices in favor of "clear-cut facts." The Virginia historian Philip Alexander Bruce, a staunchly white supremacist scholar of slavery who had also written a bleak account of the southern Negro since emancipation, told Phillips that most works on "this subject are disfigured and warped by biased opinion. . . . They are either too northern or too southern—but . . . you have struck exactly the right key. You are calm, impartial, judicial. . . . You have presented the facts as they were, in the spirit of a perfectly disinterested historian. The work is a monument of research, and equally of so fair and discriminating presentation. . . . I venture to say that you have said the final word." Phillips's detractors—among them academic historians W. E. B. DuBois, Carter Woodson, and Frederic Bancroft—mounted a sharp attack, but their words did not find a receptive audience. Even the Springfield *Republican*—once the voice of the antislavery cause—praised Phillips, comparing his work with that of neoabolitionist scholar James Ford Rhodes.[1]

Phillips may have been puzzled, even exasperated, at being compared to Rhodes, a high school–educated Cleveland iron manufacturer, who, with fellow amateurs James Schouler and John Bach McMaster and German-trained Hermann Eduard von Holst, dominated the "nationalist" school of historians whose multivolume studies celebrated the triumph of American republican ideals over southern sectionalism, states' rights extremism, and the "frightful blot" of slavery.[2] The latter phrase was used by von Holst, whose work Phillips contemptuously dismissed as a "caricature" and whose authority the young Georgian hoped to undermine—or destroy—by the weight of his own scholarly enterprises. "The history of the United States has been written by Boston and largely written wrong," said Phillips in a 1903 letter to a friend. "It must be written anew before it reaches its final form of truth, and for that work the South must do its part. . . . New England has already overdone its part."[3]

But Phillips was supremely confident that he brought more than a regional sensibility and sound intelligence to what he once called the "virgin field" of southern history.[4] As an undergraduate at the University of Georgia in the 1890s, he had been schooled in the new "scientific" history by John H.T. McPherson, whose doctoral training under Herbert Baxter Adams at Johns Hopkins University placed him in the swelling ranks of scholars who were laying the foundations of the modern profession of historical research and pedagogy. An undistinguished scholar himself, McPherson introduced Phillips to the work of Frederick Jackson Turner, his fellow student at Hopkins, whose seminal essay, "The Significance of the Frontier in American History," had been published in 1894. Turner's essay apparently struck the young Phillips with the force of revelation with its references to the "germs of processes," the "vital forces" that "lie behind constitutional forms and modifications," and "the record of social evolution"; with its metaphor of society as a "complex nervous system" undergoing "steady growth"; with its invocation of the frontier as a "crucible" in which Americans were "fused" into a "mixed race, English in neither nationality or characteristics"; with its picture of "tides" and "waves" of emigrants "impelled by an irresistible attraction" toward the free lands of the west; with its attention to geological "arteries" and the "centers of frontier attraction"; and its bold affirmation of the primacy of material forces in history. "So long as free land exists," said Turner, "the opportunity for a competency exists, and economic power secures political power."[5] During the summer of 1898, Phillips studied with Turner at the University of Chicago, and he began his teaching career at Turner's Wisconsin, where he captivated students with his lectures on the antebellum South and mined the immense southern collection at the university library.

By this time his intellectual compass was apparently set. In 1903, after the publication of his first book, *Georgia and State Rights,* and just before his appointment at Wisconsin, Phillips wrote, "A short investigation has shown me that the political history of our section has been dominated in nearly every instance by economic conditions and considerations, and it is easy to see that when an adequate history comes to be written of the South . . . it must treat southern developments largely with an economic interpretation." In another essay he wrote, "to him who would follow an economic interpretation, [southern history] is especially alluring. Material wealth was quickly translated by the plantation system into terms of social distinction and political control." As Merton Dillon has said, the young Phillips "accepted Turner's early dictum that history is an amalgam of past literature, past politics, past religion, and past economics, though even more than Turner he singled out economic interest, maintaining it to be the prime force in historical process. For Phillips, ideology and morals had no independent, objective reality. Economics and demography, his studies of antebellum Georgia taught, largely determined political behavior. His understanding of history thus placed him with the progressive historians— Turner, Charles A. Beard, Carl L. Becker—whose works for so long set the dominant interpretation of the American past." Phillips never tired of acknowledging his debt to Turner. "A deepening appreciation of the historic significance of the plantation and of the preceding frontier regimes," he told Becker in 1925, "I owe to Dr. Frederick J. Turner of the University of Wisconsin, whose constant disciple I have been since 1898."⁶

But discipleship for Phillips was not deference to great figures but a kind of inspirational or "exhilarating" force that helped shape the work of a fertile and restless mind. Turner's students, he once said, "are not content (the good ones) to walk in his steps, but are eager to blaze paths of their own."⁷ If Dillon is correct in claiming that the young Phillips embraced a species of economic determinism in his work on Georgia politics and society, it is equally clear that his emerging interpretation of southern culture—evident especially in the many essays that preceded the publication of *American Negro Slavery*—revealed his determination to depict the antebellum regime as a "living order" possessing a "natural organic life."⁸ This could signify many things. But to the mature Ulrich B. Phillips—the Phillips of *American Negro Slavery*—it signified a regime dominated by large-scale commercial agriculture, "a stereotyped economy with staple production as its cardinal feature," but profoundly, even permanently, shaped by other factors as well. In the final analysis, said Phillips, the plantation South in the days of slavery could not be described simply as an economic mechanism governed by the exploitation of bonded labor and the acquisition of material wealth. "The regime," he insisted, "was conditioned" not only by its economic relationships and by its material pursuits but "by its habitat, its products, the racial quality of its labor supply and the traditional predilections of the masters."⁹ Here, in capsule form, is the interpretive framework of *American Negro Slavery*.

The meaning of these suggestive phrases is elaborately explained in a work that even today is bound to impress the inquisitive reader as a remark-able historical and literary accomplishment. Slavery had long been a promi-nent topic in American historical writing. The nationalist historians had ex-plored in depth the corrosive controversy over slavery, which they believed had caused the disruption of the Union. James Ford Rhodes had devoted a substantial chapter of his history—the famous chapter 4—to an appraisal of slavery as a social institution rather than simply a source of sectional dishar-mony and war. Indeed, Rhodes's harsh analysis—joined as it was to a deep-seated and reflexive racism—helped shape the views of Harvard professor Albert Bushnell Hart, the descendant of an Ohio Free Soiler whose *Slavery and Abolition,* published in 1906, was written as a volume in the American Nation series of which Hart was the editor. Equally significant, beginning in the late 1880s, Johns Hopkins University became a center for institu-tional studies of slavery. In the years before the Great War, Hopkins pub-lished seven monographic studies, each exploring aspects of the institution in a single state. Some—though not all—are still consulted by serious stu-dents of slavery.[10] As I have suggested, Phillips found serious fault with most or all of these works, either because of what he saw as sectional bias and ignorance or because—as he said of the Hopkins studies—they failed to reveal "the true nature of the living order" of the antebellum regime.[11]

Even Phillips's harshest critics may agree that, as a work of the historical imagination, *American Negro Slavery* makes the Old South reappear with many—though not all—of the features of a "living order." By a resourceful and dexterous use of carefully selected and arranged primary source materi-als—newspapers, magazines, travelers' accounts, plantation diaries, account books, personal letters, works of political economy, and planters' instruc-tions to overseers—and by an interpretive scheme that becomes a broad and colorful thread in the fabric of the book, Phillips painted a picture of a society sustained in part by semitropical abundance, governed by a patriar-chal planter class, and immeasurably enriched, even ennobled, by the daun-ting challenge of caring for a population of childlike, cheerful, affectionate, loyal Negroes, whose "inert" labor diminishes the earnings of their owners while presenting a fair field for the exercise of their finer impulses. Here was a society, Phillips tells us, in which the interests of property-holders—the owners of human "capital"—were absolutely congruent with the spirit of benevolence and humane, paternal regard. The great planters, Phillips insisted, strove for a system of order that could only be maintained by the performance of fatherly duties and a mild discipline calculated to sustain the affection, fealty, and crude efficiency of their dependents.

Phillips supported his argument with what he certainly believed was ample documentation, beginning with planters' instructions, or "manuals," that he had discovered during his scholarly expeditions in the South. In the preamble to one manual, a Mississippi planter informed his overseer:

The health, happiness, good discipline and obedience, good, sufficient and comfortable clothing, a sufficiency of good, wholesome and nutricious food for both man and beast being indispensably necessary to successful planting as well as for reasonable dividends for the amount of capital invested, [regardless] of the Master's duty to his dependents, to himself, and to his God, I do hereby establish the following rules and regulations for the management of my Prairie plantation, and require the observance of the same by any and all overseers I may employ.

In another, the famous James H. Hammond of South Carolina wrote,

A good crop means one that is good taking into consideration everything, negroes, land, mules, stock, fences, ditches, farming utensils, etc., etc., all of which must be kept up and improved in value. The effort must therefore not be merely to make so many cotton bales or such an amount of other products, but as much as can be made without interrupting the steady increase in value of the rest of the property.

A fellow South Carolinian reminded his overseer

that his first object is to be, under all circumstances, the care and well being of the negroes. The proprietor . . . never can or will excuse any cruelty, severity or want of care toward the negroes. For the well being, however, of the ne-groes it is absolutely necessary to maintain obedience, order and discipline, to see that tasks are punctually and carefully performed, and to conduct the busi-ness steadily and firmly, without weakness on the one hand or harshness on the other.

And in a yet another, a Georgia planter wrote that the

best interests of all parties are promoted by a kind and liberal treatment on the part of the owner, and the requirement of proper discipline and strict obedi-ence on the part of the slave. Every attempt to force the slave beyond the limits of reasonable service by cruelty or hard treatment, so far from extorting more work, only tends to make him unprofitable, unmanageable, a vexation and a curse.[12]

Supplemented by descriptive passages from the writings of legendary an-tislavery travelers such as Frederick Law Olmsted and Harriet Martineau, the words of these planter manuals suggest the line of argument that Phillips would pursue in the chapters he devotes to the antebellum regime. "The theory of rigid coercion and complete exploitation," he contends, "was as strange to the bulk of planters as the doctrine and practice of moderation was to those who viewed the regime from afar. . . . And since chains and bolts were out of the question, the whole system of control must be moderate; slaves must be impelled as little as possible by fear, and as much as might be by loyalty, pride and the prospect of reward." He continues that the relationship between masters and slaves was "shaped by a sense of propriety, proportion and cooperation," and "based on pleasurable responsibility."[13] The laws might give planters despotic power over their slaves. But in "the actual regime [the "living order" of the South] severity was clearly the exception and kindliness the rule." The daily dynamic of "concession" and "geniality," says Phillips, made "plantation life not only tolerable but charming."[14]

Here, then, are the rudiments of Phillips's interpretation of the antebellum South as a social order conditioned by the harmonious blend of proprietary interest and paternal benevolence or restraint—what Phillips calls "the traditional predilections of the planters." Taken in isolation, however, this phrase invites misunderstanding, and some commentators, it seems to me, have failed to explain its full meaning. For in Phillips's mind, the habits of the planters are comprehensible not as universal human qualities nor even as attributes of slaveholders, but as modes of behavior evoked by the peculiar "circumstances" of the South and most importantly by "the racial character" of their chattels. Phillips's white supremacy, then, is not simply a defining feature of his understanding of slavery's benefits and the virtues of the planter class, but an analytical instrument that guides him to the cultural and moral source of the distinguishing features of southern life. In one of the most important passages in *American Negro Slavery,* Phillips mounts a brief comparative analysis of Roman and American bondage. The "heartlessness" of the Roman system, he tells us, was the consequence of owner absenteeism, the endless supply of low-priced slaves, "and the lack of difference between masters and slaves in racial traits. In the antebellum South," continues Phillips, "all these conditions were reversed: the planters were commonly resident; the slaves were costly; and the slaves were negroes, who for the most part were by racial qualities submissive rather than defiant, light-hearted instead of gloomy, amiable and ingratiating instead of sullen, and whose very defects invited paternalism rather than repression."[15]

This passage, in my mind, provides the keystone of the interpretive edifice of *American Negro Slavery.* For when he told us elsewhere that "the plausible disposition of the blacks conspired with the heat of the climate to soften the resolution of the whites and make them patient" and that "the generality of negroes insisted upon possessing and being possessed by a cordial but respectful intimacy,"[16] his aim was to complete the imaginative structure of his work not with decorative or enriching features but with the powerful buttresses that held it in place. The "racial character" of the Negro, he was certain, gave rise to southern paternalism, that is, it gave rise to the southern way of life. Moreover, the impress of the Negro—the sheer force of his presence not simply as a laborer but as a human or cultural type—was ubiquitous in the region that Phillips thought he knew so well both as a historian and as a southerner. "The separate integration of the slaves was no more than rudimentary. They were always within the social mind and conscience of the whites, as the whites in turn were within the mind and conscience of the blacks. The adjustments and readjustments were mutually made, for although the masters had by far the major power of control, the slaves themselves were by no means devoid of influence— The general regime was in fact shaped by mutual requirements, concessions and understandings, producing reciprocal codes of conventional morality." Granting "as large a degree of liberty as they thought the slaves could be trusted not to abuse" and shunning harsh punishments, the planters "were content with achieving quite moderate industrial results. In short their despotism, so far as it might properly be so called, was benevolent in intent and on the whole beneficial in effect."[17]

There was no doubt in Phillips's mind that the planters' governance of the Negroes was absolutely necessary in nurturing civility, decorum, and decency in a population still bearing the marks of barbarism. "Every white family," Phillips proclaimed at the close of the chapter entitled "Plantation Tendencies," "served very much the function of a modern social settlement, setting patterns of well-bred conduct which the negroes were encouraged to emulate. . . . On the whole the plantations were the best schools yet invented for the mass training of that sort of inert and backward people which the bulk of the American negroes represented. . . . [The] slave plantation regime, after having wrought the initial and irreparable misfortune of causing the negroes to be imported, did at least as much as any system possible in the period could have done toward adapting the bulk of them to life in a civilized community."[18] As an economic system, Phillips insisted, slavery might be deemed a failure. Tethered to cotton, shaken by the "remorseless advance of slave prices," anchored by the labor of plodding Negroes, the slave system was "a clog upon material progress." If schemes of emancipation were shunned, it was due less to the "apprehension of industrial paralysis" than from "fear of social chaos." But at bottom, concluded Phillips, plantation slavery "was less a business than a life; it made fewer fortunes than it made men."[19] Whatever the merits of this analysis, it is clear that the author had jettisoned the "economic interpretation" of history, arguing instead that racial sentiments and "racial character" were the primary determinants in the evolution of the "living order" of the South.

The publication of *American Negro Slavery* strengthened Phillips's already exalted reputation as perhaps the most brilliant and accomplished historian of American slavery and the society of the plantation states. During the next decade, he guided a number of talented graduate students at the Ann Arbor campus (among them, Dwight Dumond and Gilbert Barnes),[20] completed

Life and Labor in the Old South, the first of three projected volumes on antebellum life, and composed a series of essays that were posthumously published under the title *The Course of the South to Secession.* In 1929, Phillips
received offers from Cornell and Yale universities. He chose New Haven,
where he became an Associate Fellow of Jonathan Edwards College, often
eating in the student dining room. He was honing his essays and working
on the second volume of his projected history when he was suddenly weakened and finally killed by cancer. He died in 1934, just five years after ac-
ceding to a position that marked the pinnacle of his professorial career.[21]
Had he lived another several years, he would have witnessed the first rum-
blings of a mounting assault that finally became an intended campaign of
annihilation against what Richard Hofstadter in a 1944 article on Phillips
called "the latter day phase of the pro-slavery argument."[22]

    We can only imagine how Phillips would have responded to this on-
slaught, which culminated in the publication of Kenneth Stampp's monu-
mental study, *The Peculiar Institution,* a year after the Supreme Court's *Brown
v. Board of Education* decision overturned state-enforced school segregation
in the South, the border states, and the nation's capital. As a young man
Phillips had been described as having "an inordinate self-esteem" and a
want of "modesty" and "tact."[23] But questions of temperament aside, there
is little doubt that Phillips—not to say his professional admirers—would
have been utterly astonished by the gathering storm within a profession
increasingly influenced by the rising wave of racial egalitarianism that was
to bring the "second Reconstruction" of the 1960s. For Phillips had ample
reason to see himself as a cosmopolitan rather than a regional intellectual.
He deliberately made his career outside the South, aspiring to a stature and
influence he would not have achieved at the backwater of Tulane, where
he taught briefly before accepting the Ann Arbor appointment. Even more
important, as we have seen, he identified himself with the reigning "progressive" historians of the day and, with good reason, saw himself as a bold
and heterodox innovator. This claim may be as strong today as it was during
the era of Woodrow Wilson. In 1982 Kenneth Stampp proclaimed that
in their day, "Phillips's writings on slavery were both highly original and
decidedly revisionist." As for the claim of disinterested, scientific inquiry,
said Stampp crisply, "he was about as objective as the rest of us, and that's
not very much."[24]

    Even Phillips's racial views—familiar as the "accomodationist" white su-
premacy that George Frederickson has so ably explored—belong to a national rather than an exclusively regional context. During the late nineteenth and early twentieth centuries, as Frederickson has pointed out, a
multifarious array of outspoken white supremacists—novelists, filmmakers,
historians, journalists, sociologists, economists, scientists, clergymen, and
politicians—appeared on the national scene, finding receptive audiences in

a variety of settings ranging from universities and professional associations to the White House itself. In the society at large, few white Americans were immune to a consensual racism validated by scientific treatises exploring the "evolutionary" stages of human development and endorsed by many of the most influential public figures of the day.[25] Perhaps predictably, the nationalist historians—von Holst, Rhodes, Schouler, and Hart—were unbending and unreflective racists whose language was at times more harsh and strident than the genteel vocabulary of the Georgia-born Phillips. "The besotted and generally repulsive expression of the field hands," wrote Rhodes in his history, "their brute-like countenances, on which were painted stupidity, indolence, duplicity and sensuality; . . . the stupid, plodding, machine-like manner in which they labored, made a sorrowful picture of man's inhumanity to man." However profound the sorrow, the plight of the slaves did not make them the equal of the white men in Rhodes's eyes. Reconstruction Radicals, he contended, had misunderstood "the great fact of race" and sought "to make negroes intelligent by legislative acts." As for contemporary problems, said Rhodes in 1905, "if the negroes stop committing rape on white women," lynching would cease, and the "negro problem" would be solved. America's destiny could best be guided by "the teutonic race," added Rhodes, though the task was "made difficult enough by Cuffee."[26] Schouler referred to the "innate patience [and] docility" of slaves, and their "canine" attachment to their masters. He insisted that southern slavery functioned purely as a race institution, a system in which "the Caucasian" lorded over an "alien, uncouth-looking people" whom he "could hardly regard without mirth or contempt."[27]

If histories "written by Boston" were shaped by these reigning ideas, what then ought we to expect of the author of *American Negro Slavery,* reared in Troup County, Georgia, in the western cotton belt, the grandson of a slave owner and a man who knew planters still wedded to the ancient ways? This is a question that late century racial egalitarians can perhaps never answer in a fair and dispassionate way. But I should like to suggest a line of inquiry that may allow us to make a measured judgment of Phillips's successes and failures as an interpreter of the past. He saw himself, after all, not as a partisan nor a defender of the "Lost Cause" but as a disinterested, skeptical, scientific historian—a student of Turner, the cofounder of a school of historical inquiry determined to strip away the veil of romance, sentimentality, filiopietism, moralism, and false reasoning, which, he believed, distorted the real history of the nation. The progressives spoke confidently of interests, forces, organic structures, historical stages, exigencies, and ceaseless struggles for economic and political dominion. They commonly spoke as moral relativists who believed that people were governed by circumstance rather than principle, conscience, conviction, rationality, or adherence to a higher moral law. They placed historical actors squarely within the confining and determining structures of their socioeconomic worlds, at times perhaps diminishing their stature as they enclosed them within the durable framework of their societies. In his 1913 biography of Georgia statesman Robert Toombs, Phillips described his subject not as an individual with a will of his own but as a "type and a product" of the antebellum regime. As Merton Dillon has said, Phillips used Toombs's career to illuminate the way in which Georgians confronted "the successive problems" (as Phillips described them) of antebellum life.[28] Equally important, in his essay on the American Revolution in *The Course of the South to Secession,* he described the ideal of "natural rights" as a "philosophical gloss" in a bitter battle over "home rule—the right of a community to restrict or cast off extraneous rule." The glittering generalities of the Declaration of Independence and other writings, Phillips suggested, were "justificatory of what was being done, not explanatory of the past or necessarily prophetic of the future. They were a device newly borrowed to replace prior appeals to colonial charters and the rights of British subjects, which had served the preceding occasions none too well and would clearly not apply to the present need."[29] This analysis faithfully recapitulated the argument Carl Becker had made in his classic work, *The Declaration of Independence* (1922), a landmark of progressive scholarship. Both Phillips and Becker saw ideas—even the sanctified ideas that defined the republican faith—as mere instruments initially forged or "borrowed" to serve the exigencies of the historical moment. And they both believed that the Lockean doctrine of the inalienable rights of individuals was a finely woven garment that did not more than hide the real contest for power. This was a contest, of course, waged by collectivities—by sociopolitical groups possessing wills but hardly consciences of their own. In this scheme of things, each patriot became a "social type or product" in what might be called "the crucible" of revolution. In this scheme of things, no one occupied the higher moral ground. Men were cast in roles that they were evidently ordained or invited to play by the vast, even irresistible historical forces of the times.

Are historians immune to these multifarious forces? Does their intelligence or their professional integrity place them on an island above the stream of history? To ask such questions may be to invite ridicule from the members of a guild that has rightly abandoned any claim to absolute scientific objectivity and detachment. But I am addressing Ulrich B. Phillips, a man who, in the words of Eugene Genovese, may have come as "close to greatness" as "any historian this country has yet produced."[30] If greatness eluded him, it was perhaps because he failed consistently and rigorously to apply some of the axioms of the very history he had found so exhilarating, so liberating—the "progressive" history he had set out to write. Although Phillips was a brilliant and tireless intellectual—an explorer, an innovator, a mover of minds—he was to a considerable degree a "social type or product" of the southern world. To be sure, the invincible self-assurance he brought to his white supremacist interpretation of the Old South can only have been strengthened by the scientific or intellectualized racism that pervaded the most prestigious academic and cultural circles of the early century. In this respect, as we have seen, Phillips was a cosmopolitan rather than simply a provincial figure. But at bottom, the racial theories of a man who "loved the Old South,"[31] as Phillips did, might fairly be seen as he saw the political ideas of his historical subjects, that is, as "justificatory of what was being done, not explanatory of the past or necessarily prophetic of the future." In "The Central Theme of Southern History," Phillips wrote that "slavery was instituted not merely to provide control of labor but also as a system of racial adjustment and social order." He described the Old and the New South as a vast and diverse civilization whose white population was united by "a common resolve indomitably maintained—that it shall be and remain a white man's country."[32] That white supremacy might have a more complex character—that it might be at once a deeply rooted sentiment and a powerful "device" or ideological "gloss" that served to maintain a system of racial subjugation—was a thought that Phillips quite simply was unable to entertain. This crippling inability—anchored in Phillips's patriarchal theory of the Negro as merrymaking child—helps to explain his failure to balance his often penetrating observations about the "living order" of the South with a more thoroughgoing exploration of the crushing evils (physical and emotional) of a social system that the Kentucky-born Abraham Lincoln once described the "greatest wrong inflicted on any people."[33] Ironically, if Phillips had been a more faithful exemplar of the dispassionate scholar, he might have approached the higher moral ground on which Lincoln stood.

NOTES

1. John David Smith, *An Old Creed for the New South: Proslavery Ideology and Historiography, 1865–1918* (Athens: University of Georgia Press, 1985), pp. 268–72.
2. Ibid., p. 110.
3. Merton Dillon, *Ulrich Bonnell Phillips* (Baton Rouge: Louisiana State University Press, 1985), pp. 45–46.
4. Ibid., p. 44.
5. Frederick Jackson Turner, *The Frontier in American History* (New York: Holt, 1928), pp. 1–38, passim. The reference to "free land" is found on p. 32.
6. Dillon, *Ulrich Bonnell Phillips,* pp. 17, 22–23, 27, 29.
7. Ibid., p. 17.
8. Ibid., pp. 46, 105.
9. Ulrich B. Phillips, *American Negro Slavery* (Baton Rouge: Louisiana State University Press, 1966), pp. 331–32.

10. Smith, *Old Creed*, chaps. 4–6, passim.

11. Dillon, *Ulrich Bonnell Phillips*, p. 105.

12. Phillips, *American Negro Slavery*, pp. 261–63, 277.

13. Ibid., pp. 293–94, 296, 329.

14. Ibid., p. 306.

15. Ibid., pp. 341–42.

16. Ibid., pp. 396, 307.

17. Ibid., pp. 327–28.

18. Ibid., p. 343.

19. Ibid., pp. 391, 395, 397, 401.

20. Dillon, *Ulrich Bonnell Phillips*, pp. 114–15.

21. Ibid., chaps. 7–8, passim.

22. Richard Hofstadter, "U. B. Phillips and the Plantation Legend," *Journal of Negro History* 29 (April 1944): 121–22. Quoted in Eugene Genovese, foreword to the 1966 LSU edition of *American Negro Slavery*, p. xiv.

23. Dillon, *Ulrich Bonnell Phillips*, p. 15.

24. Smith, *Old Creed*, p. 276.

25. George Frederickson, *The Black Image in the White Mind: The Debate over Afro-American Character and Destiny, 1817–1914* (New York: Harper & Row, 1971), chaps. 7–8, 10. More virulent strands of racism are examined in chapter 9.

26. Smith, *Old Creed*, p. 116.

27. Ibid., pp. 127, 111.

28. Dillon, *Ulrich Bonnell Phillips*, p. 116.

29. Ulrich B. Phillips, *The Course of the South to Secession* (New York: Hill & Wang, 1964), pp. 18–19.

30. Genovese, foreword, p. vii.

31. Ibid., p. vii.

32. Phillips, *Course of the South*, p. 152.

33. Abraham Lincoln, "Remarks on Colonization to Black Ministers, August 14, 1862," in *Think Anew, Act Anew: Abraham Lincoln on Slavery, Freedom, and Union*, ed. Brooks Simpson (Wheeling, Ill.: Harlan Davidson, 1998), p. 121.

8

Genealogies of Race and Culture in Anthropology: The Marginalized Ethnographers

Janet Bauer

Major reconsiderations of the "nature" and "place" of race in American anthropology began to emerge in the late 1990s. At the same time, "recovery" efforts were revealing neglected work on race by earlier generations of women and minority ethnographers, who were marginalized in the profession both for their more relational approaches to understanding race, gender, and class, and their personal character and behavior.[1] Ethnographers like Ruth Landes, Zora Neal Hurston, Elsie Clews Parsons, Hortense Powdermaker, and Katherine Dunham are now viewed as having produced "thick descriptions" that capture many of the contemporary feminist and postmodern inclinations in the study of race, culture, and gender.

   A few commentators in the new debate on race have suggested that turn-of-the-century anthropologists were so successful in developing a concept of culture detached from notions of biology (and of race) that these concepts of culture were rendered ineffective for undertaking multidimensional, sociohistorical investigations of race. Did anthropology "turn away" from race simply because the anthropological concept of culture was "too weak" to promote work around the social construction of race, as Visweswaran argues (1998), or did anthropologists more central to the discipline fail to employ the analytical tools of cultural analysis in work on race, as Harrison's questions suggest (1998)? I argue here that investigating more closely the lives and work of earlier American (and African American) women ethnographers, not previously taken as central to the discipline's theorizing of culture and race, points more to a culture of anthropology that peripheralized or ignored ongoing work on race (especially by women)

and to the "weakness" of other practitioners in failing to problematize race
than to the inadequacy of anthropology's concepts of culture for understanding race. Therefore anthropology's attention to race (and gender) and
culture might have been significantly different if its genealogy of race studies included more of underrecognized early female ethnographers.

THE CONTEXT OF CULTURAL DEBATES IN EARLIER
TWENTIETH-CENTURY ANTHROPOLOGY

Recent observers agree that women and African American anthropologists
have generally been more engaged than others with the subjects of race and
antiracist writing (Lieberman 1997; Baker 1998b). However, at the turn of
the century it was Franz Boas and his student Ruth Benedict—themselves
peripheralized as a German-born Jewish immigrant and as a woman (feminist, lesbian or bisexual)—who were best known for challenging racial prejudice and discrimination directed against "immigrants, European Jews, and
American Negroes." It is useful to describe briefly the context of the cultural debates in which the earlier women who addressed questions of race
and gender in this period, from the 1920s until the 1950s, were working.

The language used by Boas and his more famous students such as Ruth
Benedict, especially in arguments against nineteenth-century scientific racism and later twentieth-century Nazi racial ideology, may have further positioned "race as biology" against "culture" in explaining difference. Benedict herself seemed to offer some answers to the question of why and how
"race continues to be one of the most prevalent social distinctions" (Visweswaran 1997, 73) when she implicated the role of class conflict and politics in this process. "Race," she suggested, "has a profound social significance. . . . It is made the symbol of cultural status and thus serves to justify
the exploitation of the weaker group" (Benedict 1940, 257). These comments point to the unfolding developments in mainstream work on culture
at the time; others have stressed these important links to current, more nu-
anced understandings of race and culture (Baker 1998b; Stocking 1968).

One could question whether the extent to which culture and race were
separated in anthropological inquiry (or seem to have been separated) reflected the particular struggles that engaged the core figures of anthropology. It may have been necessary in the early part of this century to couch
arguments about race and culture in terms asserting the disassociation between physical variations and culture in order to situate oneself in an antiracist debate. Yet the better-known anthropologists also made certain
choices about whether and how to pursue the study of race. As Williams
pointed out, in the politics of his times, Boas adhered to "assumptions of
physical anthropology and experimental psychology" even though "he

knew that whites determined the status of blacks in the American socioeconomic order and that attitudes and behavior confined blacks to a low position" (Williams 1996, 24). He also provided decreasing support for the black folklorists' work because of dissatisfaction with their forays into the symbolic interpretations with which he disagreed. And, noticeably, Benedict used few examples of the ideology of race in America in her exploration of the concept in her 1940 book on race.

Throughout the period between and after the two world wars, when the processes of culture were being theoretically refined,[2] there is ample evidence that considerations of race and culture were not entirely separated in anthropological research. Baker (1998a) and Williams (1996) have provided extensive materials on the alternative or competing discussions of race and culture, even after the "Boasian project" had begun—in the work of Du-Bois, the Howard circle, and the black folklorists. Baker, for example, recounts the different anthropological approaches used to explore African Americans' experience and their influence on "the paradigmatic shift in the understanding of race and culture taking place between the wars" (1998, 125–126).

Noticeably, these discussions of race were not incorporated into the central genealogies of anthropological history. Instead, we see a series of developments in the "evolution" of concepts of culture or cultural process—such as the expectation to conduct fieldwork outside the United States and the subsequent divergence of ethnicity and race into different fields of study,[3] as well as an increasing division of research labor between cultural anthropology and physical anthropology. The effect of this was to divert the attention of mainstream anthropology away from engagement with the underlying historical processes in the intersections of race and culture.

It might also have been necessary to await subsequent conceptual developments in order to adequately address the cultural aspects of race; it might have been necessary to allow time for the evolution of anthropological notions of culture, as our engagement with the social, historical, and economic components of cultural processes took shape in our imaginations—or to wait for "native ethnographers" here and abroad to enter the discussion. However, there were women and minority ethnographers in the United States who continued to problematize the intersections of race, gender, and culture in their studies of the Americas.

WOMEN ANTHROPOLOGISTS' GENEALOGIES OF RACE AND CULTURE DURING THE INTERVENING YEARS

Would anthropology's attention to race (and gender) and culture, or its understanding of the "complicity of racism and culture in the 19th century"

(Young 1995), have been significantly different if some of these women had been incorporated into its genealogy of race studies? Earlier women anthropologists who are best remembered for their contributions to the elaboration of culture or perhaps to gender studies did not give significant attention to racialization. And even women like Margaret Mead and Ruth Benedict, whose ethnographies, *Coming of Age in Samoa* and *Patterns of Culture,* are described by Stocking as two of the most influential of the twentieth century (Stocking 1989, 247), did not leave a prominent legacy in theorizing about gender or culture.[4]

Anthropologists and historians are now reevaluating the ethnographic contributions of other women, for example, Elsie Clews Parsons, Zora Neale Hurston, Katherine Dunham, Ruth Landes, and Hortense Powdermaker, to the discipline in which they were trained. All of them enjoyed some recognition (Parsons became president of the American Anthropological Association [AAA]), sometimes in other disciplines or subfields. But what we now recognize as the importance of their perspectives and methods at the intersection of race, gender, and culture was largely ignored during their lifetime. As outlined by their biographers and reflected in their own work, these women had some things in common, first, a commitment to the innovative study of the lives of others and the importance of both gender and race to the project that resulted in ethnographic work approaching postmodernist ethnographic experimentation. Second, they all experienced opposition to their perspectives and methods from major (largely male and often mentor) figures in the field on whom they depended for support (in the case of both Landes and Hurston, opposition came from Herskovits, who had his own perspective on how to study African culture in the Americas). They were all further marginalized because of their perseverance in their approaches and because of their ("deviant") sexual behavior—Parsons in her unusual marriage and later liaisons, Hurston for unfounded accusations of a relationship with a twelve-year-old, Powdermaker and Landes for "sexual" behavior in the field. Fourth, they all shared the vantage point afforded to social marginals (as women, often Jewish, immigrant, or African American) that fosters an interest in topics not otherwise considered important and sometimes also the advocacy of professional or social change. As with many women ethnographers, by failing to theorize much of their work and methodology, they also relinquished the primary avenue to mainstream incorporation (cf. Lutz 1995).

Men too have been marginalized by the field (cf. Lurie 1966)—particularly African American anthropologists like St. Clair Drake and others who developed important, neglected concepts like racial class (Harrison and Harrison 1999). But women's ethnographies in particular, which seemed to capture the conceptual dilemmas of anthropology in vivid and innovative ways, enjoyed even less enduring impact.[5]

One of the first women in anthropology at the turn of the century, Co-lumbia-trained Elsie Clews Parsons (1874–1941), eventually enjoyed in-fluence as a benefactor of other fieldworkers but experienced trouble secur-ing a teaching position for herself. She had been a lone voice in challenging anthropology to examine society's accepted categories and classifications. "A maturing culture struggles against its categories," she said (Deacon 1997, 129). Her marriage relationship was "modernist" and she eventually embarked on a series of extramarital relationships that may have further af-fected her standing in the field. Her biographer, Desley Deacon, describes the innovation of one of her last ethnographies, *Mitla: Town of the Souls*, as modernist in introducing characters that reveal parts of the culture and then weaving them together throughout the text (Deacon 1997, 345). Deacon further describes Parsons's work in "Hayti" as antiracist. She dismissed other views of voodoo as not fully described "probably due to the diversion of interest to one of its reputed features. . . . voodoo human sacrifice . . . the folklore of which is widespread among foreigners, white and colored, in Hayti" (Deacon 1997, 305). Parsons, the first woman president of AAA and the subject of more extensive biographical interest than other woman in anthropology, was not marginalized entirely, but her work did not be-come part of the anthropological canon. Her approaches, unique for the time, included her use of autobiography and the "self" as native informant, her interests focusing on detailed ethnography that was gathered from actu-ally living with people. Parsons stressed the need to get under their skins and challenged existing borders and classifications. Through her relational and applied interests, she was committed to "using [anthropological meth-ods] to educate the public to accept and welcome sexual and cultural diver-sity" (Deacon 1997, xiii).

The next generation of women, including Zora Neal Hurston, Katherine Dunham, Ruth Landes, and Hortense Powdermaker, formally studied an-thropology and conducted ethnographic work for most of their careers. Except for Powdermaker, they experienced minimal support and greater opposition to the ways in which they chose to pursue their ethnographic studies. Hurston and Dunham eventually found their audiences primarily through writing novels (Hurston) or through dance (Dunham) (Mikell 1999; Aschenbrenner 1999). Landes acquired her first permanent academic job at the age of fifty-seven.

Hurston was initially frustrated by the library work she was forced to pursue in graduate school at Columbia, initially as a student of Boas. Hurs-ton's biographers and commentators emphasize her commitment to an eth-nographic method she considered deeper and more thorough than that of other anthropologists and significantly tied to the black community. Hurs-ton took issue with prevailing perspectives on black culture. In her texts, particularly *Mules and Men* (1935) and *Tell My Horse* (1938), "Hurston saw black people, especially black women struggling beneath the weight of racism and discrimination and laughing to keep from crying" (Mikell 1999, 59). Her ethnographic styles included examining herself as a native, "interpreting the cultures for a nonnative audience" (Deck 1990, 246), and adopting what have come to be known as "interpretive and symbolic styles" and "reflexivity," refusing "to translate culture for the benefit of outsiders." She believed that the best ethnographers had something in common with the people they studied and saw her approach in opposition to "the Columbia anthropologists" (Mikell 1999, 58). "An intellectual and methodological visionary, she created and used the oral and literary texts long before the anthropologists of the 1970s could generate the model as an alternative to the materialist and Marxian analyses" (Mikell 1999, 59); she also believed that culture should not be emphasized to the exclusion of political relationships.

Dunham sought to integrate her interest in ethnography and dance and was encouraged to do so by her graduate mentors at the University of Chicago. For example, Aschenbrenner describes the way in which Dunham "was able to fulfill Malinowski's 'mythic charter' more completely than many anthropologists, perhaps including Malinowski himself" (1999, 145). Much of Dunham's ethnographic work through dance had a social and an educational agenda or, as Aschenbrenner describes it, through dance cultural studies became "a way of life" (1999, 151). The impact of her work in anthropology itself was marginalized by its status as performance rather than anthropological theory. She too contributed to both autobiographical (e.g., *A Touch of Innocence*, 1959) and ethnographic works (e.g., *Journey to Accompong*, 1946) that laid out her methods and experiences.

Sally Cole has described at length the "silencing of race and gender" in Ruth Landes's experiences as an anthropologist, particularly her work in Brazil, where she had gone to study race relationships. "Although anthropologists did not reopen the debate over race, Landes continued to offer theories of race in her writings on both Brazilian and American society. Because such discourse was silent in anthropology her work remained outside the disciplinary canon" (1995b, 175). Cole further observes that "the reception of *City of Women* by the discipline offers an illustration of canon-making and of marginalizing the ethnography of race and gender" (1995b, 176). Landes was frustrated in her career development partly as a result of harsh criticism from one of the shapers of African anthropology, Melville Herskovits, who reduced her work to "travel literature," not only disagreeing with her approach to studying black culture in the Americas but chastising her for her "personal comportment . . . in the field" as an attractive single woman who engaged in a relationship with a black Brazilian journalist and folklorist (Cole 1995b, 177).

Landes's position as a Jewish woman and an outsider in American society (as well as the various storytelling methods that she and her Ojibwa informant brought to their collaborative project) positioned her to see and hear certain things in Ojibwa culture (*Ojibwa Woman*, 1938) and in Brazilian candomble culture (cf. *City of Women*, 1947) that had not been recognized before (Cole 1995a; 1995b). Landes "refuses to reproduce the theoretical and rhetorical assertions of her peers" regarding candomble; rather, she portrays the "conflicting local and subjective interpretations of the meaning of candomble" (Cole 1995b, 173). "She did not portray candomble as a homogeneous phenomenon, rather she described diversity in ritual knowledge and practices among the candombles" (p. 176).

Although not recognized as a site for anthropological theorizing, educational studies is a subfield in which anthropologists have explored intersections of race and culture, as reflected in Landes's discussions in *Culture in American Education* (1965, 247): "As minorities are deterred from sharing marriage, schooling, jobs, recreation and housing with the ruling middle class, and often, therefore, do not share the respectable, standardized language, so this ruling class does not expect minorities to share the generally admitted states of suffering." Here Landes presents culture as something used for creative rather than repressive initiatives, although Landes also refers to discriminatory institutions, race prejudice, and social events as "rooted in and ramifying the whole of a society" (1965, 40).

Hortense Powdermaker's work *After Freedom* (1939), a study of race, class, and culture in a southern town, was partly influenced by her personal experiences with the "self-forgetting" cultural alienation and assimilation of her well-off Jewish community and home life (Fraser 1991). Although her notions of race and cultural authenticity perhaps contributing to her exoticization of black culture in America) were limited, she displayed innovativeness in seeking to study "negro culture" as well as the "ideology of black racial inferiority" in the United States. Although Powdermaker's fieldwork was lengthier, John Dollard's 1937 study of the same community, *Caste and Class in a Southern Town*, received more recognition. Although this incongruity must have haunted her, she rarely spoke about it (Scheper-Hughes 1991).

Powdermaker examined the diversity of relations between classes among both blacks and whites and explicated the way in which ideologies of race were played out in the lives of southerners in a Mississippi town. Some of the prejudice against her work at the time has been attributed to her working in a familiar society rather than a "strange" one (Fraser 1991). In *Stranger and Friend* (1966), Powdermaker outlined the stance she developed for moving across class and color lines in Mississippi as she investigated the racialization of oppression in everyday life; she also mused on how her status as a white woman both facilitated and hindered her work across these divisions.

Most of these women, like Powdermaker, sought to apply anthropological methods and concepts "to the investigation of problems and settings previously considered out of the purview of cultural anthropologists" (Fraser 1991, 408). It could be argued that their various positions as "other" in their own society contributed not only to the direction of their anthropology but also to the development of a different kind of empathy applied in it. Most of these women were further motivated in their anthropology by a desire to effect social change, becoming involved in subfields or activities like social work and education (perhaps to a lesser extent in Powdermaker's case; cf. Fraser 1991, 409).

This often meant innovating in methodology and stance. Parsons and Landes specifically rejected accepted categorizations; in Parsons's case this was a specific objection to the then current anthropological data collection technique of "cataloging" the culture. Landes's early Boasian ethnography became more literary (Cole 1995a; 1994). The struggle to confront the issues of ethnographic subjectivity and method not only affected Hurston's work but her position in anthropology as well (Mikell 1999). The methodological innovations made by these women reflect their struggles to find appropriate ways to transform their ethnography by incorporating their particular positionings and experience. All, for example, exercised some "autoethnographic" modes in their work, using themselves as subjects in studying their own culture. Focusing on the topics of race and gender, they struggled in various ways to "perform" their identity while demonstrating relations of power in what they were observing.

The experience of these women in anthropology itself reflects the intersection of race, gender/sexuality, and culture. Those who sought or pursued other topics or experimented with innovative methods or lifestyles were penalized by the opinion makers of the field. Dunham and Hurston in particular found a more supportive community in other fields and in the context of a segregated, black intellectual life. If the views of women like Landes and Hurston on black and African cultures had been taken more seriously, the debates between figures like Herskovits and Boas, who were interested in tracing black cultural origins to Africa (partly to counter racist arguments that blacks had no culture), and those like Hurston, who emphasized the unique developments of diaspora African cultures, would arguably have moved anthropology more quickly toward its contemporary understanding of the processes of cultural hybridization (Williams 1996, 32). And if these women's questioning of the "anthropological convention that presumes distance between observer and observed" (Fraser 1991, 405) had been deliberated, then it is at least possible that current notions of reflexive anthropology, which incorporate the relations between observers and cultural subjects into the analysis, would have influenced the study of cultures and racialization much earlier.

I do not mean to lionize these earlier practitioners of anthropology, since their works and perspectives are themselves at times problematic. Cole (1995) and Fraser (1991) point to apparent contradictions[6] and ethnographic chauvinism (the failure to problematize whiteness or white culture or the exoticization of other cultures) in the work of Landes and Powdermaker. There is also evidence that influences of mainstream anthropological thinking in their ethnographic studies may have kept them from fully realizing the potential of the directions they took in the their own work. Fraser, for example, cites passages that reflect Powdermaker's use of the language of biology and functionalism in discussing working-class whites (Fraser 1991, 410). Biographers and commentators have generally been cautious about these women's contributions to the study of race while reassessing their ethnographic contributions.

CONCLUSIONS: CULTURAL WORK ON RACE COMES TO THE CENTER

The exclusion of these "other ethnographic voices," as much as the lack of an "adequate" concept of culture, retarded attention to race at the anthropological "center." Clearly our notions of culture have evolved; to some extent, developments in the concept of culture were segregated from biological inquiry.[7] Indeed, despite the weight given to cultural approaches in anthropology generally, biological arguments continued to have specific utilitarian value. For example, in the 1950s, those who turned to anthropology and sociology to "debunk notions of racial inferiority and to demonstrate values of assimilation" in arguments for court cases (e.g., *Brown v. Board of Education*), relied primarily on the Boasian argument that race (as biology) had no relation to superiority (no power in explaining differences) as well as on Montagu's questioning the validity of the concept itself; it relied very little on the cultural arguments of anthropologists (Baker 1998, 200–205).

Various other factors, for example, lack of personal interest or cognizance of the continuing impact of race or even individual biases (such as Boas's lack of support for black folklorists), as well as specific trajectories in the field (like the "evolution" of our understandings of culture, the segregation of studies about ethnicity versus race, and increasing specialization) also contributed to the lack of cultural research on race. The recent inclusion of "native" voices in the field has strengthened interest in race and its signification that might have been achieved earlier had some of the women writing on race (especially in the 1930s and 1940s) been allowed to influence mainstream trends. The bifurcated genealogy of race and culture encompasses both the lengthy detours of those at the center working through more complex understandings of culture, identity, and power until finally pushed to return to race, and the persistence of those ethnographers who, although marginalized in the field, were in a personal and structural position to take a special interest in the way race (racism) and gender (sexism) were inscribed in culture.

New debates about racism, biology, and culture have emerged in the anthropological discussions of reactions to late-twentieth-century European immigration, demonstrating once again that Boasian arguments on learning versus biological endowment did not succeed in de-essentializing race and culture in the popular view—an issue that Benedict takes up in her post–World War II work on racism in the United States. Although the ideological forms of what is described as the new racism—a cultural essentialism directed toward people of color—demonstrate that different forms of racism may emerge differently,[8] the revived interest in studies of racism and race suggests that anthropologists are ready to apply the elaboration of different assumptions about cultural process that Stocking (1968) indicates have emerged from the history of ethnographic research.

Clearly, we understand that a concept of culture, and assumptions made about the processes of culture, have been and continue to be important, for example, in disentangling race and class while illuminating their interaction through the meanings assigned to race and the resulting unequal structures of power (or caste; Ogbu 1978). Today I would argue that most physical and cultural anthropologists understand race and racialization in terms of meanings, practices, and systems of power that reflect the intersections of culture, history, and social and economic structures.[9] In *Race: Science and Politics* (1940), Benedict herself wrote of the abstract nature of racial categories and of the difficulty in fitting people into those categories (1940, 27ff.). In other words, race is "a social invention" as Smedley calls it, or an ideology (and meanings) that perpetuates myths about physical differences and is often used to perpetuate inequalities among peoples. This is captured in a range of recent work, for example, Urciuoli's study of race, language, and class among Puerto Ricans in the United States (1996) or Nina Glick-Schiller, Linda Basch, and Cristina Blanc-Szanton (1992) on race, class, and culture in immigrant adaptation.

According to Visweswaran (1998) and Turner (response to Stolcke 1995), the Boasian tradition in cultural anthropology did not provide a concept of culture that was adequate for handling these processes, which generate "race" as we now understand them.[10] It is not entirely clear in what way they consider that concept of culture inadequate. As I have suggested in contrasting the work of earlier women and mainstream developments in notions of culture, we should examine more closely the discipline's failure to provide a social context that engages a wider range of experiences and research instead of focusing on the inability of the anthropological concepts themselves. To avoid essentializing culture or race my-self, I have highlighted anthropology's own role in propagating a notion of culture that "lends itself to essentializing" (e.g., Visweswaran 1998, 76) by excluding or disregarding the work of women and minorities. Restoring them to the anthropological genealogy requires anthropologists to further investigate the existing ethnographic writing on race, gender, and culture—avoiding, of course, the uncritical merging of race and culture which might result in what Alarcon (1996, 139) describes as the simplistic convergence of "nineteenth-century racist biologism . . . with the end-of-the-twentieth century culturalism." Maintaining what Visweswaran calls the useful "ten-sion between race and culture" is best achieved through continually reex-amining "gendered" and "raced" relationships in the field of anthropology and by reintegrating the perspectives of those on the margins—through re-consideration of their biographies or autoethnographies, as well as of the unacclaimed ethnographic texts assigned to subfields of the discipline, such as folklore, dance, and education. Theorizing with the cultural studies of authors who did not explicitly theorize their own work should be seen now as itself part of the work of anthropology.[11]

During the last twenty years or so, the incorporation of "native" (for-merly colonized) ethnographers into central discussions in the field and new turns in ethnographic methodology regarding the Other have gener-ated renewed work on culture, race, and power (cf. Stoler 1989; Viswes-waran 1994)—bringing race back into the cultural study of the oppression of Native Americans, as well as of "exoticized and racialized" former eth-nics elsewhere. Surely one reason for anthropology's renewed concern with race is the diversification of the field to include those for whom race is a lived experience. This greater participation in formulating issues of dif-ference has had a transformative influence, at least on what is currently con-sidered trend making in mainstream anthropology. If it is true that racism is such an integral part of the logic of anthropology that "culture" cannot help us transcend it, this says as much about the practitioners of anthropol-ogy as about our understanding of culture itself.

NOTES

1. These debates on the significance of race from cultural and biological points of view in anthropology became more marked about the time Yolanda Moses be-came president of the American Anthropology Association and coauthored an *American Anthropologist* article on anthropology and race with Carol Mukhopadhyay (1997). In addition to the articles on race in the *American Anthropologist* during 1997–1998, a special contemporary issue forum issue, *Race and Racism,* appeared as volume 100, no. 3 (September 1998). A special issue of *Ethos* on racialization also appeared as volume 25, no. 1 (1997). Several issues of the *Anthropology Newsletter*

likewise debated various aspects of race and cultural theory: Michael Brian Schiffer "Return to Holism," 49, no. 3 (March 1999): 64, on variability and holism; the AAA position on race, 39, no. 6 (September 1998); George Gill, "The Beauty of Race and Races," 39, no. 3 (March 1998); Helan Page, "Understanding White Cultural Practices," 39, no. 4 (1998) on aspects of power in understanding race; J. Anthony Paredes, "Race Is Not Something You Can See," 38, no. 9 (December 1997); Leonard Lieberman, "Out of Our Skulls: Caucasoid, Mongoloid, Negroid," 38, no. 9 (December 1997); Stephen Jackson, "Real Men Eat Like Us: Racial Categories in New Ireland" 39, no. 2 (February 1998); Yolanda Moses, "An Idea Whose Time Has Come Again: Anthropology Reclaims Race," 38, no. 7 (October 1997); G. A. Clark, "Pernicious Vanities," 38, no. 7 (October 1997); Audrey Smedley, "Origins of Race," 38, no. 8 (November 1997), which states the prevailing view that "all anthropologists should understand that race has no intrinsic relationship to human biological diversity and that such diversity is a natural product of primarily evolutionary forces, whereas race is a social invention."

2. We could trace these developments through attention given to "learning" paradigms, individual identity, and concepts of unconscious or unmotivated actions, which was due first to the influence of psychological research and later to the importance given to social organization, class, and power; there were subsequent turns to structural functionalism and Marxism, and then to interactionism and agency, as in the Geertzian emphasis on ideologies of culture and Bordieu's impetus to social constructionism; and eventually to feminist anthropology with a return to body/ sexuality. Each period added new insights and theorizing to our understanding of cultural processes (cf. Stocking 1992; Hatch 1983), although in the view of Kroeber and Kluckhohn (1952) there was little theorizing in anthropology before the 1930s.

3. See Banks (1996) for a comprehensive discussion of how ethnicity became linked to cultural differences and the study of other cultures while race reflected an emphasis on physical differences and the study of immigrants at home.

4. Kroeber and Kluckhohn fail to mention them in their discussion of significant developments and changes in concepts of culture (1952).

5. For discussions of the marginalization of women's careers in anthropology, see Parezo (1993a; 1993b).

6. Examples include the lack of self-consciousness about race and racialization in Landes's earlier writings on Native Americans and Powdermaker's inconsistent position on the desirability of taking up ethnographic work that was more or less distant from her own experience.

7. Kroeber and Kluckhohn's 1952 volume on concepts of culture reflects little on the intersections between biology and culture.

8. For example, Stolcke (1995) suggests that the biological link in the new European racism is contained in cultural differences in communication that are "inherent in human nature," although she has been challenged to examine the role of phenotypic characteristics in popular conceptions of foreigners (as opposed to statements by political figures).

9. See the AAA statement on race at: www.ameranthassn.org/racepp.htm.

10. It is true, however, that anthropologists have not clearly expressed what they "take for granted" about culture. See nonanthropologists like Nussbaum (1997) for more coherent descriptions of the complexities of culture.

11. These women are also largely absent from feminist genealogies of method
(e.g., the discussion of "scripts of relational positionality"), which are identified as
a 1980s phenomenon in which personal identity was used as a vantage point for
theorizing (Friedman [1998]).

REFERENCES

Alarcon, Norma. 1996. "Conjugating Subjects in the Age of Multiculturalism." In
    Mapping Multiculturalism, edited by Avery F. Gordon and Christopher Newfield,
    pp. 127–48. Minneapolis: University of Minnesota Press.
Aschenbrenner, Joyce. 1999. "Katherine Dunham: Anthropologist, Artist, Human-
    ist." In African–American Pioneers in Anthropology, edited by Ira Harrison and Faye
    Harrison, pp. 137–153. Urbana: University of Illinois Press.
Baker, Lee. 1998a. From Savage to Negro: Anthropology and the Construction of Race,
    1896–1054. Berkeley: University of California Press.
Baker, Lee. 1998b. "New Directions in the History of United States Anthropol-
    ogy." Transforming Anthropology 7, no. 1:71–74.
Banks, Marcus. 1996. Ethnicity: Anthropological Constructions. New York: Routledge,
    1996.
Benedict, Ruth. 1940. Race: Science and Politics. New York: Modern Age Books.
Caffrey, Margaret M. 1989. Ruth Benedict: Stranger in this Land. Austin: University
    of Texas Press, 1989.
Cole, Sally. 1994. "Ruth Landes in Brazil: Writing, Race, and Gender in 1930s
    American Anthropology." In The City of Women. Albuquerque: University of
    New Mexico Press.
Cole, Sally. 1995a. "Women's Stories and Boasian Texts: The Ojibwa Ethnography
    of Ruth Landes and Maggie Wilson." Anthropologica 37:3–25.
Cole, Sally. 1995b. "Ruth Landes and the Early Ethnography of Race and Gen-
    der." In Women Writing Culture, edited by Ruth Behar and Deborah A. Gordon,
    pp. 166–85. Berkeley: University of California Press.
Cox, Oliver. 1948. Caste, Class, and Race. New York: Monthly Review Press.
Deacon, Desley. 1997. Elsie Clews Parsons: Inventing Modern Life. Chicago: Univer-
    sity of Chicago Press.
Deck, Alice. 1990. "Autoethnography: Zora Neale Hurston, Noni Jabavu and
    Cross–Disciplinary Discourse." Black American Literature Forum 24, no. 2:237–56.
Di Leonardo, Micaela. 1998. Exotics at Home: Anthropologies, Others, American Mo-
    dernity. Chicago: University of Chicago Press, 1998.
Drake, St. Clair, and Horace Cayton. 1945. Black Metropolis. Harper & Row.
Fraser, Gertrude. 1991. "Race, Class, and Differences in Hortense Powdermaker's
    After Freedom: A Cultural Study of the Deep South." Journal of Anthropological Re-
    search 47, no. 4:403–16.
Friedman, Susan. 1996. Mappings: Feminism and the Geographies of Cultural Encounter.
    Princeton: Princeton University Press.
Glick Schiller, Nina, Linda Basch, and Cristina Blanc–Szanton. 1992. "Transna-
    tionalism: A New Analytic Framework for Understanding Migration." In

Towards A Transitional Perspective on Migration: Race, Class, Ethnicity, and National-ism Reconsidered, pp. 1–24. New York: New York Academy of Sciences.

Gruber, Jacob. 1966. "In Search of Experience." In *Pioneers of American Anthropol-ogy: The Uses of Biography*, edited by June Helm, pp. 3–28. Seattle: University of Washington Press, 1966.

Harrison, Faye. 1998. "Introduction: Expanding the Discourse on Race." *American Anthropologist* 100, no. 3:609–31.

Harrison, Ira E., and Faye Harrison. 1999. "Introduction." In *African American Pio-neers in Anthropology*. Urbana: University of Illinois Press.

Hurston, Zora Neal. 1938. *Tell My Horse*. New York: J. B. Lippincott.

Hatch, Melvin. *Culture and Morality: The Relativity of Values in Anthropology*. New York: Columbia University Press, 1983.

Helm, June. 1966. Preface to *Pioneers of American Anthropology: The Uses of Biography*, pp. vi–ix. Seattle: University of Washington Press.

Herskovits, Melville, J. 1928. *The American Negro: A Study in Racial Crossing*. Indi-ana University Press.

Karim, W. J. 1993. "Epilogue: The 'Nativised' Self and the 'Native.' " In *Gendered Fields: Women, Men and Ethnography*, edited by Diane Bell, Pat Caplan, and Wazar Jahan Karim, pp. 248–51. New York: Routledge, 1993.

Kroeber, A. L. 1923. *Anthropology: Culture Patterns and Processes*. New York: Har-court Brace Jovanovich, 1963.

Kroeber, A. L., and Clyde Kluckhohn. 1952. *Culture: A Critical Review of Concepts and Definitions*. New York: Vintage Books.

Landes, Ruth. 1947. *The City of Women*. Albuquerque: University of New Mexico Press, 1994. With an introduction by Sally Cole.

Landes, Ruth. 1965. *Culture in American Education: Anthropological Approaches to Mi-nority and Dominant Groups in the Schools*. New York: Wiley, 1965.

Lieberman, Leonard. 1997. "Gender and the Deconstruction of the Race Con-cept," *American Anthropologist* 99, no. 3:545–58.

Lurie, Nancy. 1966. "Women in Early Anthropology." In *Pioneers of American An-thropology: The Uses of Biography*, edited by June Helm, pp. 29–82. Seattle: Uni-versity of Washington Press, 1966.

Lutz, Catherine. 1995. "The Theory of Gender." In *Women Writing Culture*, edited by Ruth Behar and Deborah Gordon, pp. 249–66. University of California Press, 1995.

Mikell, Gwendolyn. 1999. "Feminism and Black Culture in the Ethnography of Zora Neale Hurston." In *African American Pioneers in Anthropology*, edited by Ira Harrison and Faye Harrison, pp. 51–69. Urbana: University of Illinois Press, 1999.

Modell, Judith S. 1983. *Ruth Benedict: Patterns of a Life*. Philadelphia: University of Pennsylvania Press.

Mukhopadhyay, Carol, and Yolanda Moses. 1997. "Reestablishing Race in An-thropological Discourse." *American Anthropologist* 99, no. 3:517–33.

Nussbaum, Martha. 1997. *Cultivating Humanity: A Classical Defense of Reform in Lib-eral Education*. Cambridge: Harvard University Press, 1997.

Ogbu, John. 1978. *Class and Caste in Minority Education*. New York: Academic Press.

Parezo, Nancy J. 1993a. "Anthropology: The Welcoming Science." In *Hidden Scholars: Women Anthropologists and the American Southwest*, pp. 3–37. Albuquerque: University of New Mexico Press.

Parezo, Nancy J. 1993b. "Conclusion: the Beginning of the Quest." In *Hidden Scholars: Women Anthropologists and the American Southwest*, pp. 334–67. Albuquerque: University of New Mexico Press.

Powdermaker, Hortense. [1939] 1993. *After Freedom: A Cultural Study in the Deep South*. Reprint, Madison: University of Wisconsin Press, 1993. With an introductory essay by Brackette Williams and Drexel Woodson.

Powdermaker, Hortense. 1966. *Stranger and Friend: The Way of an Anthropologist*. New York: Norton, 1966.

Scheper–Hughes, Nancy. 1991. "Hortense Powdermaker, The Berkeley Years (1967–70): A Personal Reflection." *Journal of Anthropological Research* 47, no. 4:457–72.

Stocking, George. 1968. *Race, Culture, and Evolution: Essays in the History of Anthropology*. Chicago: University of Chicago Press.

Stocking, George. 1989. "The Ethnographic Sensibility of the 1920s and the Dualism of the Anthropological Tradition." In *Romantic Motives: Essays on Anthropological Sensibility*, pp. 208–76. Madison: University of Wisconsin Press.

Stocking, George. 1992. *The Ethnographer's Magic and other Essays in the History of Anthropology*. Madison: University of Wisconsin Press, 1992.

Stolcke, Verena. 1995. "Talking Culture: New Boundaries, New Rhetorics of Exclusion in Europe." *Current Anthropology* 36, no. 1:1–24.

Stoler, Ann. 1989. "Making Empire Respectable: The Politics of Race and Sexual Morality in 20th Century Colonial Cultures." *American Ethnologist* 16, no. 4:634–60.

Urciuoli, Bonnie. 1996. *Exposing Prejudice: Puerto Rican Experiences of Language, Race, and Class*. Boulder: Westview, 1996.

Visweswaran, Kamala. 1994. *Fictions of Feminist Ethnography*. Minneapolis: University of Minnesota Press, 1994.

Visweswaran, Kamala. 1997. "Histories of Feminist Ethnography." *Annual Review of Anthropology* 26:591–621.

Visweswaran, Kamala. 1998. "Race and the Culture of Anthropology." *American Anthropologist* 100, no. 1:70–83.

Williams, Vernon, Jr. *Rethinking Race: Franz Boas and His Contemporaries*. University of Kentucky Press, 1996.

Young, Robert. *Colonial Desire: Hybridity in Theory, Culture, and Race*. New York: Routledge, 1995.

Part III

Race and the Literary Imagination

9

The Continental Fallacy of Race

Colbert Nepaulsingh
For William R. Scott, brilliant son of Sheba's race

Revolution, like charity, should begin at home. If we intend to make meaningful change in the way we conceive of race, then we ought to think seriously how best to teach human physiology to our children, even before they enter the school system. The immediacy of this task was driven home to me as I was composing this chapter. My ten-year-old son came home from school and asked me, as I was writing a sentence about race, why his nose is as it is, a question he had never posed before. I guessed correctly that some classmate of his was practicing physiognomy on him without a license.

My son's science textbook includes no discussion whatever about phenotype and genotype, no beginner's hint of what he and his classmates need to know about heredity and environment. If his classmate had been taught from infancy the difference between human physiology, the science of human beings, and physiognomy, the impossibility of knowing character from physical appearance, she might not have perturbed my son; and if I had prepared my son better, he would not have been perturbed. I thought I had taught my children about physical appearances. But I had to begin again to explain to my son why human physiology can be a useful science, and why physiognomy is an inexact, misleading, harmful, and unnecessary practice. The gap between physiology and physiognomy, I said to him, is as wide as the gap between astronomy, a defensible science, and astrology. I felt pleased that I had given my son a sufficient answer for his physiognomist.

The next day, my son came home asking why his lips are thick, and why his hair curls tightly. Again, I learned that answers, however convincing, seldom change the behavior of determined physiognomists. Maybe she likes my son, you might think; but whether she likes him or not, her remarks, her character interpretation of his body, were clearly designed to make him think less of himself and to make him think that she is superior to him in body and in mind.

And so, after yet another painful lesson, I have decided to keep a solemn promise I made a few years ago never to address the public, in speaking or in writing, unless I was also addressing my family. I must constantly repeat to myself in practice as in theory that revolution should, like charity, begin at home. As I speak and write, I must imagine that my children and their teachers (who need also to be taught) are among my listeners and readers with you. I speak and write not in public but in private space, as if at home.

At home in private, we should say nothing about race that we would not like to hear repeated and attributed to us in public. Contrary to popular misconception, race is not a topic to be whispered about; race is neither intimate nor secret nor shameful; race is normal. This simple concept of race in theory would, if practiced widely, yield revolutionary results. If I were in the bumper sticker business, I would make one that says "race is normal."

The Concept of Race is a book edited by Ashley Montagu, a contemporary author (b. 1905) of several sensitive books about race. Another of Montagu's books is entitled *Man's Most Dangerous Myth: The Fallacy of Race*. In spite of the words "dangerous" and "fallacy" in this title, Montagu's works do not deny differences among groups of human beings; they deny the powerful lies that persist about race.

Montagu reminds us that the word "race" is of recent and obscure origin (1965, 7) and that our concepts of race are "unsatisfactory" and "meaningless." Montagu also includes in his edited volume a well-reasoned 1962 article by Frank Livingstone entitled "On the Nonexistence of Human Races." The most authoritative geneticists have concluded that "from a scientific point of view, the concept of race has failed to obtain any consensus; none is likely" (Cavalli-Sforza, Menozzi, and Piazza 1996, 19). If race is nonexistent or if it is impossible for us to define race satisfactorily or scientifically, should we then abolish it?

We claim to have abolished "slavery," and we refer laudably to certain activists in the history of struggle against enlavement as "abolitionists." Yet enslavement persists in varying forms throughout the world, though not as widely as it did before. Likewise, we could attempt to abolish race, for example, by making marriage within the same race not merely illegal but as taboo and as incestuous as marriage within the same immediate family. But if any such attempt to abolish race were to succeed, the human race would have lost too much, in my opinion. The prospect of abolishing race is genocidal. If the physical elimination of one's self is suicide, then the melting-pot elimination of races, even if it were genetically possible, would be genocide. As there is a normal instinct against suicide, so too there will always be a natural, ineradicable instinct against the elimination of races. Race cannot be a static concept; races have changed and race has evolved, but race will not disappear.

Since race will persist, it is a misconception to believe that racism can be eliminated. There will always be people in every race, like my son's unlicensed physiognomist classmate, who will ignore the demonstrable, normal facts about race, preferring instead to cling to abnormal prejudices about race that provide them personal satisfaction and political power.

The common misconception, for example, that most racists are white is a demonstrably false political ploy. Racism certainly exists in the United States and Europe, for example, where many so-called whites abuse personal and political power. But racism also exists with equal virulence in so-called nonwhite countries, Indonesia, for example, where most Chinese are hated because some Chinese have economic power. And in the United States and Europe, of course, so-called white people in general are hated by many racists not called white.

This universal characteristic of racism is true not only for this century but for as long as we have recorded history. We know that the Mexicas, for example, the people we have come to call Aztecs, described themselves as direct descendants of the Nauatlaca, which means "people who express themselves and speak clearly" (Parry and Keith 1984, 1:53). For the Mexicas, however, as the Aztecs called themselves, all non-Mexicas around them were Chichimeca, which means "people descended from dogs" (Thomas 1993, xix, 37).

Distinctions that ancient Greeks and Romans made between civilization and barbarism are commonly excused as nonracist, yet Greeks and Romans considered people less than human unless they spoke their languages or organized themselves in cities like Greek and Roman cities. The word "barbarian" can be traced to Homer's onomatopoeic word *barbaraphonoi*, which means making subhuman noises like "bar, bar" (Kirk 1985, 1:260–261; Friedman 1981, 29). Augustine wrote that "a man should more gladly be with his dog than with a foreigner" *(libentius sit homo cum cane suo quam cum alieno)* (Augustine 1960, 6:148, my translation; also in Friedman 1981, 216). Long after Augustine, we still define a barbarism as an offensively inferior or impure use of language. Greeks and Romans scornfully described people according to their eating habits: lotus eaters, people eaters *(anthropophagi)*, dog-headed people eaters, raw meat eaters, and so on. Then too our words "civilized," "polite," and "urbane" are all rooted in the Greek and Roman words for "city."

Some of the people whom Greeks considered barbarians lived in northern Europe, but in Greek and Roman texts most barbarians were monstrous African and Asian races. Civilization and barbarity are prejudiced cornerstones in universal concepts of race from which the ancient Greeks and Romans were not exempt. The ancient Greek and Roman concept of race consistently and deliberately confused Africa and India and called them both Ethiopia, not because of bad geography but because of skin color; the Greek word *aithiopes* means "burned faces," and some etymologies relate the Roman name "Africa" to a Hebrew word, *apher,* for burned ashes (Hay 1957, 9 n. 3).

To correct the widespread and growing misconception that racism is congenitally and uniquely European rather than universal, we might use the dictum "all styles in all races at all times." All races have and will always have geniuses and fools, and there always will be racists in every race. Racism is like dandruff; it is a condition that can be controlled but, as far as we know, cannot be cured.

If we can conceive of race as normal, that is, if our scientists cannot define race for us clearly, then we should conceive of racism as abnormal. We should stick to our commonsense concepts of race; we should look at a person's name or hair or nose or cheekbones or eyes and, as we shake hands or embrace or kiss both cheeks or rub noses with him or her, we should say or think and mean, "I salute the ancestors who brought you into this world with the same respect that you salute the ancestors who brought me into this world with you." And then, as casually as we say "good morning" or "good evening," we should think no more about it until our next greeting. By abnormal, I mean that we will always meet people who refuse to return our greeting.

Not even legally enforced miscegenation (a word that was coined in 1864 by a New York newspapermen; see Montagu 1974, 445) can eradicate racism. Europeans were always concerned that the miscegenation that occurred in the New World, where there were few European women and an abundance of other women, would lead to a loss of European control over New World peoples. Rather than lose control to miscegenated peoples, Europeans invented rigidly hierarchical racist categories calibrated according to the quantity of so-called white blood in a human being.

In English-speaking areas of the New World, these categories were relatively few: mulatto, quadroon, octoroon, sambo, and so on. In Spanish-speaking areas, these racial categories numbered usually from fourteen to twenty, each with its unique name. In French-speaking areas, like Haiti, for example, there were at least 128 distinct categories of miscegenated human beings (Dayan 1995, 25), including a special category for a person who had one part so-called Negro blood and 8,191 parts so-called white blood (Herskovits 1937, 50).

There was no defensible logic to any of these categories; they were arbitrarily ranked solely for the purpose of maintaining control. An eighteenth-century Spanish text makes the lack of logic clear. It accepted as a fact that

Spaniards and so-called Indians are pure races but that the Negro race is somehow irredeemably impure:

> It is known [this Spanish text claims] that neither Indian nor Negro contends in dignity and esteem with the Spaniard; nor do any of the others envy the lot of the Negro, who is the most dispirited and despised. . . . If the mixed blood is the offspring of a Spaniard and an Indian, the stigma disappears at the third step in descent. . . . [but] from a Spaniard and a Negro a mulato is born. . . . [and] it is said with reason that a mulato can never leave his condition of mixed blood, but it is rather the Spanish element that is lost in the condition of the Negro. (Katzew 1996, 11)

This eighteenth-century Spanish text proves that the infamously illogical "one-drop" rule did not originate in the United States. If one drop of so-called Negro blood in a person who has 8,191 parts of so-called white blood makes that person black, then why does not one drop of so-called white blood in a person who has 8,191 parts of so-called black blood not make that person white? The one-drop rule was not intended to persuade people who think clearly; it was meant to reassure people in power that European control of other races in the New World would be maintained at all costs, however absurd.

Spanish priests in colonial America maintained three registers for recording births, baptisms, marriages, deaths, and other census data. One register was used exclusively for Spaniards, another for so-called Indians, and the third for so-called mixed bloods. Of course, because mestizos (Spaniards mixed with Indians) were redeemable as white and because the system placed optimum value on so-called whiteness, a profitable tax-collecting business arose through which mestizos could claim pure whiteness for a fee. The Spanish system became so ridiculous that it eventually had to be discarded entirely. Today, as we debate how census takers should categorize and conceptualize race in the United States, we would do well to remember the failure of the Spanish system of miscegenated categories in the colonial New World. There is no pure, unmiscegenated race.

Clearly, we misconceive color reductively as it pertains to race. Carolus Linnaeus (1707–1778) and Johann Blumenbach (1752–1840), the scientists who color coded humanity, obviously knew nothing about color and did not bother to find out what they did not know. Blumenbach died in 1840, long ago enough for us to have realized that his five color-coded categories are visibly absurd. Caucasians are not white; Mongolians are not yellow; Malays are not brown; Ethiopians are not black; and native Americans are not red. And yet we continue to use these deficient descriptors, knowing them to be offensive.

It is easier, of course, to control five coded colors of humanity than it is to accept as beautiful all the many tones of human skin. Even if these five colors were convenient for Linnaeus and Blumenbach, they ought to be aesthetically insulting to us, especially since we have makeup artists and cosmetologists who are paid well to teach us about skin tones. Colors are beautiful. It is shameful that we do not have in our racial lexicon as many beautiful and well-used words for skin color as the Inuit people have for snow.

Where did the misconceived idea originate that Europeans are pure and superior, Asians pure but redeemably inferior, and Africans irredeemably impure? Why is this continental misconception of race so tenacious, even in the age of molecular biology? One of the most abused sources for the tenacious hierarchy of continents is the Book of Genesis. Chapters 9–10 of Genesis seek to explain how the known earth was populated after its destruction by the flood from which Noah and his family were saved. This passage in Genesis is so important to common misconceptions about race that we ought to focus on ten key verses, 10:18–27:

> 18. And the sons of Noah that went forth from the Ark were Shem, and Ham, and Japheth; and Ham is the father of Canaan. 19. These three were the sons of Noah, and of these were the whole earth overspread. 20. And Noah the husbandman began, and planted a vineyard. 21. And he drank of the wine, and was drunken; and he was uncovered within his tent. 22. And Ham, the father of Canaan, saw the nakedness of his father, and told his two brethren without. 23. And Shem and Japheth took a garment, and lain it upon both their shoulders, and went backward, and covered the nakedness of their father; and their faces were backward, and they saw not their father's nakedness. 24. And Noah awoke from his wine, and knew what his youngest son had done unto him. 25. And he said: "Cursed be Canaan; a servant of servants shall he be unto his brethren." 26. And he said: "Blessed be the Lord, the God of Shem; and let Canaan be their servant. 27. God enlarge Japheth, and he shall dwell in the tents of Shem; and let Canaan be their servant."

On the basis of this passage from Genesis, maps were drawn that were called T/O maps because they show the earth as a circle circumscribing its three continents in the shape of the letter T (Hay 1957, 54, facing page 84). Japheth is Europe, Shem is Asia, and Ham is Africa. The hierarchy is derived from the fact that the Hebrew word *japheth* is part of a family of words that includes words for material enlargement, beauty, and purity; the word *shem* is related to words that mean fame, good name, untarnished reputation; whereas the word *cham* is said to be an ancient name for Egypt related to words that mean hot and black, as hot and as black as the rich soil of Egypt. In this passage, like many passages in the Bible, wordplay is paramount.

For at least twenty centuries, people have abused this passage to justify the superiority of Europeans and the enslavement of Africans. They have embellished the story to attribute to Ham all sorts of sexual perversion in the ark with animals, in order to explain their belief that the descendants of Africans have a proclivity for abnormal sex, especially for raping beautiful European women. We might tell ourselves that the few racists who abuse this passage today are dangerous but controllable. But if we are serious about reconceiving race, then we should not ignore the deep impressions this passage has made on the human psyche. Not one of the many recent books I have read about race discusses this passage adequately.

Let me engage us in a little limbering-up exercise. If you are convinced that you are not the descendant of enslaved people, raise your hand. If you know that you are the descendant of people who were called slaves, raise your hand; I am glad to see, in my mind's eye, that my children raised their hands with me to the second of these. The fact is that we are all descendants of people called slaves. Slavery has existed on whichever of the earth's continents your ancestors lived. In Europe, it was common to buy European "slaves" around the Caucasus region as late as the mid-fifteenth century. In Asia and Africa, slavery persists to this day. In the New World, the Incas, Mexica, and Maya all practiced slavery. And if you are Jewish and can claim heritage on all continents, then you know quite well what your ancestors were in Egypt.

The misconception that only Africans were called slaves is common, especially in the United States, not simply because of the Civil War and the transatlantic slave trade but especially because the sons of Ham were cursed in Genesis as the servant of servants, the slaves of slaves. But slavery respects no human color. There are ancient legends in Africa and Asia that claim, perhaps in retaliatory self-defense, that blacks owned white slaves long before whites owned black slaves (Henry 1968, 74).

Within Europe, the racial divisions between blond Teutons, dark-haired Celts, and brunette Mediterraneans reflect prejudices seeking validation in Genesis; at least one leading British scientist, James Prichard (d. 1848), referred to Aryans as the Japhethic race (Stepan 1982, 99). The divisions in Judaism among Sephardim, Ashkenazim, and Oriental Jews also derives from abuse of the story of Noah and his sons. Ashkenaz was one of the descendants of Japheth, Sepharad was a place in the land of Shem before it came to mean Spain, and Cush (now Ethiopia) was named in Genesis 10:6 as one of the sons of Ham.

Menachem Begin was once asked if the Jews who should not be called Falashas were Sephardic. Begin replied, "You ask me if they are Sephardi. I do not know. But one thing I do know: they are not Ashkenazi" (Parfitt 1985, 16). People like Menachem Begin who think of themselves as European children of Ashkenaz should always remember that many Europeans are not likely to change their opinions about Jews, no matter how often they are told that Jews are a people, not a race. For these recalcitrant Euro-

peans, Jews will always be the "niggers" of Europe, gassable Africans, too
African to ever be European. I have heard the phrase "European Jew" only
from Jews; from Europeans who are not Jews, I have always heard reference to Jews without the adjective European. Many Europeans are convinced, on divine authority, that Jews are Africans because, after all, these
"literate" Europeans read their Bible, and they know where Moses was
born. They also know that Moses did not lead the Jews out of Berlin or
Beijing.

Continental rivalry based on the story of Noah permeates other powerful
literary texts and seeps into our lexicon to soak all our minds long after we
have stopped reading the Bible, after we have stopped reading Shakespeare,
stopped reading the poets of empire like Rudyard Kipling.

We may have forgotten, but the people of Shakespeare's time knew why
Othello was supposed to be a tragedy just by hearing the title, even before
they heard a single line of the play. The full title of the play is *The Tragedy
of Othello, the Moor of Venice*. We may have forgotten that the word "moor"
derives from a Latin word, *maurus,* that means black, as in Mauritania, the
Roman name for a land of black people. As the British people forgot the
Latin that they were forced as enslaved subjects to learn, they invented the
word "blackamoor" as an emphatic tautology to remind them that the
word "moor" means "black." The German version of "blackamoor" is
Schwarzeneger (as in Arnold). Europeans knew that it was tragic for a Moor
to think he could be a European from Venice. The accompanying tragedy,
of course, is that a Jew should think he could be accepted as Venetian because he was a merchant in Venice.

The phrase "white man's burden" has slipped permanently into our lexicon about race without it being necessary for us to remember that it is the
title, influenced by Genesis and Exodus, of one of Rudyard Kipling's best-
known poems. For Kipling, the white man's burden is to reap blame, hatred, and complaints from nonwhites for making them better, just as Moses
reaped blame and hatred and complaint from the people he led.

"Take up the white man's burden— / and reap his old reward: / the
blame of those ye better, / the hate of those ye guard— / the cry of hosts
ye humour / (ah, slowly!) Toward the light:— / why brought ye us from
bondage, / our loved Egyptian night" (Kipling 1913, 79).

For Kipling, only "lesser breeds," as he called them, are born outside of
England; for Kipling, God chose white people to bear humanity's burden,
and God made Jews and other nonwhites to love bondage and oppression.
For Kipling, humanity began in England. For publishing "The White
Man's Burden" (1899) and many works of literature like it, Rudyard Kip-
ling won the Nobel Prize for literature in 1907.

Kipling died in 1936. During Kipling's lifetime British scientists forged a
phony orangoutang man and named him Piltdown, rather than accept sci-

entific evidence that we all derive from Africa. The Piltdown forgery was not exposed until the 1960s, after the scientist at the center of it (Sir Arthur Keith) was knighted for his contributions to science. Another knighted British scientist (Sir Cyril Burt) fabricated evidence to fool the world that intelligence is race and class based; his Ham-based fraud was not exposed until 1964. Science has not and will not change racial misperceptions about the curse of Ham.

What are we to do when the Bible, one of humanity's most powerful documents, is used against humanity, when a passage that is clearly intended to show the unity of all humans is abused, instead, to divide all humans into unequal continents? It does not help much to think that T/O maps are outdated and that if Noah had known about the New World, he would have had four sons, not three; racists would be quick to reply that the sons of Shem eventually walked over the Siberian landbridge to populate the New World.

In order to reconceive race in the light and in the darkness of the story of Noah, we need first to remember that Japheth's blessing ("God enlarge Japheth," 9:27) is a material blessing, not a gift of wisdom, not a spiritual gift. European enlargement has dazzled the entire world since Japheth's blessing. Superior European technology has been misconceived throughout the world to be coterminous with superior systems of thought. But mercantilism, capitalism, communism, Marxism, social Darwinism, we now know, are all fatally flawed European ideas.

The New World bowed too readily to superior technology. The Mexica, the Inca, and the Maya let themselves be conquered because they all had belief systems that expected a superior religion to superimpose itself upon theirs just as European conquerors like Columbus, Cortés, and Pizarro appeared—on schedule, according to New World calendars. It is easier for us than it was for the Aztecs, Inca, and Maya to understand in theory that superior tools and weapons do not make people like Columbus, Cortés, and Pizarro superior human beings.

A certain thinker (author of a book entitled *Mind's Bodies: Thought in the Act*) reminds us that the relationship between human minds and human bodies is dynamic and complex and cannot be made simple and hierarchical (Lang 1995). Act or technique and thought or mind cannot be related to each other as inferior to superior. The shape and color of a human body says nothing about the shape and color of a human mind. And, as Karl Popper has persuaded many of us, much of what is accepted as superior philosophy from Aristotle and Plato down to Hegel and Marx is seriously flawed. European technology might continue to dominate the world, but the presumption that European philosophy is superior has caused much harm. We should not continue to permit the technological gifts of the sons of Japheth to muddy our concept of race. Japheth was blessed with material enlargement, not with clear thinking.

To reconceive our concept of race, we need to see clearly in the story of Noah that at no time did God ever bless or curse Noah's sons. Noah himself did the blessing and the cursing; and Noah's curse and blessings are fallible, not divine. Although Ham's behavior was reprehensible, Noah himself was not completely without culpability in the incident. God told Noah to build an ark and so on, but God did not tell Noah to plant a vineyard and get himself drunk and naked.

God's opinion about race is nowhere to be found in the story of Noah; this might seem obvious to you as you hold the text of Genesis before you. But to give you an idea of how persistent the myth is that God cursed Ham and thus all black people, the entry for "Ham" in the 1995 edition of the *Cambridge Encyclopedia,* published by Cambridge University Press, attributes the curse on Ham to God: "Ham . . . one of Noah's three sons . . . After the Flood his son Canaan is cursed by God" (Crystal 1995, 543).

Those people who choose to read God's opinion about race into the story of Noah should also be reminded of the story of Moses. Moses married an Ethiopian woman, a Cushite. Cush, remember, was one of Ham's sons. Moses' sister, Miriam, gossiped about this marriage. As if to warn her not to think of objecting to her sister-in-law's skin color, God gave Miriam, and all of us, a lesson in skin color. "So you think you are white," God seemed to say to Miriam, "well, I'll show you what white skin really looks like." And when Miriam looked, her skin was "as white as snow," as white as the skin of a leper (Numbers 12:1–15).

But for every story we can find in the Bible to reconceive race, racists will find a counterstory. Because we, in this New World, were left out of the T/O maps, we should simply remove ourselves from the Old World debate about continental hierarchies, understanding the misconceived basis for that debate. We should, instead, use the New World as a stage from which to teach the Old World about race a lesson it has been unable to teach itself.

Jean-Paul Sartre once called the United States a "super-European monstrosity" (Fanon 1965, 28). The United States has often behaved (in Haiti and the Dominican Republic at the beginning of the twentieth century, for example) as Sartre claimed, assuming that U.S. superiority in technology means U.S. superiority in the realm of ideas; and the rest of the world, ignoring history's lessons, seems willing to agree that the United States is superior in thought and act.

But in the hemisphere we call America, precisely at a time when the entire world is realigning itself into continental markets (four continents this time, not three as in the T/O maps), the United States, as the leader of this new continental market, has a marvelous opportunity to teach the world an invaluable new concept of race. This new concept of race will not assume a hierarchy of continents in which America dominates Europe, Asia, and Africa. This new concept of race will not permit us to continue to speak of Europeans as the race of men and supermen while simultaneously thinking of Asians and Africans as animals—Asian tigers, African gorillas. This new concept of race will proceed upon the assumption that, whatever our phenotype and genotype, we are normal; we are not Europeans; we are not Asians; we are not Africans.

Our current continental concept of race is fallacious. We are not continentals; we are islanders. We are 29 percent land completely surrounded by 71 percent water. We are one race of humans, linked by a fragile internet, floating through an immeasurable universe on a tiny island where race should play no destructive role and where racism, like all evil things, should perish.

REFERENCES

Augustine. 1960. *The City of God against the Pagans.* 7 vols. Cambridge: Harvard University Press.

Cavalli-Sforza, Luca, Paolo Menozzi, and Alberto Piazza. 1996. *The History and Geography of Human Genes.* Princeton: Princeton University Press.

Crystal, David, ed. 1995. *The Cambridge Encyclopedia.* Cambridge: Cambridge University Press.

Dayan, Joan. 1995. *Haiti, History, and the Gods.* Berkeley: University of California Press.

Fanon, Frantz. 1965. *The Wretched of the Earth.* Translated by Constance Farrington. New York: Grove.

Friedman, John Block. 1981. *The Monstrous Races in Medieval Art and Thought.* Cambridge: Harvard University Press.

Hay, Denys. 1957. *Europe: The Emergence of an Idea.* New York: Harper Torchbooks.

Henry, Paul Marc. 1965. *Africa Aeterna: The Pictorial Chronicle of a Continent.* Translated by Joel Carmichael. Lausanne, Switzerland: Imprimeries Réunies.

Herskovits, Melville J. 1937. *Life in a Haitian Valley.* New York: Knopf.

Homer. 1928. *The Iliad.* 2 vols. New York: Putnam's.

Katzew, Ilona. 1996. *New World Orders: Casta Painting and Colonial Latin America.* New York: Americas Society Art Gallery, 1996.

Kipling, Rudyard. 1913. *The Five Nations.* New York: Scribner's.

Kirk, G. S. 1985. *The Iliad: A Commentary.* 2 vols. Cambridge: Cambridge University Press.

Kuhn, Thomas. 1970. *The Structure of Scientific Revolutions.* Chicago: University of Chicago Press.

Lang, Berel. 1995. *Mind's Bodies: Thought in the Act.* Albany: SUNY Press.

Montagu, Ashley. 1965. *The Idea of Race.* Lincoln: University of Nebraska Press.

Montagu, Ashley. 1974. *Man's Most Dangerous Myth: The Fallacy of Race*. New York: Oxford University Press.

Montagu, Ashley, ed. 1964. *The Concept of Race*. New York: Free Press.

Nepaulsingh, Colbert. 1995. *Apples of Gold in Filigrees of Silver: Jewish Writing in the Eye of the Spanish Inquisition*. New York: Holmes & Meier.

Parfitt, Tudor. 1985. *Operation Moses*. New York: Stein & Day.

Parry, John H., and Robert G. Keith. 1984. *New Iberian World*. 5 vols. New York: Times Books/Hector & Rose.

Popper, Karl. 1962. *The Open Society and Its Enemies*. Princeton: Princeton University Press.

Scott, William R. 1993. *The Sons of Sheba's Race*. Bloomington: Indiana University Press.

Stepan, Nancy. 1982. *The Idea of Race in Science: Great Britain, 1800–1960*. London: Macmillan.

Thomas, Hugh. 1993. *Conquest: Montezuma, Cortés, and the Fall of Mexico*. New York: Simon & Schuster.

10

Getting Basic: Bambara's Re-visioning of the Black Aesthetic

Margo V. Perkins

Published in 1970, Toni Cade Bambara's *The Black Woman* continues to speak to many African-American women's experiences three decades later.[1] This edited volume of critical essays, poetry, and stories by black women writers and activists is one of the earliest feminist challenges to the overtly masculinist discourse of late 1960s–1970s black nationalist struggle. Many young women who first picked up the volume in the 1970s found the work affirming and empowering. Its popularity created new spaces for critical dialogue around issues important to black women that had been largely ignored within both black nationalist circles and the predominately white mainstream feminist movement. Such issues included the impact of racism on black women's self-image, the intersection of race and class in black women's experiences (sometimes referred to as "double or triple jeopardy"), and the lack of self-determination for black women with respect to reproductive freedom and health care (the former circumscribed by black nationalist ideology equating birth control with genocide, and the latter by the unethical practices of a racist and sexist medical industry). The writings anthologized by Bambara additionally explored sources of tension between black women and white women, regressive gender role expectations and sexist double standards on the part of black men, and the too frequent tendency of nationalist rhetoric to equate black liberation with the right of black men to reap the benefits of patriarchal privilege.

Convinced that there was in fact a market for black women's writing in the early 1970s (after all, as Bambara quips, "I knew 800 million Black women all by myself"),[2] she decided to put together what became *The*

Black Woman as a way of "kick[ing] the door open."[3] The volume became a harbinger of an outpouring of fiction and critical writing by black women during the 1970s and 1980s. Given the resurgence of interest today in 1960s political and countercultural movements and the relative dearth (still) of texts about black women's experiences in nationalist struggle, it is no surprise that *The Black Woman* has been reissued in the 1990s. As a text that transgresses silences around black women's experiences during that era, it is an important resource for contemporary scholars and a cautionary tale for young black activists today who tend to romanticize 1960s black nationalist praxis.

I speak at length about *The Black Woman* because Bambara first lays out in that anthology much of her own artistic vision and activist sensibility. Her preface and two essays in the volume lay a critical groundwork for interpreting her subsequent collections of short fiction—*Gorilla, My Love,*[4] *The Sea Birds Are Still Alive,*[5] and the posthumously published *Deep Sightings and Rescue Missions*[6] (a collection of short fiction, essays, and interviews). In *The Black Woman* one gleans Bambara's uncompromising commitment to a nationalist agenda that is patently feminist. Against society's schizophrenia-inducing expectation that black women define themselves in terms of *either* race *or* gender, and the tendencies historically of nationalist rhetoric to silence women's concerns and of (white) feminist discourse to erase black women, Bambara's fiction seeks to merge nationalist and feminist impulses in ways that work holistically to affirm all aspects of black women's identity. Focusing on connections between Bambara's theorizing in *The Black Woman* and the short fiction in her last volume, *Deep Sightings and Rescue Missions,* I wish to explore the evolution of Bambara's activist sensibility and her reworking of the nationalist aesthetic to create affirming and empowering models of black subjectivity.

To be sure, *The Black Woman* is not an unproblematic collection. Some of the essayists adopt postures that can only be described as protofeminist at best. Others entertain homophobic rhetoric that should make readers of the 1990s cringe.[7] The volume is very much a work of its time. But its spirit is what interests me. In order to appreciate this spirit, some attention to the nationalist aesthetic as context is pertinent. As the civil rights movement of the 1950s and early 1960s gave way in the late 1960s to the black power movement, nationalist ideology once again gained ascendancy in black America. This renewed push for self-determination had political as well as cultural dimensions.

The 1960s produced a vibrant black arts movement that sought to connect artistic endeavors with an avowedly political agenda. Artists and intellectuals of the period revisited a series of questions in their effort to define a new aesthetic. Among these questions were: What constitutes black art? Is there, in fact, such a thing? If so, what are its characteristics? Can an essential blackness be qualified? What are the functions of black art? Is all art produced by black artists automatically black art? By what criteria should this art be evaluated? And, finally, who is qualified to do this evaluation? Larry Neal, Hoyt Fuller, Amiri Baraka (then LeRoi Jones), Ron Karenga, and others called for art in the service of revolution. As Julian Mayfield succinctly put it, black art has to be about "the business of making revolution, for we have tried everything else."[8]

Unlike black literature of previous eras, the new black literature, which aimed at the consciences of black readers, Neal maintained, was less a literature of protest (in the tradition of Richard Wright, Ralph Ellison, or Ann Petry, for example) than of black affirmation.[9] Accordingly, much of the poetry and fiction generated sought to empower black readers by celebrating aspects of black identity, heritage, idiom, and experience. In many ways more prescriptive in their formulations than black theorists of earlier periods, leading figures of the black arts movement of the 1960s also, unfortunately, dismissed art and artists deemed insufficiently black based on what now seem specious criteria. Representing one of the more extreme positions in the debate over the definition and role of black art, Ron Karenga proclaimed that the social function of any work of art was the single most important criterion for judging its worth. In his 1968 essay, "Black Cultural Nationalism," Karenga declared that

> all art must reflect and support the Black Revolution, and any art that does not discuss and contribute to the revolution is invalid, no matter how many lines and spaces are produced in proportion and symmetry and no matter how many sounds are boxed in or blown out and called music.[10]

Implicit in Karenga's assertion is the notion of art as propaganda to (in his own words) "expose the enemy, praise the people, and support the revolution."[11]

Until Bambara lost her battle with cancer in December 1995, her writing consistently reflected her deep commitment to the ideal of literature in the service of revolution. She once remarked of her own craft, "I work to produce stories that save our lives."[12] In the preface to *Deep Sightings,* Toni Morrison comments on Bambara's ability to infuse storytelling with liberatory politics:

> There was no doubt that the work she did had work to do. She always knew what her work was for. Any hint that art was over there and politics was over here would break her up into tears of laughter, or elicit a look so withering it made silence the only intelligent response.[13]

Bambara's fiction in the service of revolution embraces black cultural ways of knowing, consistent with the Nguzo Saba (seven principles of nationhood): *umoja* (unity), *kujichagulia* (self-determination), *ujima* (collective work and responsibility), *ujamaa* (cooperative economics), *nia* (purpose), *kuumba* (creativity), and *imani* (faith, specifically in black people, and the righteousness of their struggle against oppression).[14] Her audience is assumed to be other blacks to the extent that she makes no apologies or qualifications to accommodate the comfort level of readers and critics outside her own cultural frame of reference. To meaningfully engage her texts, then, readers and critics must do their homework. Other ways in which Bambara's fiction manifests black aesthetic ideals include her emphasis on the importance of history, self-knowledge, and racial memory; her internal gaze or focus within the black community (black people's relationships to white people and white society constitute the backdrop but not the focus of her work); and her skillful capturing of the rhythm, style, texture, color, and humor marking black linguistic expression.

In certain important ways, however, Bambara's artistic sensibility moves beyond these characteristics of the black aesthetic, which are found (in varying degrees of success) among other black arts movement writers' works, as well. What makes Bambara's fiction unique is that she manages to invoke the rhetoric of cultural and revolutionary nationalism while subverting its masculinist assumptions. These assumptions include the equating of nationhood with black manhood (in its most patriarchal form) and the casting of race as the sole issue relevant to the black liberation struggle. In her preface to *The Black Woman,* Bambara affirms many of the tenets of the nationalist aesthetic as articulated by Neal, Fuller, Baraka, and others, but she takes issue with some of the narrow-minded dogmatism and especially the implicit or explicit marginalization of black women. Arguing for a broader conception of what constitutes "the enemy," Bambara offers her own version of the new black aesthetic:

> What characterizes the current movement of the 60s is a turning away from the larger society and a turning toward each other. Our art, protest, dialogue no longer spring from the impulse to entertain, or to indulge or enlighten the conscience of the enemy; white people, whiteness, or racism; men, maleness, or chauvinism: America or imperialism . . . depending on your viewpoint and your terror. Our energies now seem to be invested in and are in turn derived from a determination to touch and to unify. What typifies the current spirit is an embrace, an embrace of the community and a hardheaded attempt to get basic with each other.[15]

For Bambara, this "getting basic" involves black people holding each other accountable for what liberation means and for eliminating the counterrevolutionary sexist impulses that ultimately undermine the collective liberation struggle. Bambara challenges the related assumptions that women are ancillary to the struggle and that the personal is somehow separable from the political—that what is happening at the level of individual relationships has little to no bearing on the larger liberation struggle. In "On the Issue of Roles," an essay anthologized in *The Black Woman,* Bambara cautions (black men) to the contrary:

> If your house ain't in order, you ain't in order. It is so much easier to be out there than right here. The revolution ain't out there. Yet. But it is here. Should be. And arguing that instant-coffee-ten-minutes-to-midnight alibi to justify hasty-headed dealings with your mate is shit. Ain't no such animal as an instant guerrilla.[16]

Bambara's dismissal of the notion of an "instant guerrilla" is a challenge to activists to not mistake style for substance.

Bambara's fiction repeatedly returns to the importance of self-work on the part of both men and women as critical prerequisites to effective revolutionary struggle. In "Salvation Is the Issue," an essay anthologized in Mari Evans's *Black Women Writers (1950–1980),* Bambara charges that "outrage at oppression can be a dodge, a way of avoiding calling a spade a spade and speaking directly to the issue of personal/collective responsibility and will, or speaking frankly about the fact that we participate in our ambush every day of our lives."[17] Far from letting the powers that be off the hook, Bambara called for constant vigilance in order that black people might avoid, as much as possible, complicity with the power structure in their own oppression.

Reflecting her belief that revolution is built from the bottom up, much of Bambara's fiction takes as its focus the forging of transformative relationships (across gender and across generations) that create strong, cohesive (though not monolithic) communities that will ultimately be capable of overthrowing racist, sexist, and capitalist domination. Repeatedly, these transformative relationships are forged through individual characters' commitment to self-work. At least five of the six short stories in *Deep Sightings* reveal variations on this theme. All of Bambara's stories reflect a zero tolerance for sexism and chauvinism. Women characters are, furthermore, the doers and shakers in Bambara's fiction. Unafraid to "speak their speak," they are on the front lines of the struggle, warriors in their own right, helping to organize the people alongside black men of like vision. Such portraits contrast markedly with idealized images of black women as muses or African queens (or alternatively, as mollifiers of black men's revolutionary rage) popularized in a good deal of the poetry and fiction by male writers of the late 1960s and early 1970s.

In *Deep Sightings and Rescue Missions,* the three stories "Going Critical," "Madame Bai and the Taking of Stone Mountain," and "Luther on Sweet

Auburn" all present women protagonists who are socially and politically conscious and take decisive action to transform their environments. Four principles of the Nguzo Saba are featured prominently in how the stories unfold: *nia* (purpose), *kujichagulia* (self-determination), *ujima* (collective work and responsibility) and *imani* (faith). That all three stories are set in the post–civil rights/black power eras (i.e., the early 1980s) implicitly stresses the continuing need to struggle against myriad forms of oppression and social injustice. All also suggest that this struggle requires characters to draw on spiritual as well as material resources.

The first of these stories, "Going Critical," is about the relationship between a mother (Clara) and her daughter (Honey) and the lessons Clara must pass on to Honey before she (Clara) succumbs to terminal cancer. Clara wants to be sure that Honey's inherited gift of foresight will be put to proper use once she is gone. Clara's battle with cancer is presumably linked to her exposure many years earlier to radiation during government testing of a nuclear bomb. In the story, Bambara connects environmentalism with a feminist agenda. Spiritual practices are invoked in the struggle not only to heal Clara of cancer but also to heal the debilitating social ills of the community and the pollution and poisoning of the earth. Honey's gift of sight, which Bambara asks readers to take for granted, is assumed as a common phenomenon in black folk culture. Clara must pass on to her daughter instructions on how to respect the power she has been given and to use this gift for the benefit of humankind.

In "Madame Bai and the Taking of Stone Mountain," the unnamed narrator must answer a spiritual koan put to her by Madame Bai, a Korean warrior-healer, who has been invited to present a workshop to members of the narrator's activist collective. In answering Madame Bai's koan: "Stone Mountain; what is it for?" the narrator discovers how to synthesize spiritual practice with political work in order to act on what she knows. The story is set in Atlanta during that frightening period in the early 1980s when a staggering number of black (mostly male) children in the city were mysteriously abducted and brutally murdered.

In the story, the narrator (an African-American woman) and her two companions, Tram (a Vietnamese man) and Mustafa (a Jordanian man), are accosted by a small gang of white bigots who first taunt and then physically attack Tram. The gang is outdone when the narrator and Mustafa, led by Tram, prove quite capable of physically defending themselves. Badly wounded, their assailants disperse and leave the three to continue along their way while struggling to recover their prior sense of peace. The narrator's eventual answer to Madame Bai's koan, "Stone Mountain is for the taking," symbolizes her will to fight back against the kind of bigotry and racial violence associated with the murder of black boys and the terror of white supremacists. Readers familiar with the history of Stone Mountain,

Georgia, will recognize it as the birthplace of the modern Klan, which until relatively recently remained a stronghold for white supremacy. The narrator affirms the power of the people (here meaning not just blacks but all people committed to justice and racial equality) to reclaim this monument from its historical association with racial bigotry and intolerance.

The third story, "Luther on Sweet Auburn," is about an ex–social worker (affectionately nicknamed "Miz Nap" by the Brooklyn community she served in the 1960s) who encounters, years later, an acquaintance and former gang member, Luther Owens, from the Brooklyn neighborhood. The story contrasts the narrator's own continuing activism with Luther's complacency, stagnation, and squandered potential. "Luther on Sweet Auburn," like "Madame Bai," is set in Atlanta. Miz Nap has adapted her activist work, begun in the 1960s, to accommodate changing times. No longer a community youth worker, she is now a playwright, TV producer, and soon-to-be filmmaker who designs projects that give voice to the community's concerns. Contemplating the premise for her "new play in rehearsal," she notes, "theme of hostage-keeping in U.S.—slavery, reservations, ghettos, prisons, internment camps for Japanese, GIs in stockades for organizing, cities hostages of Big Business, the whole country kidnapped by thugs. Station manager not interested. Fine."[18]

When the narrator bumps into Luther Owens moments later, she is dismayed to realize in the course of their exchange that the spirit of the 1960s literally passed him by. Twenty years later, he not only has little to show for his life (which in Bambara's terms means. what have you done for the cause?), he's also talking the same jive (as the narrator comments: "all about need and you gotta and help me"). Weary of the tenor of Luther's conversation, Miz Nap cuts to the chase: "How old are you, Luther?" she inquires. "And how did the sixties manage to pass you by, you who were in hailing distance of Brooklyn CORE?" Implicit in the question is the idea of individual accountability and responsibility. In asking Luther's age, the narrator suggests that it is long past time for him to have gotten his act together. "Luther is confused," she thinks to herself, "Thinks I'm still a youth worker. Thinks he's still a youth. Thinks this is Warren Street, Brooklyn. That is, 1962."[19] Having always assumed, by the narrator's demeanor and sense of purpose, that she was much older than he, Luther is surprised to learn at the close of the story that Miz Nap, at thirty-eight, is only five years his senior.

All three of these stories present women who are empowered, invested with a sense of purpose, and committed to uplifting their communities through progressive social action. The stories propose that activism continues to be an appropriate response to a range of contemporary issues. In "Luther on Sweet Auburn," the enthusiasm of black and foreign students gathered for a rally at Bethel Church to draft position papers and to organize around pressing issues provides the story's narrator with an (as she says) "in-the-flesh refutation of the apathetic myth, the movement-is-over propaganda."[20] In Bambara's fiction, movement for social change never ends; it merely changes its form in an increasingly broad set of issues from environmental racism to xenophobia to nuclear armament.

Bambara's focus on the importance of self-work and individual accountability in the interest of progressive social transformation is complemented by an equally strong commitment to the importance of collective work and shared responsibility. To advance individuals without advancing communities is to achieve nothing at all in terms of social change. While concern for community plays an important role in all of the stories in *Deep Sightings,* Bambara's ethic of community is perhaps most vividly revealed in the stories "Ice" and "The War of the Wall," both narrated from the perspectives of children. Bambara's frequent use of child narrators reveals her respect for children's voices and often unique ways of seeing. Both stories emphasize the importance of intergenerational bonding. In the spirit of collective work and responsibility *(ujima),* all members of the community are responsible for and accountable to each other. The elders have a duty to provide the youth with a sense of who they are (through direct lessons, their own example, storytelling, etc.), as well as to nurture and instruct them in how to live ethically in this world. The young, in turn, have a responsibility to respect and care for their elders.

In "The War of the Wall," the child narrator learns important lessons about grace and tolerance from the actions of the adults in her community. In the story, the narrator is nonplussed by the arrival of an outsider to the community who has been granted permission to paint a mural on the wall adjacent to a barbershop on Talbro Street. Attached to her childhood memories of the wall as it is, the narrator declares the "painter lady's" effort to transform the wall an "act of war." The story illustrates the community's tolerance for someone different from themselves, as reflected in their capacity to embrace the painter lady (and her project) even as her lack of familiarity with the community's social mores and conventions causes her to inadvertently offend those who extend their hospitality.

The community's willingness, despite this, to grant her physical and psychic space to create additionally suggests their appreciation and respect for artistic work. At first vexed by the adults' failure to denounce the painter lady for her repeated social faux pas, the narrator is eventually pushed to rethink her assumptions about the woman and ultimately to expand her cultural horizons, when the finished mural is enthusiastically embraced by the community. Although the painter lady is an outsider, the community's reaction to the finished mural implies that she succeeds in creating a work of art that clearly speaks to, captures, or in some way validates the community that receives it. The respect she shows the community through her art is thus returned by them through their appreciation of the work.

In the final story to be considered from *Deep Sightings,* "Ice," the narrator is incensed when the adults in her community fail to act to save a litter of pups who die of exposure to the cold while she and her classmates are at school. When they return from school, the neighborhood children discover the frozen puppies and give them a proper burial. Of course, what the narrator does not appreciate is that the adults, who are necessarily preoccupied with the weighty responsibilities of work and providing for their families, are not focused on Lady or her puppies. The adults' concern for their children and the children's concern for the puppies are simply on different levels.

The adults nevertheless indulge the narrator's fussing and insinuations about the dead puppies because they recognize that her concern emanates from something that they agree is important to nurture: an appreciation for the value of life and a sense of obligation to protect and care for those who are unable to protect and care for themselves. The narrator eventually makes an important connection between her own concern for the pups and the way her Aunt Myrtle cares for Mrs. Blue, an elderly woman in the neighborhood. Spooked by the sight of Mrs. Blue, the narrator is reluctant to voluntarily visit the elderly woman despite prodding from one of her agemates. Self-congratulatory in her own concern for the pups later that evening, the narrator looks forward to telling her own children someday the story of how she and her peers did what all of the adults in her community had failed to do. In the process of spinning the story, however, thoughts of Old Mrs. Blue interrupt her reverie.

> But what if my kids notice there's a hole in my story, I asked myself, a hole I will fall right through in the telling. Suppose they ask, "But, Mommy, didn't you go and see about the old lady?" So then I'll tell them how I put my boots back on and put them silly pot-holder mittens on too to carry one of Aunt Myrtle's casseroles down to Mrs. Blue. And with the moon pushing at my back, I'm thinking that maybe I'll sit with Mrs. Blue a while even though she is a spooky sort of person.[21]

The narrator realizes that if she wants to be able to tell the story, she must tell it right. And that means that she must also be accountable herself.

In interviews, Bambara described herself as an activist who sometimes writes. To be sure, her literary achievements constituted only one facet of a woman whose talents and interests were multifaceted. Whether working in literature or, later, predominately in film, Bambara was committed to creating art in the interests of social change. In an interview with Louis Massiah included in *Deep Sightings,* Bambara explains how the community that named her also shaped her approach to storytelling:

It was Grandma Dorothy who taught me critical theory, who steeped me in the tradition of Afrocentric aesthetic regulations, who trained me to understand that a story should be informed by the emancipatory impulse that characterizes our storytelling trade in these territories as exemplified by those freedom narratives. . . . She taught that a story should contain mimetic devices so that the tale is memorable, sharable, that a story should be grounded in cultural specificity and shaped by the modes of Black art practice—call-and-response but one modality that bespeaks a communal ethos.[22]

Bambara's artistic vision lends itself to stories that are constructed around a project of possibility. They are not only about what *is* but what *might be.* Pushing against the inertia of powerlessness and defeatism, she creates black women, men, and children who are fighters rather than victims, active subjects rather than passive objects. And while they don't always win their battles, the courage, resolution, and spirit evinced in the process present us as readers with a range of possibilities for thinking about how we choose to live our own lives.

NOTES

1. Toni Cade Bambara, ed., *The Black Woman: An Anthology* (New York: New American Library, 1970).
2. Toni Cade Bamara, interview by Louis Massiah, *Deep Sightings and Rescue Missions: Fiction, Essays, and Conversations,* ed. Toni Morrison (New York: Pantheon, 1996), 230.
3. Ibid.
4. Toni Cade Bambara, *Gorilla My Love* (New York: Random House, 1972).
5. Toni Cade Bambara, *The Seabirds Are Still Alive* (New York: Random House, 1977).
6. Toni Morrison, ed., *Deep Sightings and Rescue Missions: Fiction, Essays, and Conversations* [by Toni Cade Bambara] (New York: Pantheon, 1996).
7. The term "faggot," for instance, is used uncritically several times throughout.
8. Julian Mayfield, "You Touch My Black Aesthetic and I'll Touch Yours," in *The Black Aesthetic,* ed. Addison Gayle Jr. (New York: Anchor, 1972), 29.
9. Hoyt Fuller (paraphrasing Larry Neal) in Fuller, "The New Black Literature: Protest or Affirmation," in *Black Aesthetic,* 329.
10. Ron Karenga, "Black Cultural Nationalism," in *Black Aesthetic,* 31.
11. Ibid., 32.
12. Toni Cade Bambara, "Salvation Is the Issue," in *Black Women Writers (1950– 1980),* ed. Mari Evans (New York: Anchor, 1984), 47.
13. Morrison, preface to *Deep Sightings,* ix.
14. A brief overview of the seven principles (Nguzo Saba) can be found in, among other sources, Cedric McClester's *Kwanzaa: Everything You Always Wanted to Know but Didn't Know Where to Ask* (New York: Gumbs & Thomas, 1985), 3–7.

Bambara's work embraces concepts (e.g., the Nguzo Saba) that were also celebrated by Ron Karenga and other cultural nationalists of the late 1960s and 1970s. However, Bambara was highly critical of Karenga and his cohorts for their virulent sexism.

15. Bambara, *Black Woman*, 7.
16. Bambara, "On the Issue of Roles," in *Black Woman*, 110.
17. Bambara, "Salvation Is the Issue," 47.
18. Bambara, "Luther on Sweet Auburn," in *Deep Sightings*, p. 79.
19. Ibid., p. 78.
20. Ibid., p. 85.
21. "Ice," in *Deep Sightings*, p. 77.
22. *Deep Sightings*, p. 249.

11

Beautiful Americans, Ugly Japanese, Obsequious Chinese: The Depiction of Race in Huang Chunming's Stories

King-fai Tam

In 1974, Huang Chunming, now hailed as one of the most important writers of the nativist movement *(xiangtu wenxue)* in Taiwan,[1] published an autobiographical essay, "The Tomato Tree on the Rooftop," in which he related a childhood incident in a small village in southern Taiwan.[2] One day he discovered that a tomato plant had taken root on the rooftop of his family home. Surprised, he turned to ask his grandfather how the plant could ever get to such a high place. His grandfather explained that a bird might have eaten a tomato, and the undigested seeds might have passed out in its droppings onto the roof. Still not satisfied, Huang continued to ask, "But there is no soil on the rooftop for the plant to grow in!" At first his grandfather was unwilling to speak any further. When pressed, he finally said in a solemn tone, "When something wants to live, it'll find a way."

Not long afterward, Huang drew a picture of the tomato plant in school. In his childish hand, the plant, laden with bright red tomatoes, had become a tree that dwarfed the house on which it stood. The teacher, who came from the city, could not figure out what the picture was. When he heard that it was supposed to be a "tomato tree," the teacher, ever so sensitive about his ignorance of farming matters, thought that Huang Chunming was playing a trick on him. Angrily, he slapped Huang's face again and again, accusing him of lying and demanding him to tell the truth: "You liar! How can a tomato plant grow when there is no soil on the roof? You're lying!" His grandfather's answer came to Huang Chunming's mind, and even though he did not fully comprehend the wisdom of those words, he replied without thinking, "When something wants to live, it'll find a way." The teacher did not know what to make of such an answer and, finding words failing him, he shouted Huang Chunming down, "And if *you* don't want to live, you just keep up the backtalk."

On his way home after school that day, Huang could see from a distance the tomato tree fluttering in the wind on the rooftop long before he reached the door. There, having stood up to his teacher's bullying the whole day, Huang Chunming finally broke down and cried. The incident related in this story captures a number of recurrent themes in Huang's works: adults' cruelty to children, the tenacity of life, and the ignorance and arrogance of city dwellers. In 1974, however, Huang obviously had something quite different in mind when he concluded his essay with these words: "In this world, no seed is given the right to choose the soil in which to grow. In the same way, no one is given the right to pick the color of his skin."

Although he has written a number of stories with a racial theme, this is perhaps the only explicit remark about race that he has made outside of his creative world. On one level, this is not at all surprising, as many Chinese are either oblivious to or silent on the role race has to play in human affairs. Since China is still predominantly a racially homogenous society, it is a rare occurrence for many Chinese even to set eyes on a non-Chinese, and the same is true of people living in Taiwan. This is not to say that they do not have any opinion on racial matters but that the social setting provides little opportunity for their opinions to come to the surface.[3]

Bo Yang, the gadfly to Chinese complacency, takes a cynical view of the general absence of racial discourse in contemporary China. Don't be misled into thinking Chinese are color-blind, he warns, for "the Chinese method of dealing with racial prejudice is to sweep it under the rug. Chinese preju- dice takes the form of someone bleeding from the rectum, who walks around with both hands covering his backside and proclaiming, 'No, of course I don't have hemorrhoids. Anyone who says otherwise has ulterior motives and evil intentions.' "[4] Given the general reticence or even denial on the part of Chinese writers of racial feelings, it becomes all the more remarkable that between 1971 and 1978 Huang published four important stories that focus on interactions between Taiwanese and Americans on the one hand, and Taiwanese and Japanese on the other: "The Taste of Apples" (1972), "Sayonara, Good-bye" (1973), "The Little Widow" (1974), and "I Love Mary" (1977). An earlier story, "The Evening of the Life of Uncle Gan'geng," published in 1971, also deals marginally with the question of race but never quite achieved the wide popularity of the other four stories.

At around the same time, other Taiwanese writers also began to step into this unexplored territory. Wang Zhenhe, another nativist writer, wrote two novels that have been compared to Huang Chunming's works. The first one, *Rose, Rose, I Love You*, is a burlesque about an English teacher who brings together the four major brothels in Hua Lian in eastern Taiwan to stage a spectacular welcome for the American GIs who are arriving at Taiwan for R and R.[5] His other novel, *The Portrait of Beautiful People*, describes a group of travel agency employees whose only dream in life is to emigrate to the United States. Even as they join a protest against the U.S. government for orchestrating the expulsion of Taiwan from the United Nations, they seek ways to move their assets to the United States.[6]

Even writers who are more concerned with other social matters include in their works scenes of the interaction of races. Chen Yingzhen, while investigating the influence of international corporations on life in Taiwan, came up with "The Midnight Freight Train," in which the hero of the story agonizes over the humiliating situation of working in an American firm. In a moment of revelation toward the end of the story, he resigns from his position, shouting obscenities at his American colleagues as he storms out of his office and catches a train to the south of Taiwan in the company of a woman who has silently endured the advances of an American superior.[7] Yet another example is Wen Rui'an, who is well known for his new martial arts novels. He describes in one of his stories two local ruffians who roam the streets of Taipei at night and randomly choose an American student on whom to practice the punches and kicks that they learn at a martial arts school.[8] Before going into the reasons for Taiwanese writers' sudden fascination with the question of race, I summarize three of Huang Chunming's stories, which perhaps best exemplify how the race question is approached in Taiwan.[9]

"The Taste of Apples" (1972)

Ah Fa, a construction worker, is run down one day by a car driven by a Lieutenant Graham of the U.S. military. While Ah Fa lies unconscious in an American hospital, his legs broken, the American embassy, fearing an outbreak of anti-American sentiment, moves quickly to contain the incident by offering compensation to his family. Ah Fa's family, it turns out, lives in abject poverty. With the breadwinner now incapacitated, the family's livelihood is in jeopardy. The children are too young to understand the full significance of the tragedy, yet they know enough to be afraid. The oldest daughter, especially, begins to worry that she might be taken away from her parents and put up for adoption. For the wife, Ah Gui, the greatest worry is her youngest daughter, a deaf-mute. Despite her wariness of the Americans, she is nevertheless surprised by the solicitousness of the American officer who comes with the sad news. Under Lieutenant Graham's instructions, the officer arranges for them to visit Ah Fa in the American hospital, which they would normally not be allowed to enter. More surprises are in store for them there. The cleanliness and the "whiteness" of the hospital dazzle them. (Huang Chunming inserts the ironic subtitle "The White House" in this section of the story.) The walls are immaculately white, as are the beds, the uniforms of the doctors and the nurses, the sinks and tiles in the bathroom. Even the toilet paper, which they pocket in big wads so that they can use it at home, is whiter than any kind of paper they have even seen. When an American nun appears by Ah Fa's bedside in her white habit, speaking perfect Chinese, they think they can see wings with white feathers coming out on her shoulders. For a brief moment, they get a glimpse of Heaven, which only the Americans can provide. The American embassy offers extremely generous terms of settlement. Not only do they guarantee the family's future livelihood, they offer to send the deaf-mute daughter to a special school in the United States. Ah Fa is speechless at this lucky turn of events. Looking at the stack of banknotes the Lieutenant leaves on his chest, he utters in confusion first his thanks and then his apologies for causing the American officer so much trouble. Finally the family is left alone. As he watches his family snacking on the American food brought by the lieutenant, Ah Fa reflects on his good luck of being knocked down by an American car. Losing his legs is all worth it, he thinks. He then asks his wife to hand him an American apple, the taste of which he still has to try.

"Sayonara, Good-bye" (1973)

Huang, the main character of the story, receives a call from his employer, who asks him to accompany seven Japanese business associates to Jiaoxi, his hometown, for a sex vacation. After protesting futilely, he agrees to be the guide and the translator for the Japanese visitors, even though he realizes that he is no better than a pimp in the eyes of the Japanese. The seven Japanese businessmen turn out to be veterans of World War II. Although Japan lost the war, it has now turned to economic aggression, and these seven businessmen still regard Taiwan as a Japanese colony. They expect to be entertained, proudly declaring to Huang that their one goal in life is to sleep with a thousand women. Huang is disgusted at their shameless admission of lechery but, fearing for the security of his job, he refrains from openly rebuking them. Instead, he tries to make the best of the situation by taking advantage of his role as translator to poke fun at them. Instead of looking out for their interests, he looks out for the prostitutes and on their behalf exacts a higher price from the Japanese. Huang sees a chance to teach these arrogant Japanese a lesson on the second day into the trip, when a student approaches them after overhearing their conversation on the train. The student claims that he wants to go to Japan to study and would appreciate a chance to learn something about Japan from the Japanese visitors. An idea begins to form in Huang's head: he would play his translator's trick again. First, he presents the Japanese as college professors, in whose voice he then questions the student's motives in going to Japan. Why does he choose Japan when his specialty is Chinese literature? Is he completely honest with himself when he claims that he wants to go because he is interested in examining rare editions available only in Japan? How many rare editions available in Taiwan has he perused? Is he not drawn more by the life of comfort in Japan than the academic resources that the place has to offer? In turn, when he translates for the student, he turns all his fawning remarks about Japan into angry accusations of Japanese aggression. Are the gentlemen now touring Taiwan veterans of World War II? Did they fight on the China front at that time? Why is there no apology from Japan for the rape of Nanking?[10] What do they have to say about the present Japanese economic expansionism? In the end, both the student and the Japanese businessmen are properly humbled. The student gets off the train, vowing that he would consider seriously the well-meaning advice from the "professors." As for the Japanese, now that they have been brought face-to-face to their shameful actions during the war, they become uncharacteristically quiet for the rest of the trip.

"I Love Mary" (1977)

Chen Shunde, who prefers to be called David Chen, inherits a dog named Mary from his American superior, Raymond, after the latter returns home to the United States. David's wife, Yuyun, who was once bitten by a dog, tries to object but gives in when David argues that it will help his career to take care of his superior's dog. The real reason, however, is that he is proud to own a dog that once lived with an American family. When Mary jumps around in the backseat of his car, he imagines other drivers on the road throwing glances of admiration. With an American dog under his charge, he feels as if he is one step closer to being an American. Before leaving for the United States, Raymond's wife gives careful instructions about caring for Mary. David Chen is to speak to Mary only in English. She has to be fed beef and expensive dog food. Most importantly, David should never let any Chinese dog mate with Mary. The responsibility of taking care of Mary now falls on the shoulder of Yuyun, who first has to overcome her fear of dogs. Mary, for her part, seems to take special delight in making Yuyun's life miserable, breaking pots in the kitchen, killing plants in the yard, relieving itself on the rug, and pulling and tripping her on their daily walk. When she complains to David about the dog, he invariably takes the dog's side, and the relationship between husband and wife becomes strained to the limit. Then, one day, the unspeakable comes to pass. Mary goes into heat, escapes from the backyard, and mates with a stray dog. When he hears the bad news, David rushes home from the office in less than ten minutes. He pulls his wife up from her chair and slaps her repeatedly, accusing her of being selfish and deliberately sabotaging his career. His wife is at first ridden with guilt but soon calms down. She puts the question to her husband with sobering clarity: "Do you love me? Or do you love the dog?" Totally irrational now, David howls in reply, "I love Mary!" He then dashes out the door with a bat in his hand and beats the stray dog savagely until it dismounts and runs for safety. Later that day, David returns to an empty house. His wife has left him and taken the children with her. In David's mind, her departure only confirms his belief that she has betrayed him. He goes into the living room, looks up the telephone number of a vet to arrange an abortion for Mary.

Each story in its own way gives the reader a glimpse of the historical context in which the racial imagination in Taiwan should be understood. The 1970s saw the influx of Japanese and Americans into Taiwan on an unprecedented scale. Although the U.S. government was already making plans to withdraw from Vietnam in the early 1970s, the number of U.S. soldiers arriving in Taiwan was still at its peak. At the same time, American and Japanese businessmen arrived in droves as international corporations burgeoned. Neither military nor business personnel are known for cultivating better understanding between races, but what gave a negative tone to the racial discourse in Taiwan in the 1970s more than anything else was a series of diplomatic setbacks that Taiwan suffered during that period, beginning with the expulsion of Taiwan from the United Nations in 1971. Following what is now known as ping-pong diplomacy, Nixon visited China in 1972, setting off a series of negotiations that culminated in the termination of diplomatic relationship between Taiwan and the United States in 1979. Earlier, Japan had acknowledged the Chinese Communist Party as the legitimate government of China, and Taiwan consequently severed its diplomatic relationship with Japan in September 1973. It is understandable that Taiwan should feel betrayed and beleaguered in those years.

Yet if the Taiwanese harbor feelings of resentment against the Americans and the Japanese (the rest of the world does not seem to interest the Taiwanese literary imagination in the least at this time), they distinguish between the two. Repeatedly, in Huang Chunming's stories, for example, Americans are let off rather easily. They may appear naive, insensitive, bumbling, and even oblivious to the trail of destruction they leave behind, but they are on the whole free of malice, very much in the character of innocents abroad. The Japanese, on the other hand, are the object of intense hatred; their portrayal in Taiwanese literature is reminiscent of what Ian Buruma has to say about descriptions of Nazi officers in his childhood reading in Belgium: evil yet ridiculous.[11] Most surprising of all, however, is the portrayal of the Chinese. With rare exceptions, they appear not as the underdog in an unfair racial competition (as one might expect) but as the pathetic group unaware of their being exploited by the economic and diplomatic order of the 1970s. Instead of standing up to the Japanese and Americans, they can only think of pursuing their own gain and are willing to give up their self-respect in the bargain.

The cover of the 1979 edition of "I Love Mary" best illustrates Huang Chunming's view of the Chinese.[12] Executed in the extravagant style of cartoons, the panels of pictures on the cover show a well-dressed Chinese man in suit and tie, variously holding a leash or newspapers in his mouth, rolling on the floor and exposing his belly to be scratched, sitting on his legs, his tongue hanging out, and raising his hands in supplication. The sarcasm of the picture is unmistakable. The man, no doubt David Chen in the story, is here compared to a dog, groveling in front of its master outside of the picture. The two lines on the bottom panel of the cover read in a mixture of Chinese and English: "Come" is *lai,* "go" is *qu,* and "nice dog" is *"hao gou gou"*—the very few English words that David Chen tries to teach his wife so that she can make herself understandable to the dog.

Different races, therefore, evoke different reactions from Huang Chunming. If the negative portrayal of the Americans and the Japanese can be attributed to Taiwan's diplomatic setbacks, two questions remain to be answered: (1) Why are Americans (i.e., white Americans; other ethnic groups are not even considered here) and Japanese depicted so differently? and (2) What about the Chinese for whom Huang seems to reserve his utmost contempt (there being few insults more vicious than comparing a person to a dog in Chinese)?

Finding answers to these questions leads us to consider the long history of Japanese aggression against China in the first half of this century and the Japanese colonization of Taiwan from 1896 to 1945. That period could be characterized as a dark age for Taiwan. Historians continue to unearth evidence of ruthless exploitation of the Taiwanese at the hands of the Japanese in those years. Yet, much as many would like to deny it, the overall impression left behind by the Japanese colonization period is mixed. There was a general sense of jubilation among the Taiwanese populace when Japan was defeated at the end of World War II, but soon it became increasingly clear that the Nationalist government, which came from the mainland to resume sovereignty in 1945, was bureaucratic, inefficient, and corrupt. Consequently, people began to look back with a mild nostalgia on the relative orderliness of the Japanese colonial days—a feeling that continues to surface every now and then.[13]

Our search for answers may lead us even farther back, to the late nineteenth century, when, according to Frank Dikotter, the distinction between

Chinese and non-Chinese, which had up to that time been couched in terms of culture, sovereignty, and lineage, began to take on racial under-tones.[14] Frank Dikotter points to several important intellectuals of the period, including Liang Qichao and Yan Fu,[15] who, in the process of introducing Western thinking into China, privileged social Darwinism in their analyses of world affairs. The implication of the phrase *wu jing tian ze, shi zhe sheng cun* (species vying for nature's selection, and survival for those who can adapt), with which Yan Fu prefaces his translation of *Origin of Species,* became the driving force behind all kinds of reform measures undertaken by China at the end of the Qing dynasty. In this hostile environment, Liang Qichao and others presented a world made up of five races: white, black, red, brown, and yellow. How these five colors correspond to the different races in the actual world varies from theorist to theorist and from time to time,[16] but there is a general consensus on one particular point, namely, the future of the world is to be determined by an intense contest for dominance between the white and the yellow people.

Three things are worthy of note about this topography of the races. First, the other three races, brown, red, and black, are dismissed as inferior. They are either extinct already or are on the way to becoming extinct. They are relevant to the future of the human species only insofar as they provide an example of what the yellow race might become if it did not participate in earnest in the Darwinian competition for survival. Second, the superiority of the white race is a given, and Liang Qichao and others proceed to describe its attributes as industrious, adventurous, and civic-minded—qualities that Chinese would do well to acquire. Third, the Japanese, as members of the yellow race, are regarded as a possible ally of the Chinese in this contest for racial dominance, in spite of the many ups and downs the relationship of the two peoples had undergone in the past.

At various points in Chinese history, Japan has been considered either as sharing the same culture and same ancestry *(tong wen tong zhong)* with China or, conversely, as presenting a threat to the security of China. Japanese aggression, on the one hand, has been cited as an illustration of Japanese arrogance and treacherousness. Even the geography of Japan, shaped like a caterpillar, has been described as a geomantic sign that Japan is driven in some predestined way to consume China, which has the shape of a peony leaf. On the other hand, the legend of the expedition of Xu Fu and the one hundred young boys and one hundred young girls who set out for the east in search of ambrosia for the first emperor of China (reigned 221–209 B.C.E.) is cited in favor of the unity of the two peoples. Xu Fu reached Japan, so goes the story, but never returned. The one hundred boys and one hundred girls then became the ancestors of the Japanese people. More credibly, Chinese speak of the many instances of Chinese cultural influence on Japan, including the state Confucianism of the Tokugawa period. The ambivalent memory of Japanese colonization in Taiwan, for all its historical specificities, may well in the end be just the latest chapter of the history of alternating feelings of friendliness and hostility between the two people. Given this background, the Japanese arrival in Taiwan in the 1970s evoked feelings that defy simplistic characterization. Behind the castigation, ridicule, and demonization to which Japanese are subjected in Taiwanese literature, there is always an explicit or implicit sense of disappointment that the Japanese seem to have forgotten that they share the same fate as the Chinese race. As latecomers to Taiwan, Americans are not held to a similar expectations. Their superior status is taken for granted, and their superciliousness therefore is not as hard to take. They are let off easy, in other words, precisely because they, unlike the Japanese, do not share the same fate with the Chinese. Though not necessarily welcome, the American presence does not upset the racial taxonomy to which many Chinese consciously or unconsciously subscribe. To quote Samuel Chu in his study of a different period, "White nations were 'outside the pale' so to speak, while the Japanese, being a yellow people, 'ought to know better.' "[17]

All the more so, for that matter, ought the Chinese. And this is perhaps why Huang Chunming reserves his most biting satire for those Chinese who indeed should know better. Ah Fa, the victim of the traffic accident in "The Taste of Apples," wins our sympathy, but that is because his life does not afford any choice other than to grab what is offered to him. Huang in "Sayonara, Good-bye" is depicted in a much more ambiguous light. The tricks he plays on the Japanese businessmen provide only slight comfort, and the so-called lesson he teaches them promises to be short-lived. Yet he demonstrates enough self-doubt and irony that in the end it is difficult to dislike him. David Chen in "I Love Mary," however, who refuses to answer to his Chinese name and prefers an American dog to his wife, illustrates the worst of the Chinese in Huang Chunming's eyes.

In his biography of Huang Chunming, Liu Chuncheng speaks admiringly of the compassion of Huang's creative world, in which judgment is withheld on all human foibles and errors, with two exceptions: the "insatiable tycoons and industrialists, and the Westernized intellectuals."[18] The term "Westernized intellectuals" is a shorthand reference to those who are relatively well educated and reasonably familiar with the ways of the West. They have close association with Westerners, grow enamored with their lifestyle, and imagine that they themselves could cross the racial lines to become whites. Westernized intellectuals of the kind just described are even more disturbing than the Japanese. Instead of closing the gap between the white race and the yellow race, they have chosen to side with the opponents and regard themselves as a notch higher than other Chinese. In the end, they are living proof that the Chinese have not only failed in the competition of the races but they have, infuriatingly, gone about the competition in the wrong way.

When Huang reflects on the tomato plant that grows on the roof of his childhood home, he is not therefore advocating a color-blind society at all. More likely, concerned as he is with social justice and fairness for all, he nevertheless subscribes to the view that there is a destiny waiting for each race. Since we, like a tomato seed, are not free to choose the color of our skin, any attempt to deny our race would be futile. The competition for survival in the 1970s has changed in nature; for Taiwan, military invasion has been replaced by economic aggression, but the lines of alliance and opposition remain very much the same. On the one hand, white is still pitted against yellow and, on the other, yellow remains just as divided as before. In this regard, Huang's stories illustrate, among other things, the persistence of nineteenth-century racial discourse in Taiwan.

NOTES

1. The movement of nativist literature has had far-reaching repercussions on the development of literature since the 1970s in Taiwan. Though still a matter of divisive debate, the movement can be described as an attempt to redirect the literary gaze from developments in the West to those in Taiwan. For an English treatment of the subject, see Yvvone Sung-sheng Chang's *Modernism and the Nativist Resistance: Contemporary Chinese Fiction from Taiwan* (Durham, N.C.: Duke University Press, 1993).

2. Huang Chunming, "Wuding shang di fan qie shu," in *Dengdai yi duo hua di mingzi* (Taipei: Huangguan, 1989), pp. 32–44.

3. Frank Dikotter, however, shows convincingly that "attitudes about skin color and physical characteristics are of great antiquity in China" (*The Discourse of Race in Modern China* [Stanford: Stanford University Press, 1992], pp. 1–30); some scholars even challenge the very assumption of the racial homogeneity of Chinese society, pointing out the presence of non-Chinese in Chinese society in early history, to say nothing of the many different ethnic groups that preserve their distinct ways of life in various parts of China. For a recent compilation of the discussion of ethnicity in China, see Stevan Harrell, *Cultural Encounters on China's Ethnic Frontiers* (Seattle: University of Washington Press, 1995). In Taiwan, most research on ethnicity is carried out by the Institute of Ethnology of the Academia Sinica, which publishes studies on the subject. See, for example, Chen Chung-min, Chuang Ying-gchang, and Huang Shu-min, *Ethnicity in Taiwan: Social, Historical, Cultural Perspectives* (Taipei: Academia Sinica, 1994).

4. Bo Yang, *The Ugly China and the Crisis of Chinese Culture*, trans. and ed. Don J. Cohn and Jing Qing (North Sydney: Allen & Unwin, 1992), p. 94.

5. Wang Zhenhe, *Meigui, meigui, wo ai ni* (Taipei: Yuanjing, 1984). This book is available in English translation: Howard Goldblatt, trans., *Rose, Rose I Love You* (New York: Columbia University Press, 1998).

6. Wang Zhenhe, *Meiren Tu* (Taipei: Hongfan, 1982).

7. Chen Yingzhen, "Yexing huoche," in *Yehxing huoche* (Taipei: Yuanjing, 1979), pp. 233–89.

8. Wen Rui'an, "Tie xian quan," in *Jin zhi xiazhe* (Taipei: Changhe, 1977), 100–133.

9. Huang Chunming's stories have been reprinted many times in many anthologies. For this paper, I have consulted the three-volume collection entitled *Huang Chunming xiao-shuo ji*. The first volume covers the period from 1962 to 1968, the second from 1969 to 1972, and the third from 1973 to 1983. Each volume has its own title as well: the first is entitled *Qingfangong di gu shi,* the second, *Luo,* and the third, *Shayonala Zaijian.* All the volumes are published by Taipei: Huangguan, 1985. "The Taste of Apple" can be found in the second volume, pp. 137–72; "Sayonara, Good-bye" and "I Love Mary" can be found in the third volume, pp. 13–82 and pp. 213–80, respectively. Howard Goldblatt has also translated other stories by Huang Chunming. See *The Drowning of an Old Cat and Other Stories* (Bloomington: Indiana University Press, 1980).

Although "The Little Widow" is often mentioned together with the three stories I discuss in this chapter, I have omitted it from my analysis because Huang Chunming departs from the race theme very early in the story. Beginning with the depiction of several Taiwanese bar girls who are in constant contact with American GIs, the story then turns to a romance between an American soldier and a Taiwanese woman, finally offering a character study of the American soldier, especially his traumatic experience of shooting his friend by mistake in an army camp. In my judgment, this story includes no sustained treatment of the racial theme.

10. The rape of Nanking is well documented in a recent book: Iris Chang, *The Rape of Nanking: The Forgotten Holocaust of World War II* (New York: Basic, 1997).

11. Ian Buruma, *The Wages of Guilt* (New York: Farrar Straus Giroux, 1994), pp. 6–7. See also John Dower, *War without Mercy* (New York: Pantheon, 1986), chaps. 4–5. The illustrations (pp. 181–190) also include pictures from war propaganda in the West during World War II in which Japanese are portrayed as either superhuman or subhuman beings.

12. Huang Chunming, *Wo Ai Mali* (Taipei: Yuanjing, 1979).

13. For a succinct treatment in English of the Japanese occupation of Taiwan, see Harry J. Lamley, "Taiwan under Japanese Rule, 1895–1945: The Vicissitudes of Colonialism," in *Taiwan: A New History,* ed. Murray A. Rubinstein (Armonk, N.Y.: Sharpe, 1999). Wan-yao Chou's dissertation, "The 'Kominka' Movement: Taiwan under Wartime Japan, 1937–1945" (Ph.D. diss., Yale University, 1991) focuses on the three campaigns conducted by the Japanese colonizers in the last decade of their sovereignty over Taiwan to "turn Taiwanese into Japanese" *(komika).* She further attributes the birth of the "Taiwanese consciousness" (which enables Taiwanese to see themselves as distinct from Chinese mainlanders) partly to their disillusionment with the rule of the Nationalist government and partly to the impact of the indoctrination of the *kominka* campaigns. See, especially, pp. 4–10, 222–31.

14. Frank Dikotter's analysis as summarized in this paragraph can be found in *The Discourse of Race in Modern China* (Stanford: Stanford University Press, 1992), 73–96, passim.

15. Liang Qichao (1873–1929) is a noted intellectual who is perhaps best known in the West for his role in the abortive Hundred Days Reform in Qing China in 1898. His illustrious career in many fields included work in journalism through which he systematically introduced the affairs of the Western world to Chinese readers. Yan Fu (1953–1921) received his education in England. He devoted himself to the work of translation, including *Origin of Species* and *The Wealth of Nations*.

16. As Frank Dikotter has pointed out, "Racial frontiers could easily be reassigned. The Vietnamese and the Filipinos provide a case-study of the phenomenon of inclusion and exclusion. Both peoples were usually classified as 'brown', but during the struggle against the French the Vietnamese suddenly found themselves described as 'real yellows' who would 'never allow themselves to become meat on the white race's chopping board'. They would fight the French devils *(fagui)* until not one single 'hirsute, ash-eyed white man' remained in their country. The Filipinos, normally excluded as black savages, were portrayed as the 'spearhead of the yellow race's fight against the white race' during their struggle against the United States in 1898. Japan's success in emulating the West was ascribed to the fact that its race had 'originated from China' " (*Discourse of Race*, pp. 84–85).

17. Samuel C. Chu, "China's Attitudes toward Japan at the Time of the Sino-Japanese War," in *The Chinese and the Japanese: Essays in Political and Cultural Interactions*, ed. Akiro Iriye (Princeton: Princeton University Press, 1980), p. 81.

18. Liu Chuncheng, *Huang Chunming Qian Zhuan* (Taipei: Yuanshe, 1986), p. 263.

12

From Colonialism to Immigration: The French School in Francophone African Fiction

Sonia M. Lee

Il n'y a pas de colonialisme sans racisme.

—Aimé Césaire

In her book *Race in North America,* Audrey Smedley states, "Accepting the fact that race is a cultural construct invented by human beings, it is easy to understand that it emerged out of a set of definable historical circumstances and is thus amenable to analysis as are other elements of culture."[1] I propose to begin here by stating briefly the set of historical circumstances responsible for the construct of French racism as it developed in the colonies and point out some of its cultural particularities. I will then show the effect that racism had on some of the writers of the former sub-Saharan French African colonies as it appears in their work, particularly in the Bildungsroman so popular in the 1960s. The coming-of-age novel invariably deals with the French school system, which the state used to try to eliminate the native culture in order to "adapt" the native populace to the colonial power and eventually "assimilate" them into French culture. In spite of the official rhetoric, the politics of integration came much later in the African colonies mostly as a result of the moral dilemma posed by World War II. This social problem, which remains an issue today, was further exacerbated by the economic problems posed by immigration.

I do not intend to retrace the history of French racism or to delve into its diverse manifestations but simply to give an overview of its evolution, mostly in regard to sub-Saharan Africa as France went from colonialism to

immigration. By the end of the nineteenth century, the French colonial
empire was well established and by 1930 was second only to the British. At
the onset of the empire, France bought into the racial theories that pervaded Europe at the time, mainly the belief in the cultural and moral superiority of the white race, which bore the burden of civilizing and saving
the world. These racist theories also preceded colonization in order to justify the slave trade. However, from the beginning important thinkers opposed these theories, for example, Montaigne. In his sixteenth-century
essay "Des Cannibales" he argued that civilization is a question of viewpoint and no culture is necessarily superior to any other. In the eighteenth
century Montesquieu stated with great irony that "it is impossible for us to
suppose these creatures to be men, because allowing them to be men, a
suspicion would follow, that we ourselves are not Christians."[2] Although
the French Revolution had forbidden the slave trade, it would be abolished
only in 1848 with the Second Republic. Meanwhile colonization continued and reached its peak during the Second Empire. However, with the
advent of the Third Republic in 1870, the colonial enterprise became
somewhat more difficult to justify, and blatant racist theories were no
longer convincing the opposition. Colonialism was then redefined according to republican ideology and values. Liberty, fraternity, and equality, although impossible to overlook, were kept in the background while republican universalism was brought to the forefront with the rationalization that
eventually, in a very distant future, natives would become French citizens.
In official discourse, the notion of race and racial inequality was abandoned
for that of culture. France had a civilizing mission and had to impose its
universal principles, its language, and its culture on the empire. This belief
in the "civilizing mission" continued until World War II, when it was no
longer possible to believe in the moral and cultural right of France to colonize people who had died, as they had already done in World War I, to
regain the country's freedom and, most of all, its honor. By the 1960s, the
empire was a memory, replaced by postcolonialism, which is still with us
today. The most lasting and possibly the most important impact of French
colonialism manifested itself in the schools, which is often referred to as the
"second conquest." The schools were also the locus of the most pernicious
and flagrant racism. In Africa the colonial conquest had met a constant resistance, and it became evident to the Third Republic that military forces
alone would not be sufficient to achieve colonization. The natives had to
be won to the French enterprise and persuaded to participate in its administration. In fact French sub-Saharan Africa, which covers an enormous territory, was divided in two federations: French West Africa, composed of
eight territories —Mauritania, Senegal, Guinea, Ivory Coast, Benin (Daho-
mey), Burkina-Fasso (Haute-Volta), Niger, and Mali (French Sudan),
whose administrative capital was Dakar; and French Equatorial Africa,

composed of four territories—Tchad, Central African Republic (Ubangi-Shari), Gabon, and Republic of Congo (Middle Congo), whose administrative capital was Brazzaville. After World War I part of Cameroon became a protectorate and was considered a part of French Equatorial Africa. In order to administer the empire, a law was passed in 1894 to form the Ministry of Colonies; in 1946 it became the Ministry of Overseas France, which in turn became the Ministry of Cooperation in 1961, the evolution of its official titles reflecting the evolution and then the demise of the empire.

From the middle of the nineteenth century onward, the French government considered education a major means of colonization; because of budgetary constraints, however, the implementation of this goal rarely lived up to the political rhetoric. Nevertheless, as early as 1854, General Faidherbe, governor of Senegal, created and imposed what was called the *école des otages* (the hostages' school). Every African chief had to send one of his sons to the French school—as a sign of submission to the empire but also to create an educated collaborating class. This rule was strongly resented by the African elite, but it was ruthlessly applied nonetheless. As the French African empire reached its peak, the French government became acutely aware of the competing British presence on the continent and in "a letter published in Revue de l'enseignement colonial Eugene Etienne states that the overseas extension of the French language and culture constituted 'a measure of national defense.'"[3] Thus in 1903 France started to control and regulate the colonial school, establishing a regime of education in Africa combining "heart and reason, duty and interest."[4] Until after World War II, however, very few Africans were admitted to the colonial schools; the recruiting policy was restricted to either the sons of the African elite, veterans of World War I, and the sons of civil servants. Furthermore, education was mostly at the level of primary schools. The colonial power, whose political vision often differed from that of Paris, was also conscious of the dangers in education. The purpose of the school was mostly to serve the authorities by providing interpreters and low-level civil servants to help run the empire. For example, at the level of language, the French that was taught in colonial schools was very basic, since the reason to teach French was not to introduce the natives to the glory of French literature but to ensure that they could follow or give orders. As for secondary education, it was even more restrictive; up to the post–World War II period, it existed mostly in Senegal, which was the colonial showcase of the African empire. Furthermore, until 1944, two very different diplomas sanctioned the end of secondary school. To the Africans the minister of education gave "un brevet de Capacité Coloniale" and to the French the then very important Baccalaureat. Nevertheless, after World War I, Africans' attitude toward the colonial school changed drastically and they demanded to attend in greater numbers. Various reasons explain this change of attitude (what some ob-

servers have seen as a desire to assimilate), which produced the first generation of African intellectuals as well as the now famous Négritude movement that sprang from the assimilating policies of French colonialism.
Assimilation offered several plausible benefits: being able to work as a civil
servant (a position of some power), gaining access to French citizenship,
and, most important, escaping forced labor, which remained in place until
1944. But this essay is about the second generation of African intellectuals,
or the generation of 1928, as it is often called. Following the footsteps of
the pioneers of Négritude, this new generation of African writers (who
ironically were a credit to the republican teaching of the French school)
was fully conscious of its political and cultural predicament. As subjects of
a colonial power whose so-called civilizing mission had been seriously
questioned by the economic and moral bankruptcy brought on by World
War II, they became acutely aware of the contradictions between the tenets
of French civilization and its praxis. Using its fiction writing, this preinde-
pendence generation put colonialism on trial and exposed, often with bitter
irony, its arrogance and the misery it brought to the continent. Along with
denouncing colonialism, this new generation of writers expressed the identity crisis that they were experiencing.

The novel became a principal medium by which to explore this lost
identity, and the colonial school appears as the main culprit. As Samba Gadjigo states in his study *Ecole blanche—Afrique noire* (White School—Black
Africa), "the colonial school was not only an instrument of assimilation but
rather of destruction of one culture to be replaced by an other. In the colonial school, the native had no past, only a present. His own culture was
either ignored or belittled. His place in history began with colonization as
a subject of the empire."[5] It was also evident that the school and the state
shared the same political purpose: colonizing the mind, according to the
Kenyan writer N'gugui Wa Thiongo. This perception of the school recurs
throughout the fiction of the time as a tragic leitmotif of irretrievable loss.
This existential anguish of an elite that saw itself as a cultural hybrid—as
the product of two irreconcilable worlds—is debated on the philosophical
level in Cheikh Hamidou Kane's moving novel *L'Aventure ambiguë (The
Ambiguous Adventure)* (1961). The young protagonist, Samba Diallo, member of the noble family of the Diallobés, is torn between the Islamic teaching of his spiritual master, Thierno, and the teaching of the rational and
godless French school. His inner conflict, which the young man cannot
resolve and which will lead to his tragic end, provokes many interesting
debates between diverse characters in the novel. It is Samba's aunt, "the
most royal lady," who most eloquently expresses the dilemma of colonized
Africa when she breaks the traditional silence of women to address the people, advising them to send their children to the French school so they will
"learn to forget them." She understands that the only way to survive and

to resist those "who came and won even though they were in the wrong" is to beat them at their own game, and that means a French education. This cruel message—send them to school so they will learn to forget you—echoed throughout the continent and can still be heard today, although somewhat differently now, in the new colonial space that we call immigration. To illustrate this resemblance, I would like to briefly analyze two novels written almost thirty years apart: *Mission to Kala* by the Cameroonian writer Mongo Beti and *Le Gone du Chaâba (The Kid from the Chaaba District)* by the Beur (Algerian immigrant) writer Azouz Begag.[6] In comparing these two novels, I hope to demonstrate the enduring theme of cultural hybridity perpetuated by the school and demonstrate that things have indeed changed in thirty years, allowing for at least some optimism.

In *Mission to Kala* Mongo Beti shows that after World War II, the program of the colonial school had improved to include more than basic skills. In the Brazzaville conference of 1944, De Gaulle proposed the French Union with some promises of association, which did not, however, succeed politically. Assimilation was now in full swing at least for those who were going to school; the curricula in the metropolitan and the colonial schools were no longer so far apart. Mongo Beti's style is a bittersweet testimony to the new colonial school: his novel of alienation is itself written in an impeccable and sophisticated French. *Mission to Kala* tells the story of Medza, a young Cameroonian who has just failed his Baccalaureat, as many African students did. We meet him as he is going home to his village to spend the school summer holidays. When he gets home, he is summoned by the elders and sent on a mission to Kala, a village far into the bush, to retrieve the wayward wife of a villager, Niam. Medza who does not have a clue about how to do this and does not want to go (after all he is on vacation), but he has no choice in the matter; he has been chosen for the task because he is an educated man. The elders are convinced that his education will impress the "country bumpkins" of Kala enough to pressure them into sending back Niam's wife. Medza fails in this mission. Niam's wife is her own person and will return to her silly husband when she is ready. But his stay in Kala makes Medza understand that his French education has deprived him of his childhood and that although he knows a lot about France, he knows nothing about his own culture. The novel is a first-person narrative told by an older Medza reminiscing about this particular summer, when he went to Kala. The narrator addresses the young men of his generation who "have travelled the same road as I, and made an almost identical journey up a very similar river."[7] His words refer all those who went to school, got a French education, and lost their soul in the process. He then continues his imagined conversation with his school mates:

Do you remember how cheerful we all were as we left the Native School the day after that solemn prize-giving? In fact, I found it difficult to disguise my

bitterness from you. It was lucky that we had friends with us such as that extraordinary chap Daniel, whose irrepressible wit and high spirits took me out
of myself, and stopped me doing what the romantic poets would describe as
"meditating on my sad destiny." Do you remember how Daniel always used
to say that his ancestors weren't Gauls but Bantus, and had stayed Bantus ever
since? And his prediction that wherever there was a negro, there would always
be some European colonial to kick his backside?"[8]

This passage, occuring at the beginning of the first chapter, sets the tone
of the text while underlining some of the highlights of Medza's curriculum:
the romantic poets, French history, and the realization that under colonial
rule he will always be a second-class citizen. As the story progresses, we see
everything through Medza's eyes, which are French eyes. He could be an
anthropologist exploring the African bush, making comments on the amaz-
ing things that he is witnessing. This detached viewpoint, expressed in a
sophisticated French full of Western references, is often very witty and
amusing and does provide comic relief to an otherwise tragic story. As he
travels to Kala on the chief's bicycle, Medza compares himself to Pizarro
the conquistador. His arrival at Kala goes unnoticed because a native ball-
game is in progress and Zambo, who is the star athlete, turns out to be
Medza's cousin. Medza describes the game with the emotional distance of
an outsider: "Having first taken a bird's-eye, panoramic view of the scene,
I now began to examine it in detail. The first thing that caught my eye was
a great hulking devil in the Kala team, who had such enormous muscles
that I concluded he must have bought them on the instalment system."[9] It
turns out that Zambo is everything that Medza is not but would like to be:
an athlete, a lady's man, a hard drinker, and a happy man at ease with his
surroundings. And yet to Medza's dismay, a dismay akin to that felt by an
explorer as he meets the natives for the first time, Zambo is looking up to
him, so proud of his little educated cousin: "Try to imagine a poor insignificant creature, an ex-conquistador retreating . . . in some confusion, a
mere failed student once more, who is confronted with the spectacle of a
young god falling down at his feet and worshipping him."[10]

Zambo becomes Medza's African alter ego. As they go through many
adventures together, he functions as a constant reminder to Medza of his
colonized split personality. But Zambo is not the only one who admires his
cousin. Medza soon discovers that the villagers are in awe of him because
he is an educated man, assuming that his education must give him power.
Every night Medza must go to someone's house and answer questions and
explain the white man's knowledge. These evenings, of questions and answers between the common folk and the westernized boy whom they see
as the Trojan horse that will help them beat the colonial system, reveal to
Medza the extent of his alienation and his powerlessness. They oblige him

"to explain a point which I had never let myself think about, the very idea of which terrified me: my future and that of all my generation."[11] Although Beti's generation achieved independence, the author felt, at least when he wrote the novel, that the tragedy of his generation was like "that of a man left to his own devices in a world which does not belong to him, which he has not made and does not understand."[12] For Beti's hero, the French school was like "an ogress," a monster that robbed African children of their youth and of their culture just to spit them back into a foreign hostile world where they would be strangers forever. This cultural angst expressed so movingly by many Francophone African male writers remains, however, the particular experience of a masculine elite. Later on in the 1970s, when women writers appeared on the literary scene, they perceived the school very differently from their male counterparts in regard to education as the only road to emancipation and self-discovery. It is true that in Africa women's writing came on the wings of independence and, by that time, the French school had changed considerably. But it must be underlined that women writers as a rule had little nostalgia for the past and the bygone traditional values that had hardly recognized them. A Western education, in this case a French one, gave women writers a voice and a means to break the patriarchal imposition of silence.

This changing perception of the French school is also evident in the literature of immigration, particularly the writing of Algerian immigrants in France known as "beurs."[13] Algerian immigration stems directly from colonialism and represents the most important immigrant population in France today. Furthermore, the tension and bitterness resulting from the Algerian liberation struggle, which ended in 1962, still lingers in France today, mostly perpetuated by former French residents of Algeria who had to leave the country at the time of its independence. To further complicate matters, Islamic Algerians are perceived by the French as problematic in regard to their integration into the culture and have thus been the main target of French racism. All things considered, it interesting to examine the place of the school in Beur writing in comparison to colonial literature.

Thirty years after the publication of Mongo Beti's novel, French Algerian Azouz Begag barely fictionalized his own childhood as an immigrant living in France, recounting his experiences with the French school in a first-person narrative whose narrator-protagonist bears the name of the author. The other characters in the novel are based on people known to the author who retain their real names; this proved to be a problem for Begag, as most of them were not pleased to be on public display. The text comes with a glossary of dialect Arabic terms as well as a translation of the deformed French spoken by the hero's parents. The child protagonist, Azouz, tells his story in a simplistic and slangy French, a far cry from Medza's sophisticated, assimilated prose. In fact Azouz is not assimilated and not even integrated.

His family lives in a shantytown on the outskirts of Lyon, France's second largest city. Like Beti's hero, Azouz does not know much about his own culture, only that he is an Arab and that under the circumstances this is a liability. Although the text describes in detail Azouz's life in the shanty and his social interaction with the people of his own social class, an important part of the novel is dedicated to his life as a schoolboy. Most of the time, he does not relate to the teacher's lesson, especially when it speaks about morally coded and civic behavior. Azouz knows that his behavior and that of the Arabs in the project do not coincide with the teacher's values; he is ashamed of his behavior, of his address in the city, and of his poor French. All this makes him decide that he does not want to be who he is socially: "I don't like being with the poor and the bad students of the class. I want to be among the best like the French.¹⁴" After working very hard, Azouz moves to the head of the class. But unlike Medza, who was admired for his education, Azouz is told by half of the Arabs in the class that he is no longer an Arab because he behaves like a French kid. Like most immigrant children, Azouz belongs to two worlds, and a moment comes when he must choose one over the other. Azouz is hurt by the ostracism of his Arab friends but he is not deterred. He has no doubt about his "arabity"; he paid for it, he says, with "a little piece of himself," which he had to surrender under very painful circumstances. He had gone through the "rite de passage" without which one is not an Arab, and he feels that his identity is branded in his flesh. But he does not want to be a poor Arab, and the only way out of poverty passes through the schools. And yet there is very little connection between the school where he studies and the shantytown where he lives and plays. Like Medza, Azouz does not know much about his cultural background. He can quote Baudelaire but cannot read Arabic; after all, he was born in France but never set foot in Algeria. If he were to go to his parents' village, he would be as lost as Medza was when he went back into the bush. But in his case the French school teaches him about Algeria and makes him feel that it is possible to be French and Algerian at the same time. The school helps the boy find a cultural modus vivendi "between two different parts of the self: one which identifies with the secular values of contemporary France, and one which, through the family home, remains engaged with the Islamic traditions of north Africa."¹⁵

One of Azouz's teacher (aptly named Loubon) was born in Algeria, where he used to teach before independence. He speaks and writes Arabic and teaches Algerian culture to his class. Although Azouz feels somewhat embarrassed to be singled out, thanks to this special teacher he gains self-confidence and writes a well-constructed essay on racism for which he earns an A. This new face of the French school system is corroborated by opinion polls taken among the immigrant population. Does this mean that we have come full circle? The French school has changed from an ogress to a nourishing mother? At the end of the novel, Azouz's family moves to a better part of town; we can assume that if all goes well they will climb the social ladder. The message, which is very common to Beur and immigrant literature, seems to be that integration has begun. But has it? I offer an ambiguous conclusion. Surely, it is a fact that the French school system has changed drastically since the end of colonialism and particularly since 1968, which was a watershed moment for France. The cultural revolution of 1968 did away with the old traditional nationalistic thinking, replacing it with a new, liberal vision of France as a nation and a new, rather permissive moral code. To the extent that this is true, integration and cultural pluralism should be on the horizon. But the spirit of 1968, which is still with us in many ways, has been heavily impeded by the economic crisis of the 1970s and the high unemployment that resulted from it. This economic crunch has exacerbated traditional French xenophobia. An opinion poll on racism that appeared in the leftist magazine *Le Nouvel Observateur* of October 1996, 45 percent of the French were classified as racist. On the up side, a different poll, conducted among the immigrants, showed that 85 percent of them thought that the antiracist organizations were doing a good job; 79 percent had the same opinion about the school system; 76 percent thought that the police were racist but that the judges and the governmental agencies were not. On the down side, the level of unemployment among the young of Algerian background is 40 percent, more than twice the national rate. This figure is particularly alarming in view of the fact that the level of education among young Algerians equals that of their French counterparts.[16] So, even if we can assume that the French school has come full circle in its mission to integrate its foreign population, we also have to face the fact that it has not yet entirely succeeded in "civilizing" the natives.

NOTES

1. Audrey Smedley, *Race in North America* (Boulder: Westview, 1993), p. 16.

2. Quoted by Ashley Montagu in *Man's Most Dangerous Myth: The Fallacy of Race* (New York: Oxford University Press), p. 50.

3. Jerry B. Bolibaugh, *French Educational Strategies for Sub-Saharan Africa: Their intent, Derivation, and Development* (Stanford: Stanford University Press), p. 25. Most of the information concerning the French Colonial school comes from his text.

4. Samba Gadjigo, *Ecole blanche-Afrique noire* (Paris: L'Harmatten, 1990), p. 53.

5. Ibid., p. 13.

6. Mongo Beti, *Mission to Kala* (New York: Colliers, 1957); Azouz Begag, *Le Gone du Chaâba* (Paris: Seuil, 1986).

7. Mongo Beti, *Mission to Kala*, trans. Peter Green (New York: Colliers, 1971), p. 5.

8. Ibid., p. 20.

9. Ibid., p. 43.
10. Ibid., p. 46.
11. Ibid., p. 104.
12. Ibid., p. 213.
13. The word "Beur" is a construct of French Algerian popular speech based on the word "Arab" inverted.
14. Begag, *Le Gone du Chaâba*, p. 60.
15. Alec. G. Hargreaves, *Voices from the North African Immigrant Community in France* (New York: Berg, 1991), p. 20.
16. Michèle Tribalat, "Faire fi des a priori idèologiques," *Mars* 6 (1996): 94.

Part IV

Race or Class: Which Is It?

13

Economics and Motivation: (Dis)Entangling Race and Class

Andrew J. Gold

This chapter is about disentangling race and class within economics, and it addresses two of many potential areas in which "race matters" and in which race and class are implicated. In one—housing—race matters relatively more; in the other—employment—race now matters relatively less. An additional aim of this chapter is suggest caution when imputing reasons for racial outcomes. Relying on the work of T. C. Schelling to discuss integration and separation in housing, I hope to show that what is observed as "hypersegregation" in cities does not necessarily imply preferences for hypersegregation on the part of whites or blacks. In regard to employment and housing, I will contrast the consequence of "race" as a low-cost (even if biased) carrier of class information versus race as bigotry or taste based animus. I distinguish between two motivational differences for race-based decisions: one, rooted in animus, is clearly and properly called "racist"; the other, rooted in information, or "fact," I prefer to call "race-based decision making"; perhaps "racialist" is the better word. Changing racist decisions requires changing hearts; changing racialist decisions requires changing facts. Complete change requires changing both.

LABOR MARKETS

In spite of blacks' disproportionate disadvantage because of the recent decline in demand for low-skill labor and changes in the geography of jobs away from inner cities, I believe that William Julius Wilson is largely correct about "the declining significance of race"[1] *in labor markets,* in the sense that current racial *discrimination* no longer plays the predominant explana-

189

tory role it once did, especially for younger cohorts, in the labor market.[2] Studies by economists that carefully separate the influence of race from class origins and other premarket influences of productivity largely support his thesis. After controlling for premarket influences and proxies for expected productivity, *for those in the labor market,* there is a decline in what can be attributed to race and more that can be attributed to initial social class or other nonlabor market causes.

Relative income gaps, even unadjusted for background differences, have been falling at least since the 1940s, as tables 13.1–13.3 show. The figures shown in these tables are unadjusted for years of schooling, proxy measures of productivity, and so on. When Richard Freeman made those adjustments to answer his question, "Black Economic Progress after 1964: Who Has Gained and Why?" he found that

> young blacks from more advantaged family backgrounds have made especially large gains in the market to such an extent that family background has become a much more important determinant of black socioeconomic position than in the past. As a result of the decline in black-white economic differentials and the enhanced impact of family background on black educational and economic attainment, *background differences appear to have become a more important impediment than market discrimination for attainment of black-white parity among the young.*[3]

These findings don't say that in the aggregate blacks and whites are likely to have the same income but that blacks and whites of similar background are likely to.[4] Of course, it is precisely those backgrounds that differ, though less so than ever before when it comes to education. Nor was the optimism evenly distributed, since the convergence varied by age (younger more than older) and skill groups (better skilled more than less skilled). To repeat, "blacks from more advantaged backgrounds made greater gains in the market than those from less advantaged backgrounds."[5] Where you started on

Table 13.1　Average Job Status for *Employed* Adults, 1940–1980

	Socioeconomic Index		
Group	1940	1960	1980
Black men	16	21	31
Black women	13	21	36
White men	30	36	40
White women	36	39	43

Source: Hochschild p. 40 after Farley and Allen.

Table 13.2   Relative Occupational Position of Nonwhite Workers Ratio of Nonwhite to White Index of Occupational Position

	1950	1964	1969	1997
Male	.76	.80	.84	.89
Female	.49	.69	.80	.92

Source: Freeman, *Black Economic Progress after 1964: Who Has Gained and Why?*

the social escalator mattered in a way that it had not mattered before. In the prewar period, you could not be sure the intergenerational escalator went up at all.

Another recent reappraisal reached the same conclusion: "Background differences appear to have become a more important impediment than market discrimination" because of the increase in premium for skills learned in school. This has adversely affected blacks more than whites, given measured skill differences. "As a result, differences in school quality or family and socioeconomic background that lead to differences in the acquisition of human capital are highlighted and now have an even greater impact on economic outcomes than they did in the past."[6] Schooling, not labor market discrimination, has become of primary importance.

Additional evidence comes from Urban Institute audit studies that used matched pairs of testers to test for equal treatment in hiring. These audit studies found equal treatment 80 percent of the time, a far cry from what might have been found in the 1940s. Different treatment occurred in 20 percent of the interviews. Of those (20 percent) treated differently, 14 percent favored whites, whereas 7 percent favored blacks, which would have been unimaginable fifty years ago.

The overall decline in labor market discrimination as an explanation for labor market difference is good news, not unalloyed good news, but good news nevertheless, since there are fairly sizable differences in background and performance on tests of achievement that still matter to labor outcomes.[7]

This reduction in labor market discrimination should not be thought of

Table 13.3   Percentage Ratio of Black to White Annual Earnings (Age 15 +)

	1939	1959	1979	1984
Male	44	53	66	65
Female	40	61	101	99

Source: Jaynes, "The Labor Market Status Of Black Americans," *JEP* Fall 90.

as easily won; just think of Jim Crow, labor riots, and civil rights struggles. But labor market discrimination can be made to bend to the law. Getting beyond labor market discrimination to background social class conditions requires change of a different sort—a retail sort, less amenable to law. At the lower tail of the income distribution, it becomes increasingly more difficult to move past a poverty or an equality goalpost.[8] Henry Louis Gates states it more elegantly:

> Starting around the time of Bakke (1978), . . . in one of the most curious social transformations in the class structure in recent history, two tributaries began to flow, running in two distinct rivers of aspiration and achievement. By 1990, the black middle class, imperiled though it might feel itself to be, had never been more prosperous or relatively more secure. Simultaneously, the pathological behavior that results from extended impoverishment engulfed a large part of a black underclass that seemed unable to benefit from a certain opening up of American society. . . . and for the first time ever, their inability to benefit seemed permanent.[9]

It may be helpful to step back for a longer view that provides both perspective on progress and reasons for persistent inequality using figure 13.1, which will carry much of the weight of the narrative.

Taking here the longest of runs, from the Civil War to the recent present, we can see a fairly continuous record of decline in a schooling gap measured by years (not quality) of schooling (▲), relative literacy (●), relative wages (■), and relative school enrollment rates (+). "In 1850, 56.2 percent of school-aged whites and 1.8 percent of school-aged blacks were enrolled in school. . . . Thirty percent of nonwhites were literate in 1870, as compared with 91.3 percent of native whites. . . . By 1969, the literacy rates were 96.4 percent and 99.3 percent for nonwhites and whites respectively."[10] On the eve of World War II, 1940 wages of whites were 84 percent above those of blacks, compared to 32 percent forty years later (unadjusted for human capital differences). These raw numbers understate some important differences. From 1950 to 1960 roughly 1.5 million blacks migrated north and west from the South. About 50 percent of northern and western blacks at that time were born in the South. Consider data from Mississippi for 1939–1940 (table 13.4):

The data do not even begin to address all the inequalities between blacks and whites in terms of days in school, hours per day, and so on. If we are considering class legacies, one factor is the educational background of forebears. But that is not all. There are financial legacies as well, and figure 13.2 from Mulligan gives us a view of that.

Here the two inequalities are expressed in terms of black–white net worth (▲) and relative home ownership rates. The disparity in wealth and

Figure 13.1   Black–White Education and Wage Gaps, 1850–1985

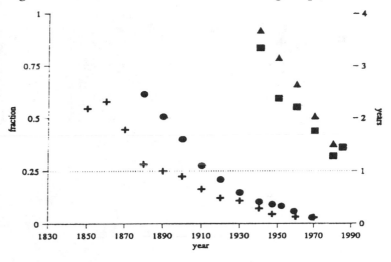

■ in (white-black wage ratio) (left scale)   ▲ white minus black years of schooling (right scale)
✚ white minus black school enrollment rate (left scale)   ● white minus black literacy rate (left scale)

Source: Mulligan, "Parental Priorities and Economic Inequality," *Evolution of Economic Inequality,* p. 177.

the consumption that wealth permits has been slower to come together than income or educational differences. Wealth is terribly important not only for the financial cushion it brings but, in the face of imperfect human capital markets, for educational finance. Wealth may of course capture other aspects of inherited capital that money alone does not measure.[11] Since class has a legacy, some of it reflected in the illustrations above, we should not be surprised to find lingering class consequences. Families pass on their advantages only incompletely so that there is some equalization over time. But the kind of disadvantage we are considering here, which has

Table 13.4   Mississippi School Data, 1939–1940

	Average Expenditure per Classroom	*Average Salary Paid*
White schools	$784	$821
Black schools	$154	$235
New York City	—	$2604

Source: Batchelder, "Decline in the Relative Income of Negro Men," *QJE,* November 1964.

Figure 13.2   Indicators of Black-White Wealth Gaps, 1940–1988

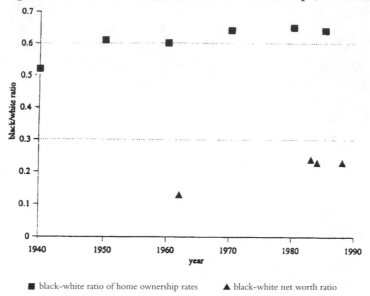

■ black-white ratio of home ownership rates   ▲ black-white net worth ratio

lasting parenting and educational effects, makes the probability of full equality in the near future rather remote.

Although issues of race seem to be with us as much or more than ever before, discrimination in economic life has diminished. This decline in discrimination based on race is especially marked in labor market contexts because employers have an incentive to reasonably, though not precisely, estimate the expected productivity of potential employees.

Gary Becker, Nobel Prize winner and holder of a chair in economics and sociology, demonstrated forty-one years ago in *The Economics of Discrimination*[12] that more prejudiced employers (who ignore the productivity of black employees because of bigotry) will have less profitable businesses than unprejudiced employers in competitive markets. Even so, for social and political reasons (including prejudiced labor unions), competitive market forces alone were not sufficient to erode discrimination and segregation in labor markets.[13] It took the cataclysmic effects of World War II, court decisions like *Shelly v. Kramer* (restrictive covenants in 1948), *Brown v. Board of Education* in 1954, Rosa Parks and Freedom Rides, the civil rights revolution and civil rights tragedies, to bring legal, migratory, and social changes that made nondiscriminatory decisions even more profitable, if only to avoid legal liability.

Perhaps in consequence of these real changes, economists' explanations for differential outcomes in labor markets, for the most part, have moved away from a basis in bigotry or, more precisely, "tastes for discrimination," in which "race" is a matter of "taste." Current explanations are based in statistical discrimination, network, and cultural externalities in which the primary emphasis is on the information cost faced by an employer who finds it profitable to disentangle the information that race conveys from other markers of expected productivity. Race still matters, but it is now subject to underlying *group* reality rather than animus, which makes race less important but salient. The bad news is that this residual effect of race is harder to eliminate totally because information-based discrimination doesn't have the same undermining dynamics that taste-based discrimination has.[14] Prejudicial views can be subject to powerful undermining cascades, but information is not similarly subjective (although it too can be read with biased eyes). Ideas, tastes, and the lure of profit are contagious; information is not. (That is an exaggeration, since the "heuristic of social proof," that bias in cognitive processing which takes social agreement on facts as proof of their truth, suggests that even the perception of facts may be contagious.[15] In hiring decisions, relying on the heuristic can be costly.) For information-cost reasons, it may be costly to completely discount average group productivity differences related to race, even though in labor markets, in contrast to housing (which I discuss below), it now pays to get it largely right. It may not be legal or moral to take average productivity differences related to race into account, but there is a powerful incentive to do so by "unbiased" profit maximizers—those for whom profit is the single motive.[16]

Joleen Kirschenman and Kathryn M. Neckerman's " 'We'd Love to Hire Them, But . . .': The Meaning of Race for Employers"[17] provides insight into the tangle of race and class in a context in which productivity signals are fuzzy because of the generally poor reputation of the public schools. Their study pertains to Chicago employers who hire entry-level employees in the inner city as well as the suburbs. Many of the employers exhibited concern about hiring blacks in relation to skill levels such as reading ability and problems of increased tension that mixed or heterogeneous workforces seemed to bring.[18] Most employers, not all of whom were white, had generalized notions about race negatively associated with blackness, which also related to class, residence in the inner city, and poor schooling. "Some mentioned that they passed over applicants from Chicago public schools for those with parochial or suburban educations."[19] Race—though not race alone—appeared to be a shorthand for the perceived experience of employees:

Regardless of the generalizations employers made, they did consider the black population considerably heterogeneous, which made it more important that they be able to distinguish "good" from "bad" workers. Whether through skills tests, credentials, personal references, folk theories, or their intuition, they used some means to screen out the inner-city applicant. . . . And black applicants, unlike their white counterparts, must indicate to employers that the stereotypes do not apply to them . . . by demonstrating their skill or by adopting a middle-class style of dress, manner, and speech or perhaps (as we were told some did) by lying about their address or work history.[20]

Without more information, it is hard to know whether these views reflect taste-based bias or an accurate generalization of experience. That it might be a generalization is suggested by "the four year gap between blacks and whites on national tests. The average black 17 year old scores the same as the average white 13 year old."[21] Certainly some of the expressed views are not in conflict with other studies of inner-city life as some (but not all) live it. That is, employer generalizations may have that "kernel of truth," though not necessarily statistical accuracy, that leads to statistical discrimination hurtful to those on the upper end of abilities. Without question, this makes life much more difficult for those who are stereotyped and carries ramifications. Picking up a concept from dual labor market theory, "antagonisms among workers and between worker and their employers are likely to diminish productivity. Thus employers' expectations may become self-fulfilling prophesies." This is especially likely since "qualities most likely to be proxied by race are not job skills [easily measured] but behavioral and attitudinal attributes—dependability, strong work ethic, and cooperativeness—that are closely tied to interactions among workers and between workers and employers."[22] For many entry-level jobs it is precisely those hard-to-measure attributes that matter.

There may be other reasons why firms may prefer homogeneity in the workforce. Language or communication barriers can make a mixed workforce less productive than a homogeneous one. Alternatively, homogeneity may affect the internal costs of decision making in a firm.[23] There are, of course, less benign reasons why heterogeneity might "spoil" productivity, relating to the problem of identity and the perceived "productivity" of black employees. Whites who expect deference from blacks may retaliate against black supervisors or coworkers (or require wage premiums). Literature from social psychology suggests the existence of what may be an unconscious form of prejudicial behavior. Katz, Goldston, and Benjamin in a 1958 experiment on biracial work groups found "deferring" behavior on the part of black team members; whites exhibited dominating behaviors. In a follow-up experiment (Katz and Cohen), assertiveness training and other techniques were used to modify the performance of black subjects. Not only did whites prefer the untrained (less assertive) black partner, but whites who had the assertive partners "downgraded the partner's ability and tended to reject him as a future coworker." This literature on "interaction disability" suggests that "productivity" is not a simple mechanical relationship independent of the identities and expectations of the parties on the "team."

A recent article on diversity in the workplace suggests that these results may still be valid despite years of experience with more integrated workplaces. Tsui, Egan, and O'Reilly in a study of three organizations' work environments in entry-level positions found that "white individuals in the (white) homogeneous units express[ed] the highest degree of attachment and a systematic decline in the attachment of majority members as the proportions of minorities increased." In general they report higher attachment to homogeneous rather than heterogeneous workplaces but the effects are not racially symmetrical. "For whites, increasing distance from others in the work unit is related to lower attachment, while for nonwhites, being different in race has no effect on attachment to the organization."[24] It is not hard to imagine how these psychological dispositions of whites, rooted in identity differences, make themselves felt toward blacks.

It is possible for some discrimination to exist side-by-side with equal market outcomes for equivalently skilled blacks and whites. First there is the signaling burden mentioned above—the need of those in the upper end of the skill distribution (and employers) to distinguish themselves from lower-average-skill compatriots balanced by the fact that given a sufficient number of employers who hire without bias, blacks can achieve equal income in the face of some discriminatory treatment. Still, "the fact that blacks and whites with above-average scores on the Armed Forces Qualification Test (AFQT) now seem to earn relatively equal wages does not mean that they live in a color-blind world. Anyone who imagines they do should spend a day talking to well-paid blacks."[25]

HOUSING

Despite expressed reductions in the negative attitudes of whites toward blacks in general or toward blacks as neighbors in particular, integration has not increased nearly as much in housing markets and spatial segregation as it has in labor markets. In housing and schooling, in contrast to markets for labor, most whites may not find that it pays to disentangle race and class; these markets do not include the same offsets to gross and incorrect stereotyping that exist in labor markets and thus offer fewer potential gains to individuals who resist stereotyping. For a variety of reasons, the distinctions they do make suggest avoidance rather than attraction. Still, some progress has been made. Isolation of blacks from whites in general has finally declined from peak 1970s levels.[26] Isolation is greater between blacks and whites than between whites and any other group but is also high between blacks and other ethnic groups. Social-class segregation is less extreme than racial segregation and is now as extreme in the black community as it is in the white, which indeed lies behind Wilson's underclass thesis. Differences in the social class composition of the races mask the obviousness of that.[27]

In what follows I address the question of why racial segregation is so prevalent in spite of widespread evidence that whites are far less racist than they used to be in their *expressed* preferences.[28] To do this I first approach the explanation theoretically rather than empirically in order to illustrate how difficult inferring preference can be.[29]

Suppose that you were confronted with the hypothetical living arrangement described in figure 13.3, in which the #s and 0s appear segregated from each other. A reasonable inference is that the #s and 0s do not want to live together. If you try to imagine the preferences that created the outcome—assuming noncollusive action by the #s or 0s—you are unlikely to come up with the preferences shown below (figure 13.4).

In fact, the outcome in figure 13.3 resulted from an initial random distribution (figure 13.5) in which nine out of forty-five were initially "dissatisfied" (with their nine-square neighborhood), given the preference assumptions just displayed. Yet individual motion started by these nine, contingent upon what each other person separately did, created the strongly segregated pattern. This is quite general for simulations of individual moving behavior. Sometimes you get more segregation than you "bargained" for, wanted, or needed. Indeed, with many socially contingent behaviors you can get

Figure 13.3   Hypothetical Living Arrangements

```
        #  #  0  #  #

     #  #  #  0  0  0  #  #

     #  #  0  0  0  #

     #  0  0  0  0  0

     0  0  0  #  0  0  0

        0  #  #  #  0  0  0

        #  #  #  #

        0  0  #
```

Source: T. C. Schelling, *Micromotives and Macrobehavior* (New York: Norton, 1978).

Figure 13.4   Preference Assumptions

If only one neighbor, it must be a like person (# or 0)
If two neighbors, one must be alike (e.g., ##0 or 00#)
If three, four, or five neighbors, two must be alike
If six through eight, three must be alike

Source: T. C. Schelling, *Micromotives and Macrobehavior* (New York: Norton, 1978).

outcomes that conflict with the underlying preferences that produce it (Kuran). Expanded simulations from *Growing Artificial Societies*[30] show that Schelling's initial simulations are not a fluke but a general consequence of individual, contingent motion in the face of even, nonextreme preference. As Schelling points out, the process of aggregation produces a result apparently more extreme than underlying preferences would suggest.

A little "racial arithmetic" will show why it is difficult to get integrated results when integration or tolerance is defined differently by two groups. The arithmetic, again from Schelling, considers the possibilities for arrangement in a population composed of ten blacks and ninety whites when there are ten towns to live in. Alternative preferences are shown on the left side and possible outcomes on the right side of table 13.5. (Note that the index of dissimilarity, a widely used but not exclusive index of segregation, is wildly sensitive to small differences from perfect integration.)[31]

We know a great deal about housing markets, which involve more than individual preferences as they are expressed above. Historically, whites have demonstrated their strong preferences through a variety of collusive, exclu-

Figure 13.5   Initial Random Distribution

–	#	–	#	0	#	–	0
#	#	#	0	–	0	#	0
–	#	0	–	–	#	0	#
–	0	#	0	#	0	#	0
0	0	0	#	0	0	0	–
#	–	#	#	#	–	–	0
–	#	0	#	0	#	0	–
–	0	–	0	–	–	#	–

Source: T. C. Schelling, *Micromotives and Macrobehavior* (New York: Norton, 1978).

Table 13.5   Assumptions: 10B, 90W; Ten Towns

Preferences	Outcome
White preference >90%	Presence → Voluntary integration impossible
Black preference = 20% White preference = 80%	→ 5 Intregrated towns (2B, 8W) 5 Segregated towns (10W) (Dissimilarity index = .5)
Black preference = 50%* Whites indifferent	→ 2 Integrated towns (5B, 5W) 8 Segregated towns (10W) (Dissimilarity index = .88)
Black preference = 30% White preference = 80%	→ No compatible towns or some Blacks must stay away *or whites must act collectively to restrict flight or resist entry*
Black preference = 50% White preference = 70%	→ Unstable integration, some Entrants must stay away for stability *or whites must act collectively to restrict flight or resist entry* (if stability enforced at 70/30, dissimilarity index = .55)

*Modal choice in most surveys

sionary devices up to and including violence to preserve white neighborhoods (as they did white jobs).[32] Initially (ironically as it may seem) southern segregation was actually less severe than northern. As political and social controls on social distance collapsed, however, southern segregation increased toward northern levels, probably as a substitution of distance for the "social controls" that earlier kept blacks "in their place." Overall, for a variety of reasons, segregation increased until its peak in the late 1960s and early 1970s. Violence still occasionally occurs and so does racial steering and some vestiges (although this is contested) of mortgage discrimination; even so, levels of isolation and segregation overall have begun to fall to prewar levels.[33] This change reflects the growing black middle class, the increasingly multicultural nature of major population centers, and change in ideas referred to earlier—the war, civil rights revolution, and so on. It is easy to forget how rigid the discriminatory boundaries actually were, and how viciously enforced.

However, even with weakened racial preferences and declines in exclusionary force, the racial arithmetic shows that integration is not easily attained. Although white flight and tipping has diminished, other ethnic groups continue to react differently to blacks.[34] Regions of overlapping preference or mutual tolerance exist (as do integrated neighborhoods), but they are not yet sufficient[35] to make integration a norm.[36] This situation has been summarized by Anthony Downs in the *Brookings Review:*

> Given these disparate views [of integration] blacks will continue moving into a partly integrated neighborhood beyond the fraction that keeps the neighborhood desirable to whites. That causes other whites to stop moving in, and the inevitable turnover in neighborhood residents, (about 16–20 percent in most areas) results in more blacks moving in but no more whites are willing to do so. Eventually, the neighborhood becomes almost entirely black—thus racially segregated—even without anyone's explicitly desiring such segregation.[37]

Perhaps we can expect white tolerance to grow as it dawns on whites that the black middle class is growing, suburbanizing, and becoming self-perpetuating. Even in Detroit, a city where the underclass created Devil's Night,[38] a Halloween ceremony of burning down one's own housing units, whites now appear more willing to live among blacks than previously.[39] Perhaps these changed views will eventually form a cascade, changing white preferences and behavior more than they already have.

Still, don't expect the waters to part all the way just yet. It is not only prejudice or preference but inference in the face of information cost that keeps blacks and whites apart. The differences in the average background of blacks and whites and associated group-linked behaviors support "kernel-of-truth" stereotypes and racialist decisions that result in separation.[40] Housing choices and locational preferences involve expectations about property-value increase or decrease, peer groups for children, what kind of stores will locate profitably in the neighborhood, what kind of music one will heard from neighbors' stereos, how easy neighboring relations will be, how safe one will feel, how the neighborhood will be viewed by others whose response then determines future property values, and what redistributive burdens one will face. Another important expectation involves what kind of classmates one's children will have in school. (System-wide standards can be easier or harder to maintain, depending on how important groups of students do with respect to those standards; when large, politically strong and visible groups don't meet the standard, it is easy for the standard to give way, creating a signaling problem for the better students who cannot differentiate themselves from the worse students with whom they are lumped together, and so on.) Many of these factors influence whites (and high-income blacks) to favor separation from the majority of blacks.

If, for example, many whites do not prefer to live among blacks, that preference will be expressed in the price people can expect to receive for their property as neighborhoods change from white to black. During an initial phase of transition, prices actually rise (assuming no collective action to prevent sales) as blacks who desire to move in pay a premium for whiter neighborhoods; eventually, however, that premium becomes a discount in value for the whites who stay.[41] Whites gain by selling early and lose by selling late, since the heretofore white neighborhood premium disappears as more and more whites sell. It is a self-fulfilling value collapse to be sure, but one in which the individual white, who may even prefer integration, is caught. Without benefit of collective action,[42] whites in transition areas are caught in an n-person prisoners' dilemma in which it makes financial sense to sell early even if they wish to remain in an integrated neighborhood. Knowing that the value of my house depends on what my fleeing neighbors are doing, I am better off joining the rush. In this manner, the least tolerant exert disproportionate impact.

Like all Prisoners' Dilemma situations, individuals are not necessarily able to achieve their preferred cooperative outcome, which could be a stable integrated neighborhood of the 80 to 20 or (stretching it) 70 to 30 kind. One cannot infer, then, extreme segregatory preferences from a segregated outcome. If integration now requires collective action to be feasible (where before segregation relied on collective action), an inference of underlying motivation from uncoordinated action is unwarranted. It is not rational to be the last white left in order to preserve an integrated neighborhood. If whites know what social scientists know, that "as minority composition rises above 20 percent neighborhoods move more quickly toward minority dominance" and that "the bi-polar distribution of neighborhoods—with tracts clustered at the high and low level of minority representation is confined to structural types containing blacks," the individual in a neighborhood nearing the 20 percent figure may reasonably begin looking over his shoulder even if he prefers an integrated neighborhood.[43]

The effect of collective action may be observed in figure 13.6.

George C. Galster's work, as exhibited graphically in O'Sullivan's *Urban Economics*,[44] illustrates the effect of collective action in the form of affirmative marketing in Cleveland. The Morland area, not far from areas of black concentration, was a middle-class section of the affluent, white Shaker Heights suburb, whose schools were separate from Cleveland's. The community association that controlled a large number of properties used its position to maintain an integrated balance in this desirable middle-class area. As figure 13.6 suggests, they were successful both in attracting blacks when they were "too few" and successful in avoiding tipping, which would overtake the nonmanaged areas that form the datum of the chart.

So far I have treated white housing preferences as purely racial, that is, unexplained except in racial terms and thus necessarily irrational or racist. And surely this is true to some extent. "Whites interpret a videotaped shove as violence when the shover is black, but playing around when the shover is white."[45] Whites are less likely to see blacks and Hispanics as hard-

Figure 13.6   Changes in the Racial Composition of Cleveland Neighborhoods, 1970–1980

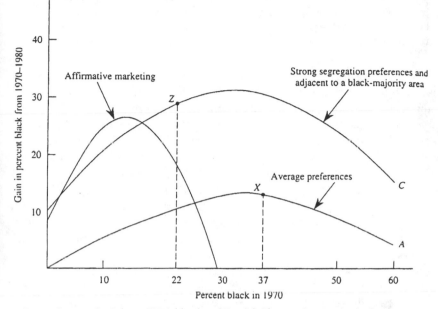

Source: George C. Galster, "Neighborhood Racial Change, Secregationist Sentiments, and Affirmative Marketing Policies," *Journal of Urban Economics* 27 (1990), pp. 344–61.

working, intelligent, or even as patriotic as themselves.[46] But whites also have more black friends than ever before and express less concern over interracial marriage.[47] And so the question arises of whether, and to what extent, racism dominates decision making and market consequences in housing. At least one other (possibly related) fact is the impact of crime.

IMPACT OF CRIME

Individual interracial friendship and relations are one thing, but integration requires a communal or collective acceptance of mostly unknown neighbors. Since mixed neighborhoods have often been transitional (when they have existed at all), whites do not have much collective experience to go on. Outright racism kept that from happening in the past, but a current factor, real or imagined, is concern with crime. That concern itself is a reality that taints the innocent and the guilty combined—as is captured by Richard Epstein:

An individual will find it rational to lock his house even if he thinks that 99 percent of the population would *not* steal his goods if the house were left unlocked. The possessions in the house can be stolen only once. The lock, therefore, is not put on the door because of the *average* run of humanity, which may be quite high. Rather, this decision is driven by the conduct of the *marginal*, in this case the *worst*, individuals within the group.[48]

The race/class/crime connection is not a figment of white imagination; although blacks are the primary victims of crime, a fair amount of crime is interracial. For robbery, rape, and assault, whites were the victims of blacks 53.8 percent of the time, compared with 46.2 percent for black victims. Blacks made up 2.4 percent of the victims of white-originated crime.[49] Within cities, the correlation between poverty, race, and crime is also apparent. For example, a study of crime in Dallas found a correlation of $+.61$ between violent crime and percentage black, a correlation of $-.54$ with percentage males in white-collar occupations, a correlation of $-.45$ with an area's median income.[50] These correlations are not likely to go unnoticed and, unfortunately, *the most visible indicator* is race when class clues are not obvious.

Crime is partly a question of propinquity and opportunity; it may not be surprising, then, that "blacks in *non*poor and near-poor neighborhoods report losses that are twice as high as those reported by whites in nonpoor and near-poor neighborhoods. . . . the losses of blacks in neighborhoods with poverty rates of less than 10 percent are among the very highest rates reported of any group."[51] Whites attempt to protect themselves from interracial crime "partly by black-white residential separation since recent evidence suggests that most offenders tend to commit crimes in areas near to where they live."[52] Maintaining a distance from those areas makes good risk-avoidance sense, since "journey to crime apparently displays the distance-decay characteristics of most spatial interaction. . . . As predictable from the rational criminal model, the rate of distance decay varies inversely with the value of the potential booty at the destination." For example, "one third of juveniles apprehended in Philadelphia committed offenses within one quarter mile of home; three quarters, within one mile of home."[53] (Violent crime is a more localized affair than property crime.)

Clearly, local poor have less impact than the "surrounding" poor. "Neighborhoods in which the accessibility to the surrounding poor is one standard deviation above the mean have property crime rates 2 to 4 standard deviations above the mean."[54] "The crime rate in a neighborhood can rise as a result of the entry of lower-status families in a neighborhood several miles away."[55] It is reasonable, then, to be concerned not only with immediate surroundings but also with indicators of change some distance away, next door."

Figure 13.7   Probability of White Population Loss

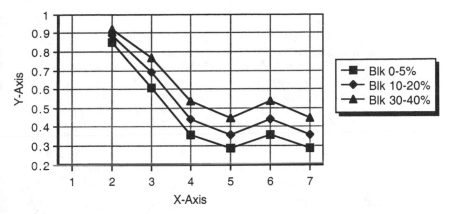

Source: Massey and Denton, *American Apartheid*, p. 79.

Based on Douglas S. Massey and Nancy A. Denton's *American Apartheid* (table 3.5, p. 79), figure 13.7 gives the probability of white population loss in census tracts between census periods as a function of distance: less than five miles, five to ten miles, ten to twenty-five miles, and more than twenty-five miles from the nearest black neighborhood. Clearly, low black entry produces some white population loss (no matter how small), a greater probability of loss with increasing proximity to a black neighborhood, and a loss that grows in response to a larger percentage of black entry. For whites there is the assumption of safety in distance.

Given the data on crime, whites are likely to believe that the risks of crime increase if they remain in areas that become poor and black. Blacks may well believe the same, especially as they are more heavily victimized. The heavier victimization of middle-class blacks probably stems from a reduced ability to separate themselves socially from crime-prone neighbors. Blacks do try. There is about the same degree of spatial separation of high- and middle-income blacks from poorer blacks as there is between high- and middle-income whites and poorer whites.[56] But "because the black and white distributions of education, occupation, and income differ greatly, blacks are exposed to neighborhood mixes different from those of whites, even when the levels of social class segregation are identical."[57] Perhaps it is for this reason—"black-white differences in income, not because of racial differences in residential segregation by class"—that the black middle class is overrepresented among victims of crime.

Whites are not likely to be concerned with the criminal victimization of blacks insofar as they are able to "comparison shop" risks and avoid them.[58] They are not likely to separate victim from victimizer in the process of generalization—a process made all the cruder from lack of contact and knowledge.

> More than a tiresome slight, the notion that one could not tell blacks apart bespeaks the intricate way urban dwellers scan their environment, sift visual and other clues for forecasts of danger, and make guesses about the intentions of strangers. People generalize from experience to reduce uncertainty and manage alarm. Employers, pedestrians, and homeowners do not operate on the presumption of innocence that lies at the core of legal reasoning. They associate individuals with classes of events and merge past incidents with hunches about repetition."[59]

Whether it is called overgeneralization, stereotyping, a tiresome slight, or outright racism, such generalization has consequences for the victims of the generalizer. Blacks are well aware of the wariness of whites, find it more than tiresome, and suffer from the consequences—the psychological burden that blacks feel in their interactions with whites and the race and class isolation that have been well documented by Wilson and others.[60] It is hard to get a precise estimate of the cost of isolation, but Cutler and Glaeser have estimated the overall costs of racial segregation by comparing social outcomes in cities with more and less segregation (holding other variables constant, of course). On a variety of indexes, the most segregated cities have the worst outcomes. For example, cities with segregation below the mean show single motherhood rates of 45.4 percent compared to 40.4 percent in high segregation cities. Their "estimates suggest that a one standard deviation reduction in segregation (13 percent) would eliminate one-third of the *gap* between whites and blacks in most of [their] outcomes."[61]

Additional evidence comes from the Gautreaux program in Chicago which, beginning in 1976, has undertaken to disperse public housing residents to the suburbs—as close as it is possible to get to an experiment.[62] The Gautreaux program takes screened public housing tenants and offers some of them an opportunity to move out of the projects into scattered-site, Section 8 housing in the city or suburbs—the location largely a function of availability, not deliberate choice by tenants. Although the sample is not random, neither is it atypical of many of the Chicago public housing residents. "Although both groups started from the same baseline, after moving, suburban residents were 13 percent more likely to have jobs than city movers."[63] The "suburban effect" was even greater for those who had no prior work experience. No difference occurred in hourly wages or hours worked. Control variables that negatively affected the outcome were "internal locus of control" and long-term welfare subsistence—so called culture of poverty variables that simple relocation is unlikely to overcome.

Equally interesting, the respondents felt that suburban living had helped them find greater employment, not only because of the increased number of jobs available but also because of the greater safety of the suburbs for work trips and the reduced fear of leaving their children in the suburbs, compared with the projects. The new suburban locations were not nirvana—travel was difficult, babysitters were harder to find, and competition for some jobs was stiffer—but seem to have mattered in a positive way. Reducing segregation by 13 percent won't be easy, and reducing the lingering effects of social class and racial isolation won't be easy: witness the slow pace of Yonkers's version of *Gautreaux*. Still, blacks are suburbanizing, segregation is falling, and the next census may bring some optimistic news.

CODA

I think it is not wrong to use the term "tragedy" to describe the current state of the unfulfilled promise of a world in which race does not matter. It is a tragedy for the victims[64] and a moral tragedy for the "victimizers." Both are trapped (not identically to be sure) by a history that began in slavery. Reinforced by racism pure and simple, separation is now supported by racialist decisions that make integration difficult (though no longer impossible) to achieve. Exploring the effects of racial and now race/class separation would require another chapter, but suffice it to say that recent estimates of the effect of racial separation are not minor. It is morally correct to argue that each white, individually, needs to act differently (and many do), but self-interest and the legacy built into the race/class nexus militate against relying on individual decisions to quickly or easily erase class/race distinctions. Collective solutions might push progress forward, but they presuppose both a "technological" ability to erase class effects and a willingness beyond what the white majority may deem acceptable.[65] Although white motivation may have moved from "racist" to "racialist," it has not moved to a willingness to give up white advantages to engage in "nonrace" behavior. It has not moved far enough to put us in one another's shoes so that institutions are fashioned to eliminate the need or desire for racialist decisions. It has not moved far enough to erase the enduring legacy of class that had its roots in white behavior of a most egregious sort that continues in part because of the racial separation from which blacks and the underclass in particular suffer from.[66] Moving beyond this legacy will not be easy, but it remains a moral imperative.

Perhaps it is realistic to close on this summary judgment from Orlando Patterson's *The Ordeal of Integration:*

> The objective economic, sociological, and political record clearly demonstrates that this painful period of transition has not been in vain. In almost all areas of life, progress—sometimes quite dramatic—has been made in surmounting the ingrained and institutional evils of racism and oppression. Only a fool or bigot would deny that a great deal remains to be done.[67]

NOTES

1. William J. Wilson, *The Declining Significance of Race* (Chicago: University of Chicago Press, 1980).
2. Convergence by Cohort.

Figure 13.8   Black Weekly Wage As a Percentage of White Weekly Wage (Adult Males, 1940–1980)

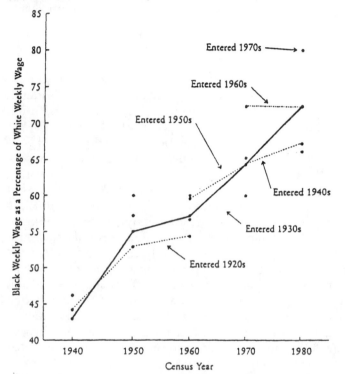

Source: James P. Smith and Finis R. Welch, "Black Economic Progress After Myrdal," *Journal of Economic Literature* XXVII (2) (June 1989), constructed from data in table 8.

3. Richard Freeman, "Black Economic Progress: Who Has Gained and Why?" in *Studies in Labor Markets,* ed. Sherwin Rosen (Chicago: University of Chicago Press, 1981), p. 248. Author's emphasis.
4. In searching through old references and notes, I came upon these poorly documented (early 1960) notes on a study either by Sexton or Bond that, perhaps as vividly as anything academics are likely to encounter, illustrate the effect of class:

Number of male workers required to
Produce One Merit Scholar Winner   *Occupation*
12,627   Professional, technical

37,153	Managerial
77,632	Sales workers
366,270	Service workers
3,581,370	Laborers

5. Freeman, "Black Economic Progress," p. 256.

6. June O'Neill, "The Role of Human Capital in Earnings Differences between Black and White Men," *Journal of Economic Progress* 4, no. 4 (Fall 1990): 43.

7. "In 1997 black high school seniors from families with annual incomes between $70,000 and $80,000 scored an average of 472 on the verbal component of the SAT, compared to an average of 487 for whites from families whose income was less than $10,000 per year." Glenn Loury, comments on "The Black White Test Score Gap," *American Prospect* 41 (November December 1998): 69.

8. W. Locke Anderson, "Trickling Down," *Quarterly Journal of Economics,* November 1964.

9. Henry L. Gates, "The Best of Times, the Worst of Times," *Brookings Review,* Spring 1998, p. 6.

10. Casey Mulligan, *Parental Priorities and Economic Inequality* (Chicago: University of Chicago Press, 1997), p. 178.

11. Given the roots of these wealth differences in the most egregious forms of injustice, in my view, a case can be made for reparation.

12. Gary Becker, *The Economics of Discrimination* (Chicago: University of Chicago Press, 1957).

13. George Akerloff in "A Theory of Social Custom" shows that if "reputation" is in the utility function of decision makers, they may find it in their interest to follow a social code even at personal financial cost. First, they may deeply believe in the code and thus have a large psychological stake in overcoming it, but even those who do not believe in the code, face serious social risks from bucking it. Akerloff makes a similar argument in his "Economics of Caste," where the cost of breaking caste assumptions is "outcasting." The rigidity of the caste system can be enhanced when "governmental regulator-regulatee nexuses and political machines are held together by a caste-outcaste structure. . . . Codes may ultimately disappear if enough come to disbelieve in them. Nothing suggests that this needs to be a quick or easy process. George Akerloff, "A Theory of Social Custom" and "The Economics of Caste and of the Rat Race," in *An Economic Theorist's Book of Tales* (New York: Cambridge University Press, 1984).

14. "Suppose that blacks and whites do in fact differ in productivity, at least on the average. This is in turn due to some causes, perhaps education, perhaps cultural differences; but the cause itself is not observable. Then the experience of employers over time will cause them to use the observable characteristic, race, as a surrogate for the unobservable characteristics which in fact caused the productivity differences. This is a market-based explanation which does not require tastes for discrimination" (Kenneth Arrow, "Comment," *JEP,* Spring 1998, p. 97).

15. It is easy to see that two separate communities could easily have biased perceptions of each other, neither of which may be accurate yet the bias of social proof makes difficult to erode these "fact" beliefs. We all too easily adopt the views of those around us. Even academics with tenure. The reasons for this are nicely ex-

plored in Timur Kuran, *Private Truths, Public Lies: The Social Consequences of Preference Falsification* (Cambridge: Harvard University Press, 1995).

16. I have not discussed either customer-based discriminatory preferences or complementary labor–based discriminatory preferences, both of which can result in discriminatory outcomes (Becker, *Economics of Discrimination*). Discriminatory preferences by customers are more important in personal services, where customer contact matters. Union bigotry has been well documented but has subsided as an explanatory force.

17. Joleen Kirschenman and Kathryn M. Neckerman, "'We'd Love to Hire Them But . . .': The Meaning of Race for Employers," in *The Urban Underclass,* ed. Christopher Jencks and Paul E. Peterson (Washington, D.C.: Brookings Institution, 1991).

18. It was noted that this concern explicitly occupied only a minority of firms. But employers who valued teamwork among their low-skilled workers "were twice as likely to have racially and ethnically homogeneous workforces in the sample job" (Kirschenman and Neckerman, "Meaning of Race," p. 227).

19. Ibid., p. 215.

20. Ibid., p. 231.

21. Diane Ravitch, quoted in Tamar Lewin, "How Boys Lost Out to Girl Power," *New York Times,* December 13, 1998, sec. 4, p. 3.

22. Kirschenman and Neckerman, "Meaning of Race," p. 231.

23. Richard A. Epstein, *Forbidden Grounds: The Case against Employment Discrimination Laws* (Cambridge: Harvard University Press, 1992), pp. 60–69.

24. Tsui, Egan, and O'Reilly III, "Being Different: Relational Demography and Organizational Attachment," *Administrative Science Quarterly* 37, no. 4 (1992): 549 (electronic version).

25. Christopher Jencks and Meredith Phillips, "The Black White Test Score Gap," *American Prospect,* November–December 1998, p. 71.

26. Segregation in housing markets is greater between blacks and whites than it is between most groups of whites and a dominant white "other." For example, in 1980, while the segregation index between blacks and those of English ancestry in Chicago stood at 85 (100 is perfect segregation), the segregation index between Russian background and English ancestry was about 62, between Japanese and English 60, between Italian and English less than 50, and between Swedish and English about 27. In addition, during the development of most of the literature, measured segregation of most groups decreased while segregation between black and white hardly changed. Reynolds Farley, "Residential Segregation among Blacks" in *The Urban Underclass,* ed. Jencks and Peterson (Washington, D.C.: Brookings Institution, 1991), p. 284.

27. Ibid., p. 285. Indeed, "controlling for family income, segregation was greater among blacks than among whites."

28. One explanation is that whites are not to be believed; but the decline in expressed racial preference tracks other evidence based on voting, tipping, and the increasing prevalence of integrated neighborhoods.

29. Based directly on T. C. Schelling, *Micromotives and Macrobehavior* (New York: Norton, 1978).

30. Joshua Epstein and Robert Axtell, *Growing Artificial Societies: Social Science from the Bottom Up* (Washington, D.C.: Brookings Institution, 1996).

31. For example:

2B 8W, 3B 7W, 5B 5W, OB 10W . . . ⇨ Dissim index of .766
1B 9W, 3B 7W, 6B 4W, OB 10W . . . ⇨ Dissim index of .73
1B 9W, 2B 8W, 7B 3W, OB 10W . . . ⇨ Dissim index of .727

32. This sorry mess is well documented in Douglas S. Massey and Nancy A. Denton's *American Apartheid: Segregation and the Making of an Underclass* (Cambridge: Harvard University Press, 1993) for those unfamiliar with this history.

33. Figure 13.9.

Figure 13.9   Index of Isolation, 1890–1990

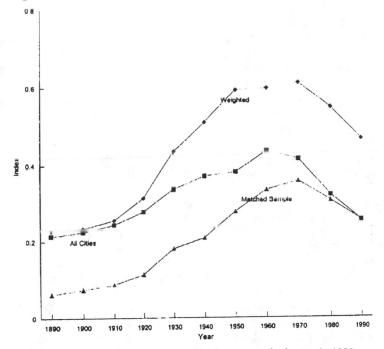

Note: Matched sample mean is normalized to unmatched mean in 1990.

34. Douglas S. Massey and Nancy A. Denton, "Patterns of Neighborhood Transition in a Multiethnic World: U.S. Metropolitan Areas, 1970–1980," *Demography* 28, no. 1 (1991).

35. W. A. Clark, "Residential Preferences and Neighborhood Racial Segregation: A Test of the Schelling Segregation Model," *Demography* 28, no. 1 (1991).

36. In a study of twenty-six metropolitan counties in Florida, out of a group of 1,637 census tracts, thirteen were found to be integrated and stable from 1980 to 1990. This study used a more careful definition of stable integration. Richard Smith, "Discovering Stable Integration," *Journal of Urban Affairs* 20 (Winter 1998): 1.

37. Anthony Downs, "How America's Cities Are Growing," *Brookings Review,* Fall 1998, p. 10.

38. Ze'ev Chafets, *Devil's Night: And Other True Tales of Detroit* (New York: Random House, 1990).

39. John Kain, "An Assessment of the Adverse Impacts of Housing Market Discrimination and Suggestions for Policy," Association for Public Policy Analysis and Management Research Paper, September 1994, p. 22.

40. This is not to deny the role that raw racism as animus may play or racism reinforced by stereotypes.

41. This very roughly describes the (Muth–Bailey) equilibrium border model. Martin Bailey, "Effects of Race and Demographic Factors on the Values of Single-Family Homes," *Land Economics* 42 (May 1966): 215–220; and Richard Muth, *Urban Economic Problems* (New York: Harper & Row, 1975).

42. A basis for the disequilibrium border model unless whites individually raise their prices to blacks who buy. The latter hypothesis, which preserves individual rather than collective action, is not plausible over the longest run and certainly not plausible once transition is under way. The disequilibrium model has greater predictive accuracy for the postwar period through the 1960s. It accurately predicts the crowding and housing shortage that occurred from postwar migration of blacks to the North and the West. It is not the more plausible model in the 1980s and 1990s.

43. Massey and Denton, "Patterns of Neighborhood Transition," p. 51.

44. Arthur O'Sullivan, *Urban Economics,* 3d ed. (Chicago: Irwin, 1996), p. 398.

45. Jennifer Hochschild, *Facing Up to the American Dream: Race, Class, and the Soul of the Nation* (Princeton: Princeton University Press, 1995), p. 116.

46. Ibid.

47. Stephan Thernstrom and Abigail Thernstrom, *America in Black and White: One Nation, Indivisible* (New York: Simon & Shuster, 1997), pp. 521–25. "Less concern," not "no concern." *The New Republic* (November 23, 1998, p. 10) reported that in the November 1998 election 38 percent of South Carolinians voted to keep interracial marriage illegal in spite of its being a legally dead issue. They also cite a national study in which 45 percent of whites "approved" of interracial marriages, whereas 16 percent would still ban it.

48. Richard A. Epstein, *Forbidden Grounds: The Case against Employment Discrimination Laws.* In general, I do not support the thrust of Epstein's book.

49. Thomas Edsal and Mary Edsal, *Chain Reaction: The Impact of Race, Rights, and Taxes on American Politics* (New York: Norton, 1991), p. 236.

50. Martin T. Katzman, "The Supply of Criminals: A Geo-Economic Examination," in *Crime Spillover,* ed. Simon Hakim and Geroge F. Rengert, *Sage Research Series in Criminology* (Beverly Hills: Sage, 1981), 23:120.

51. Gerald Jaynes and Robin Williams, *A Common Destiny: Blacks in American Society* (Washington, D.C.: National Academy Press, 1989), p. 471. The material does not indicate whether these are blacks and whites in the same or in different neighborhoods. One suspects different ones.

52. Ibid., p. 465.

53. Katzman, "Supply of Criminals," p. 122.

54. Ibid., p. 130.

55. Ibid., p. 132.

56. For individual whites or blacks, the level of crime will be a classic public good (or bad) little affected by their own individual behavior per the logic of the collective dilemma. Flight, not fight, is the more likely response for those with the choice. Not everyone, of course, makes that choice and those who do not are properly regarded as neighborhood heroes.

57. Contrary to popular belief, studies have found that "controlling for family income, segregation was greater among blacks than among whites" (Farley, "Residential Segregation," p. 285).

58. Suttles, in describing the control sought in city life, speaks of "uniform cultural forms which are required by the mechanics of life itself. The quest for a good community is among other things, a quest for neighborhood where one does not fear standing at arm's length from his neighbor, where one can divine the intent of someone heading down the sidewalk, or where one can share expressions of affect by the way adjacent residences dress up for mutual impression management" Gerald Suttles, *The Social Construction of Communities* (Chicago: University of Chicago Press, 1972), p. 234. This surely holds true for both blacks and whites. Facing what Naison described as an "outlaw culture" in some inner city neighborhoods wracked by recent violence, one Chicagoan said, "It's the worst I've ever seen it. Just going out at night to get something, I can't tell you when I last did that. If I ain't got it by nightfall, I don't get it." Mark Naison, "Outlaw Culture and Black Neighborhoods," *Reconstruction* 1, no. 4 (1992): 128.

59. Reider, p. 86.

60. See Jencks and Peterson, *Underclass Phenomenon,* for a good review that gives some but not full support to Wilson. See especially Crane's essay on contagion.

61. Cutler and Glaeser, "Are Ghettos Good or Bad?" *QJE* 112 (August 1997): 864, emphasis mine. Literature on spatial mismatch support their conclusions. For my view of the harmful the consequences in education, see Andrew J. Gold, "In the Aftermath of *Sheff*—Considerations for a Remedy," *Connecticut Law Review* 29, no. 3 (1997).

62. James E. Rosenbaum and Susan J. Popkin, "Employment and Earnings of Low Income Blacks Who Move to Middle-Class Suburbs," in *Urban Underclass,* p. 348.

63. Ibid.

64. "In 1990, 2,280,000 black men were in prison, or probation, or parole while 23,000 earned a college degree. That's a ratio of 99 to 1, compared with a ratio of 6 to 1 for white men" (Gates, "Best of Times," p. 7).

65. Take, for example, John Roemer's recent estimate that it would take a six- to tenfold increase in educational expenditure aimed at black students to equalize incomes (or a 50 percent decrease in expenditure enjoyed by whites). So strong is the class legacy. Clearly both outcomes are politically unfeasible. The reason for this large estimate is that educational expenditure has low marginal impact in overcoming class differences. "The Relative Merits of Different Educational Opportunity Reforms from the Point of View of Equality of Achievement" (paper presented at the APPAM Twentieth Annual Research Conference, New York, October 1998).

66. I believe that the burden of social class integration is on whites and not on

blacks alone. This is so not only for moral reasons but the obvious fact of numbers. The white middle class vastly outnumbers the black middle class. For a discussion of ghetto rebuilding versus ghetto dispersal, see the original John Kain and Joseph Persky, "Alternatives to the Gilded Ghetto," *Public Interest,* Winter 1969.

67. Orlando Patterson, *The Ordeal of Integration: Progress and Resentment in America's "Racial Crisis"* (Washington, D.C.: Civitas Counterpoint, 1998), p. 1.

14

Race and Class:
Why All the Confusion?

Johnny E. Williams

In many sociological studies, class and race are understood to be independent of each other; consequently, researchers tend to focus on one or the
other without examining their combined effects.[1] This is problematic because it does not afford researchers the opportunity to investigate the depths
of the interpenetration of race and class in the United States. Such an investigation might help shed light on how race not only conveys tangible advantages for whites but also naturalizes the class-based manner in which
society is ordered in the United States.

For the purposes of my analysis, race is defined not as a "natural" or
biological attribute but as a socially and historically constructed concept by
which members of society endow human skin color variations, which have
no intrinsic meaning,[2] with meanings that reinforce a hierarchy of privilege
and power in society. Class is defined as a system of stratification in which
unequal allocation of resources and opportunity for social advancement is
supported by cultural myths that naturalize inequality.[3] Although these
concepts are conceptually distinct, they are related in interesting and com-
plicated ways. As I will demonstrate below, class issues are often concealed
in racially coded language and meanings. Racial stereotypes are frequently
used to reinforce a system of class inequality while class stereotypes are used
to reinforce a racial hierarchy. These confusions are not puzzling when we
examine the dynamics that create them.

In this chapter I attempt to contribute to the race/class debate by examining the ways in which (1) class issues (i.e., poverty, welfare, economic
inequality) are concealed in racial terms,[4] (2) race and class inform and sustain one another, and (3) those with various types of power have vested
interests in creating and sustaining the confusion between race and class. In

other words, we gain a better understanding of American society not by trying to disentangle race *effects* from class *effects* but by observing how they interact in our culture and politics. Before proceeding with this discussion, I briefly review some of the various approaches scholars use to examine the relation between race and class.

THEORETICAL APPROACHES TO
UNDERSTANDING RACE AND CLASS

Social scientists usually take either a reductionist[5] or a relational approach when examining race and class. Theories of reductionism treat racial phenomena as epiphenomena of other social factors such as ethnicity[6] or class. The ethnicity variant of reductionism attempts to reduce race to an element of ethnicity in an effort to explain how ethnic identity facilitate or inhibit ethnic group incorporation into the majority culture. The theoretical assumption is that ethnic psychological, cultural and status differences disappear with assimilation. The chief theorists of the ethnicity theory, Gunnar Myrdal (1944), Milton Gordon (1964), and Nathan Glazer and Daniel Patrick Moynihan (1970), all contend that when subordinate racial groups are given an opportunity to assimilate, they can carve out their own place in society through hard work, patience, and thrift that will ensure their socioeconomic success and acceptance in society. Myrdal succinctly makes this point in his book *An American Dilemma* when he suggests that despite the considerable racial hostility directed at blacks:

> If America in actual practice could show the world a progressive trend by which the Negro finally became integrated into modern democracy, all mankind would be given faith again—it would have reason to believe that peace, progress, and order are feasible. . . . *America is free to choose whether the Negro shall remain her liability or become her opportunity.*[7]

The ethnicity theoretical variant of reductionism is problematic because it denies the significance of institutional discrimination in preventing socioeconomic success.

A second type of reductionism, the class variant, explains race as an outcome of relations deriving from the creation and distribution of material resources, specifically, economic processes. Three general approaches, or perspectives, are included in the class variant[8]: (1) market based, in which race appears as an anomaly or market imperfection that interferes with the equilibrating tendencies of the market; (2) stratification, which views race as a product of extraeconomic factors that play important roles in maintaining and modifying systems of stratification for the distribution of resources;

and (3) class conflict, which maintains that race is a product of capitalist economic interests that seek higher profits and more secure controls over the labor process through strategies that pit white and black labor against each other (Bonacich 1976; Omi and Winant 1994). Though these are all very interesting and insightful approaches, my analysis is concerned with the more general premise of class reductionism. A chief theorist of class reductionism is sociologist William Julius Wilson who, in his book *The Declining Significance of Race*, argues that socioeconomic factors are increasingly replacing race as a determinant of black life chances due to economic changes fostered by a shift from "goods producing" to "service producing" activity and state-sponsored civil rights initiatives. As a consequence of these changes, Wilson argues, low-skilled blacks find themselves in social and economic contexts with a narrowing opportunity structure that limits their ability to secure a decent standard of living. Wilson's approach is problematic because it treats economic processes as impersonal forces that are imposed on society without human choice, thus ignoring the significance of consciously constructed racism in shaping social and economic life (Bonacich 1976; Reed 1988). When racial concerns are reduced to economic issues, one cannot discern how racial and economic imperatives are conceptually distinct but interdependent forces.

A quite different theoretical approach to race and class is taken by relational theorists (Pettigrew 1980; Pinkney 1984; Willie 1989; Omi and Winant 1994; Winant 1994). These theorists, the chief critics of reductionism, see race as an irreducible component of social structures that pervades social life. That is, they contend that race and class are so interrelated that race is not a side issue that can be resolved through assimilation and/or more structural opportunities. They argue that research should shift from efforts to parcel out the effects of race and class to focus on understanding and explaining their interpenetration (Collins 1990; Griffin 1995, 92). Relational theorists see race as an irreducible and central organizing feature in political and cultural life that shapes cultural discourse and economic opportunities.

W. E. B. Du Bois (1903), Frantz Fanon (1967), Michael Omi and Howard Winant (1994), and Joe Feagin and Hernàn Vera (1995) are some of the chief theorists of the relational approach. They contend that society is suffused with racial meaning to which we are all subjected. Omi and Winant maintain that racial subjection

is quintessentially ideological. Everybody learns some combination, some version, of the rules of racial classification, and racial identity, often without obvious teaching or conscious inculcation. Thus we are inserted in a comprehensively racialized social structure. Race becomes "common sense"—a way of comprehending, explaining and acting in the world.[9]

Omni and Winant contend that ongoing interpretation of our experiences in racial terms shapes our relations to the institutions and organizations through which we are imbedded in the social structure (Omi and Winant 1994, 60). Since we live in a society that is racially aware, it is impossible to represent race discursively without simultaneously locating it in a social structural context. Nor is it possible to organize, maintain, and transform social structure without simultaneously engaging in racial signification (Omi and Winant 1994, 60). Thus racial meaning is diffused throughout society and used by people as a means to comprehend and explain social difference such as the food we eat, the clothes we wear, the music we play, and the way we walk and talk (Omi and Winant 1994). Hence relational theorists contend that social structural positions like class frequently are racially assigned by cultural discourse because race serves as a marker of status in the social structure (Fanon 1967; Winant 1994).[10] Jacqueline Rahlins, a South Philadelphia homemaker, understood this well when she remarked,

> I have the desire to do all kinds of things, but I got to have the opportunity to do them. I can't jump out there and say "I'm going to do it." Because there's somebody out there to stop me. There's always hindrance; regardless what you started there's a hindrance. Because if I could jump right out there and say I'm going to do this and that, I wouldn't be living in this neighborhood. . . . These higher persons, if they had any mercy, we wouldn't be here in this neighborhood.[11]

CONCEALING CLASS WITH RACE

Although the relational approach offers important insight about the interpenetration of race and social structure, it has not paid much attention to developing an analysis of the social processes that hide and racially code class. In this study, Antonio Gramsci's (1971) concept of hegemony is integrated with the relational approach to explore the dynamics of how race and class get constructed as race. Gramsci understood hegemony as the conditions necessary in any given society for the achievement and consolidation of rule (Winant 1994, 67). The ruling class consolidates its control over subordinates through systems of ideas and practices that are elaborated and maintained through such social mechanisms as everyday interactions, the media, politics, family, and education.[12] After subordinates are persuaded that the existing system of ideas is fair or natural, these ideas become their *commonsense* ways of thinking and acting that legitimate the way society is organized. For example, racial segregation that systematically undermines black life chances in the United States maintains its legitimacy among

Americans in part through an interpretation of this phenomenon not in structural terms but in an individualistic perspective that both ruling and subordinate groups value. Thus it is easy for a vast majority of Americans to believe that the disproportionate number of blacks who are stuck in "ghettos" are there because of factors intrinsic to them (e.g., differences in values and habits within the group) rather than because the social structure provides different groups with unequal opportunities (Jackman and Jackman 1983). Such an explanation of inequality works to the benefit of the advantaged group, since it leaves the social structure free from scrutiny.

The structural inequalities of race and class both involve processes of institutionalized struggle over power, status, and wealth through a complex of practices and ideologies whereby the dominant group takes advantage of subordinate groups (Dugger 1996). Specifically, each mode of inequality possesses a set of enabling myths that culturally defines inequality to make it seem natural to both subordinate and dominant groups. These myths contribute to the development and maintenance of public thinking and perception that construct class as race. This is evident in the "race-coded" nature of contemporary welfare politics. Although welfare is defined in income or class terms, white Americans' perceptions of welfare are strongly shaped by race and stereotypical beliefs about the black work ethic, particularly the work ethic of black welfare recipients (Gilens 1996, 600). That is, whites' evaluations of welfare are steeped in racial considerations that are not limited to poor blacks or blacks on welfare but extend to blacks in general (Gilens 1996). According to Gilens, this racial view of welfare is far more important in shaping whites' opposition to welfare than class considerations because beliefs about blacks appear to dominate whites' thinking when evaluating welfare (Gilens 1996, 598). Thus hegemonic enabling myths work to bolster the advantaged position of dominant groups by (1) promoting the belief that societal institutions function equitably for everyone; (2) creating the otherness of the oppressed; (3) creating a fear and dread of the unknown, of the other, in the minds of individuals; and (4) making it possible to deny that institutional inequalities occur by encouraging the oppressed to blame themselves (Dugger 1983, 33). Thus the major mechanism of inseparability of race and class is the hegemonic process.

SUSTAINING RACE AND CLASS

Enabling myths are sustained by everyday conversations and institutional texts (i.e., newspapers, television, songs, books, films, etc.) through which people convey, legitimate, or indeed conceal or deny inequality (van Dijik 1992, 87–89). We can get a sense of how this process works from a discussion between a journalist and an expert on computer usage that was aired on National Public Radio in October 1998. The journalist asked the expert about his findings regarding low-income students' access to computers. The expert, who was never asked to designate the race of low-income students, failed to acknowledge that he was only answering part of the question when he replied, "the data revealed that though low-income *minority* students did not own computers, they had about the same access to computers and the internet as white students." What was really revealing about this conversation was the tacit legitimacy the journalist gave the expert when he made no effort to point out that his question was about income, not race. Thus through their public discourse the journalist and computer usage expert seemed to be suggesting to themselves and to the public that "white" is a signifier of economic virtue.

Everyday discussions that conflate race and class have the consequence of helping to maintain existing social arrangements. For example, elite colleges committed to diversifying their student body often fail to consider the effects that such variables as low Scholastic Achievement Test (SAT) scores and financial considerations will have on their recruitment efforts. Thus the recruitment efforts of many colleges flounder when their diversity rhetoric is not accompanied by innovative changes in admissions criteria and additional financial funding for new students. This outcome is related to the fact that (1) many students in the targeted groups attend schools in poor inner-city districts whose academic environments are devoid of courses that prepare them for college entrance examines and (2) most students cannot afford to take outside preparatory classes.[13] Although the low SAT scores are a problem of class, they are not presented as such. The college discourse suggests that its inability to racially diversify the student body is a "personal trouble" of the targeted student group rather than a "public" class issue.[14]

The ability of race and class to mask and reinforce each other is currently being exposed by a lawsuit filed in February 1999 by five civil rights organizations[15] on behalf of 750 black, Latino, and Filipino American students who had high school grade point averages of 4.0 yet were denied admission to the University of California at Berkeley. These students were denied admission by a U.C.–Berkeley admissions policy that favors applicants who take advanced placement courses in high school. Since such courses tend to be offered in wealthier suburban schools and not in the inner-city schools the plaintiffs attend, many students from wealthier families start off with an advantage over poor students in the admissions process. Though the unfairness of the U.C.–Berkeley admission policy at first glance appears to be only about socioeconomic status, it is also about race. The residential segregation of black, Latino, and Filipino students can be used, as the U.C.–Berkeley policy demonstrates, as an institutional apparatus to support both racial and class discriminatory processes. Massey and Denton sum it up this way: "To the extent that white prejudice and discrimination restrict the residential mobility of blacks and confine them to areas with poor schools . . . and low educational aspirations, segregation undermines their social and economic well-being."[16]

In the United States it is virtually impossible to separate racial from class interests because hegemonic cultural ideas like "the American Dream," which suggest that socioeconomic success results from actions and traits under one's own control, are premised on racial meanings and practices (Hochschild 1995, 30). The idea of the American Dream is used to project a positive self-presentation and negative other presentation that allows one to claim responsibility for achieving or not achieving success. Those who achieve success are viewed and view themselves as role models; those who fail are devalued and represented as negative others. Creating the otherness of those who fail allows people to explain failure in terms of personal dys-functions so that they can maintain their belief that social arrangements are fundamentally just (Hochschild 1995, 31). Thinking along these lines is commonplace and is often extended to perceptions of subordinate racial groups, with adherence to the belief that group members' lack of success is based on factors intrinsic to them rather than to the social structure. For example, although many blacks face unfair race and class barriers to success, many (e.g., *Black Enterprise* magazine publisher, Earl Graves) assert that individuals are responsible for their own success:

> Each day we must work to break down the barriers of racism by showing that we can be the best whether we are making deals on Wall Street or delivering goods on Main Street. . . . We must acknowledge and confront the obstacles and put forward our maximum effort. We must not run or hide if we want to ultimately achieve our goals.[17]

Thus failure, especially the disproportionate numbers of blacks and Latinos who fail to achieve success, is usually not interpreted in structural but individual terms that stress an alleged "lack of will or effort" on the part of the unsuccessful other to work for success (McLaughlin 1993, 365).[18]

People daily engage in unconscious and conscious private and public discourses that are permeated with racial and stereotypical beliefs. These beliefs help them construct a consensus about individual rather than structural causality of inequality that victimizes and benefits them. This consensus diverts many Americans, especially whites, who are keenly aware of their precarious socioeconomic position, from thinking of their situation in terms of worker exploitation by corporate capital. Rather, their attitudes about class inequality are heavily fashioned by cultural myths of individualism and race that turn their attention away from corporate capitalists, whose quest for profit is the source of white economic distress, toward subordinate racial groups with whom they compete for employment. Whites who accept this cultural discourse believe that their economic advantages are deserved and earned and that government policies like affirmative action, which seeks to remedy limited aspects of structural inequality, unfairly give unqualified racial groups an unearned competitive advantage in the job market. In effect, race is used as a means to reinforce the advantaged position of white beneficiaries using a discourse that reconciles in the minds of both victims and beneficiaries a social system that is fair and legitimate; it teaches beneficiaries that their advantages are deserved and earned (Dugger 1993).

In essence, everyday talk and institutional practices frequently code class issues with racial discourses that are constructed as institutions and meaning systems that guarantee tangible (i.e., social, economic, and political) and intangible (i.e., positive self-presentation, ordering of life) advantages for groups and individuals designated as white (Griffin 1995). The end result of this process is expressed in large inequities such as current black/white household income gap (blacks, with an average income of $25,050 a year versus whites, with an average of $38,972), which is explained as a consequence of a "skills mismatch" rather than employment discrimination and underemployment, even though income differences persist even when black skills are the same as whites (Census Bureau, 1998).[19]

VESTED INTEREST IN CONFLATING RACE AND CLASS

Groups and individuals with various types of power have vested interests in encouraging people to avoid understanding how race and class work together to structure life and obscure power relationships. The construction of race and class as race is frequently employed by politicians to divert attention away from transforming structures by using cultural discourses, which suggest that inequality is the result of unfair advantages or can be solved by small social-structural reforms. The former technique was used effectively in a 1992 reelection ad for Senator Jesse Helms of North Carolina, which showed a pair of white hands on the television screen holding and reading a job rejection letter. The ad announcer informs viewers that the person was not hired because an unqualified affirmative action beneficiary filled the position. The ad ended by assuring voters that voting for Jesse Helms protected them from losing a job to affirmative action. The ad effectively portrayed the pro-affirmative action stance of Helms's black opponent, Harvey Gant, as a threat to whites' privileged class position. Moreover, it helped to convince whites in North Carolina who voted for Helms that employment in the state was scarce because of the unfair advantage that affirmative action gave "unqualified" blacks. In other words, the campaign advertisement kept whites so narrowly focused on race that it obscured their ability to identify with blacks in their same class situation and diverted their attention from power relations in the market that contributed to the scarcity of jobs.

The small structural reform technique is best illustrated by President Bill Clinton's 1998 dialogue on race with a panel of journalists on public television. After one panelist asserted that many people think that racial differences are actually class differences, the president quickly acknowledged the correlation between race and class status but suggested a solution for erasing these differences that was contingent on the very economic structure that creates and maintains the inequity. He stated: "I think that the point I want to make is to whatever extent you can have an economic approach that embraces people of all races, if it elevates disproportionately—racial groups that have been disproportionately depressed, you'll help to deal with the race problem" (PBS *Dialogue on Race,* July 8, 1998). On the face of it, the president's comment seems to express an enlightened view that seeks to effect structural change, but in actuality his comment renders structural sources of inequality invisible by indirectly expressing his belief that impersonal economic processes afford depressed racial groups better opportunities to realize economic success. The important point about the president's comment is that it denies the significance of racism in shaping economic success by encouraging people to believe in economic expansion as the panacea for racial inequality. Although this logic is contradictory—considering that capitalism requires some form of inequality to exist—the president seized it as a means to persuade people that global economic expansion is good for the social well-being of all people.

One of the most memorable constructions of race and class as race occurred during the media portrayal of the O. J. Simpson trial. Although O. J. Simpson's celebrity status provided him with the resources to afford very competent and high-priced defense lawyers, the media (i.e., newspapers, magazines, television, etc.) chose to deemphasize the role that class played during the trial. The economic structure of the media forces it to tap into the sensationalistic aspect of stories like the O. J. Simpson case in order to attract big audiences to sell to advertisers whose revenue is the media's primary source of profit.[20] For this reason, the media may have been inclined to frame the O. J. Simpson saga in the sinister image and convoluted history of race that reflected America's obsession with race. This racial obsession sells newspapers. The media were far less likely to represent the O.J. case in class terms because class, unlike race, was not as appealing to audiences who make sense of their reality primarily in racial and not class terms.

The obfuscation of class using racial discourse often obscures important information that explains social differences. For example, every year when SAT scores are released, the breakdown by race is presented, showing an enormous gap between blacks and whites. However, we rarely ever see a breakdown of scores by class, which would also show enormous gaps between rich and poor that could help explain the differences in scores between races (Kahlenberg 1995, 5). According to Richard Kahlenberg, we do not see the breakdown by class because organizations like the National Association for the Advancement of Colored People (NAACP) and the author of *The Bell Curve*, Charles Murray, have a vested interest in framing the figures in terms of race. The NAACP cites the statistics as evidence that more needs to be done to close the race gap while Murray presents them as evidence of intractable differences (Kahlenberg 1995, 5). Because there is no powerful, organized group to talk about class or to push for class policies, race by default becomes the primary means that we use to talk about inequality; in doing so we obscure other categories for talking about and understanding inequality.

CONCLUSION

Throughout this chapter, I have tried to demonstrate that it is impossible to talk about race without talking about class for the simple reason that these two forces of inequality are substantively interdependent while also being conceptually distinct. That is, race and class are so linked in identity, interests, and meanings that attempts to disentangle them are virtually hopeless. This fact does not curtail efforts to employ discourses in which class antagonisms are displaced by racial differences, which assume central social and political significance in our society. Such a discourse confuses discussion of inequality to the point of fostering the belief that inequality is natural and that its causes are individual rather than structural. This disposition obviously impedes the development of remedies for inequality that would disclose rather than obscure power relations.

NOTES

1. See Griffin 1995 for further elucidation about this research problem.
2. Cross-cultural racial labeling illustrates well why race should be considered a sociopolitical process rather than a biological or scientific process. For example, people classified as black in the United States would be classified as "coloured" in South Africa.
3. The cultural system of class allows dominant economic groups to take advantage of subordinate groups by supplying the former with a rationale, which asserts that beneficial market competition, not differential economic advantage, is the best way to distribute income and wealth.
4. There may be other tendencies; however, the question my study addresses

is, when race and class are at work together, why, more often than not, is this relationship constructed as race?

5. I borrowed this term from Howard Winant (1994), who uses reductionism to convey how some theorists contend that racial dynamics are manifestations of other, supposedly more significant, social factors.

6. In this chapter ethnicity is defined as socially constructed expressions of culture and a sense of peoplehood that provide people with a sense of belonging to a group.

7. Gunnar Myrdal, *An American Dilemma* (New York: Harper, 1944), 1021–22. Emphasis original.

8. My aim here is not to provide an in-depth analysis but a brief overview of the various approaches to give the reader a sense of the diversity of perspectives within the class variant. For a more detailed discussion of the various class approaches, see Winant 1994.

9. Omi and Winant 1994, 60.

10. Fanon (1967) makes this argument in "The Negro and Language" section of his book *White Skin, Black Masks* when discussing the importance the colonized placed on mastering their colonizers' language.

11. Hochschild 1995, 73.

12. According to Dominic Strinati (1995), Gramsci's theory of hegemony suggests that subordinate groups accept the ideas, values, and leadership of the ruling group not because they are mentally or physically coerced into doing so but because concessions are made by the ruling group to subordinate groups. The culture that sustains hegemony thus expresses in some way the interests of subordinate groups.

13. In a recent article Tony Schwartz (1999) does a nice job explaining the correlation between income and SAT scores.

14. I borrowed the concepts in quotes from C. Wright Mills (1959), who makes a distinction between personal troubles and public issues of the social structure to convey how individuals contribute to shaping their society and the course of its history while simultaneously being made by society and its historical processes.

15. The five groups are the Mexican American Legal Defense and Educational Fund, the National Association for the Advancement of Colored People Legal Defense and Education Fund, the Asian Pacific American Legal Center of Southern, the Lawyers' Committee for Civil Rights, and the American Civil Liberties Union of Northern California.

16. Massey and Denton 1993, 150.

17. Hochschild 1995, 82.

18. This line of thinking manifested itself once in a conversation I had with a fellow graduate student. After viewing and accepting the rationale of a CBS News *60 Minutes* segment on the relationship between Asian families and educational success, she constructed a racially based explanation to explain why black children are less successful in education than other students. She suggested that black familial structures, unlike those of other racial groups, failed to provide children with the necessary support and values they needed to succeed. My classmate had absorbed the individualism associated with "the American Dream" to such an extent that without much thought about her comments, she provided us with a positive self-

representation of herself as successful and a negative representation of blacks as racial others whose lack of values was the sole reason for their low educational achievement. Moreover, by labeling blacks as the unsuccessful other, my classmate relieved herself of her dread and fear of being identified with the unknown other when she told me she "was glad her family had stressed the importance of academic achievement." Basically her rationale was so suffused with racial and class meanings that it was almost impossible to ascertain whether race or class interests drove her to focus on racial group behavior rather than on economic processes, environmental constraints, or political structures as a legitimate explanation for group variation in socioeconomic achievement. (Cf. Hochschild 1995, 36).

19. For further elucidation about racial income gaps, see Fainstein 1987.

20. See Weaver 1994 for a more involved understanding of how media sell audiences to advertisers.

REFERENCES

Bonacich, Edna. 1976. "Advanced Capitalism and Black/White Relations in the United States: A Split Labor Market Interpretation." *American Sociological Review* 41:34–51.

Collins, Patricia Hill. 1990. *Black Feminist Thought: Knowledge, Consciousness, and the Politics of Empowerment.* Boston: Unwin Hyman.

DuBois, W. E. B. [1903] 1997. *The Souls of Black Folks.* Reprint, Boston: Bedford Books.

Dugger, William M. 1996. "Four Modes of Inequality." *Contributions in Economics and Economic History* 178:21–38.

Fainstein, Norman. 1986/1987. "The Underclass/Mismatch Hypothesis as an Explanation for Black Economic Deprivation." *Politics and Society* 15:403–51.

Fanon, Frantz. [1967] 1991. *White Skin, Black Masks.* Reprint, New York: Grove.

Feagin, Joe R., and Hernán Vera. 1995. *White Racism: The Basics.* New York: Routledge.

Gilens, Martin. 1996. " 'Race Coding' and White Opposition to Welfare." *American Political Science Review* 90:593–604.

Glazer, Nathan and Daniel Patrick Moynihan. 1970. *Beyond the Melting Pot.* 2d ed. Cambridge: MIT Press.

Gordon, Milton M. 1964. *Assimilation in American Life.* New York: Oxford University Press.

Gramsci, Antonio. 1971. *Prison Notebooks: Selections.* Translated by Hoare Quintin and Geoffrey N. Smith. London: International Publishers.

Griffin, Larry J. 1995. "How Do We Disentangle Race and Class? Or Should We Even try?" *Work and Occupations* 22:85–93.

Hochschild, Jennifer L. 1995. *Facing Up to the American Dream: Race, Class, and the Soul of the Nation.* Princeton: Princeton University Press.

Jackman, Mary R., and Robert W. Jackman. 1983. *Class Awareness in the United States.* Berkeley: University of California Press.

Kahlenberg, Richard. 1995. "Class, Not Race: Toward a New Affirmative Action." *Current* 375:3–6.

Lehrer News Hour. 1998. "Remarks by the President in PBS Dialogue on Race." July 8.

McLaughlin, Neil. 1993. "Beyond 'Race vs. Class.' " *Dissent* 40:362–68.

Mills, C. Wright. 1959. *The Sociological Imagination.* New York: Oxford University Press.

Myrdal, Gunnar. 1944. *An American Dilemma.* New York: Harper & Brothers.

National Public Radio Weekend Edition Saturday. 1998. Interview with Computer Usage Expert. October.

Omi, Michael, and Howard Winant. 1994. *Racial Formation in the United States: From the 1960s to the 1990s.* 2d ed. New York: Routledge.

Pettigrew, Thomas F. 1980. "The Changing—Not Declining –Significance of Race." *Contemporary Sociology* 9:19–21.

Pinkney, Alphonso. 1984. *The Myth of Black Progress.* Cambridge: Cambridge University Press.

Reed, Adolph L. 1988. "The Liberal Technocrat." *The Nation* 246:167–70.

Schwartz, Tony. 1999. "The Test under Stress." *New York Times Magazine,* January 10, 30–35, 51, 56, 63.

Strinati, Dominic. 1995. *An Introduction to Theories of Popular Culture.* New York: Routledge.

U.S. Census Bureau. 1998. *Current Population Survey, March Supplement.* Washington, D.C.: Government Printing Office.

Van Dijik, Teun. 1992. "Discourse and the Denial of Racism." *Discourse and Society* 3:87–118.

Weaver, Paul H. 1994. *News and the Culture of Lying.* New York: Free Press.

Willie, Charles. 1989. *Caste and Class Controversy on Race and Poverty: Round Two of the Willie/Wilson Debate.* Dix Hills, N.Y.: General Hall.

Wilson, William Julius. 1978. *The Declining Significance of Race.* Chicago: University of Chicago Press.

Winant, Howard. 1994. *Racial Conditions. Politics, Theory, Comparisons.* Minneapolis: University of Minnesota Press.

15

Race and Medicine: The Black Experience

Priscilla Kehoe

The scientific community needs to reevaluate the meaning and intent of the ethnic and racial divisions of our species. Many disciplines hold that there is no biological basis for the concept of race, viewing it instead as a reflection of societal categories rather than readily defined scientific ones (Blackburn, this volume). Physical anthropologists long ago ceased their attempts to classify Homo sapiens into various races of subspecies. However, the disciplines of medicine and epidemiology continue to ascribe biological meaning to racial designations, arguing that race is useful for explaining the prevalence of certain disorders as well as for distinguishing groups of people. Yet the racial classifications they incorporate in their studies are not based on rigorous scientific criteria but on bureaucratic categories, such as those used in the U.S. Census (Cooper, Rotimi, and Ward 1999, p. 62).

As C. Seymour-Smith states, race is a concept that imputes physical, psychological, and moral characteristics to members of a category and thereby justifies a discriminatory system (1986). Because we live in a world in which racial designations assume unfortunate significance, researchers must grapple with the scientific import of race while not forgetting its societal meaning. The medical community, including researchers, educators, and practitioners, should take into account the destructive effects of racism and how it may complicate the understanding of diseases as they affect minority groups (Cooper, Rotimi, and Ward 1999).

Carl von Linne (Carolus Linnaeus) began classifying Homo sapiens by race in 1758. Race was first applied in medicine by German anthropologist and anatomist Johann Blumenbach in 1775 (Witzig 1996). He classified humans into five divisions: Caucasian, Mongolian, Ethiopian, American, and Malay. Both men actually stated that humans constitute one species and that their proposed categories were arbitrary. These concepts and categories have not been laid to rest, despite the knowledge that phenotypic and bio-chemical varieties do not correlate in a simplistic manner with genotypic differences (Cavalli-Sforza, Menozzi, and Piazza 1994; Witzig 1996). The term "race" varies in interpretation and definition, with most anthropologists concluding that the term is vague and only has significance when it represents a closely inbred group in which all family lines are alike. This condition may be seen in pure breeds of domesticated animals but not human types in large populations (Boas 1938).

It is generally agreed, therefore, that race is an unscientific social construct, created from social perceptions and lacking a scientific foundation. More recent definitions tend to use anthropological criteria, defining some three hundred "races," as in the 1990 U.S. Census. This broader interpretation of the term "race," as offered by the *Taber's Cyclopedic Medical Dictionary* (1993), parallels ethnic categorization, in which a group of people within a cultural system are given special status based on specific traits such as religion, language, culture, or appearance. The medical literature incorporates the terms "white" and "black" to describe particular races of people, thus classifying individuals according to perceived skin color. Such classification is unscientific because complexion hue can be environmentally altered and does not fit a primary color scheme (Rensberger 1990). Complexion density ranges from light (albino) to very dark and varies as much within any one defined group. Thus grouping by skin color has no scientific meaning when the result is construed as a race or an ethnicity (Witzig 1996). Even terms such as Caucasian, Mongoloid, Negro, Anglo, Hispanic, and Oriental, for example, contain groupings that represent aspects of geographic, linguistic, and phenotypic groupings that encompass hundreds of ethnic entities and are so broad as to be medically insignificant (King 1981). And yet modern-day medicine uses some of these classifications as acceptable descriptive labels for patients and as a significant aspect of diagnosis and treatment of disease (Witzig 1996).

Medical students are exposed to a wide variety of texts, including some that do not mention race (Gelehrter and Collins 1990), some that specify three major racial groups (Thompson, McInnes, and Williard 1994), and some that list race as a factor without specifying what it is (Bates 1991). The seventeenth edition of *Taber's Cyclopedic Medical Dictionary* (1993) defines race as "a distinct ethnic group characterized by traits that are transmitted through the offspring." Another meaning is "a taxonomic classification of individuals within the same species who show distinct genetic characteristics." The *Mosby Medical Encyclopedia* (1994) states that race is "a vague, unscientific term for a group of genetically related people who share some physical traits." *Mosby's Guide to Physical Examination* (1995, 1999) states that race is a physical, not cultural, differentiator based on a common heredity, with color, head shape, and stature as identifying characteristics. In fact, however, genetic research shows that most variation occurs between two individuals from the same ethnic group; less than .01 percent of the variation between humans in total genetic material can be attributed to differences in "race" (King 1995).

Mosby's Guide to Physical Examination (1995, 1999) explains that recognizing health beliefs and practices that differ from those of the Judeo-Christian, Western perspective influences the ability to care for a wide variety of individuals. The *Textbook of Physical Diagnosis* (1994) has a section on ethnic and cultural background and points out that stereotyping by race, lifestyle, culture, and religious background can be detrimental. The authors point out that African Americans are a heterogeneous ethnic group with no prototypic "black." In the third edition (1998) of this textbook, the authors paradoxically state that despite great intragroup variability, knowledge of race, culture, and religion can be used to better understand the patient. Unfortunately, they go on to define "race" according to the definition in *Webster's Collegiate Dictionary* (10th ed.) as "class or kind of people unified by a community of interests, habits, or inherited physical characteristics." The authors of the textbook provide no further clarification, except to add at the end of the section that "ethnicity . . . is often used as a polite word for race."

In the seventh edition of the textbook *Physical Examination and History Taking* (1999), the authors discuss challenges that the clinician may experience in taking a history on sensitive topics. Individual bias about race, drug use, and homosexual practices are possible barriers in the patient–physician interview. They go on to advise the clinician to "do some reading about the life experiences of ethnic or racial groups that live in your region." Race is not defined, but culture is explained as "a system of shared ideas, rules, and meanings which individuals inherit or acquire." It is unclear how ideas, rules, and meanings are inherited. Many textbooks inform their readers at some length about "racial and ethnic" variations in the population, but others do not discuss them at all (Greenberger and Hinthorn 1993), even to the extent of invalidating them. With medical students and clinical residents referring to such a wide variety of texts, many are likely to be practicing medicine with inaccurate inferences and misinformation about human differences.

On the positive side, the most recent *Mosby's Guide to Physical Examination* (1999) informs the clinician that "racial differences can have an impact on the care of individuals even in the absence of financial differences." Although the term "racial" remains undefined and vague, the authors go on the explain that "whites" are more likely to receive invasive cardiac procedures and tests compared with "blacks," implying that a variety of social, cultural, and clinical factors are at work in the differential implementation of health care. Some of the newer texts pair the terms "race" with "ethnicity" while emphasizing the need for medical and health professionals to be informed of and sensitive to this more current sociocultural categorization.

Ethnicity can provide important information to studies of population differences that may be important to health and well-being (Caldwell and Popenoe 1995). The term "ethnicity" itself, however, is imprecise, with great variations in geography, migration, housing and employment patterns, dietary preferences, and genetic ancestry. Both race and ethnicity are social constructs and are subject to similar types of biases (Senior and Bhopal 1994); more often than not, racial and/or ethnic group labels are used that further confuse matters, since they are both ill defined and conceptually dissimilar. Ethnicity is complex, and with a growing population of multiethnic groups in the United States, the general concept of ethnicity has become simplistic and difficult to utilize in the health management of individuals.

Despite the vagueness of the terms "race" and "ethnicity," they are commonly used variables in medical research. Many researchers attempt to control for ethnic group or cultural differences during analysis (McKenzie and Crowcroft 1994). Unfortunately, patterns of disease, response to treatment, and the use of services are increasingly being explained in ethnic or racial terms. This is troublesome because in many studies, the categories of race and ethnic group are rarely defined, and terms are used inconsistently and are often assigned arbitrarily (Sheldon and Parker 1992). Race is often used interchangeably with ethnicity or culture, although race is thought to be biologically determined and ethnicity and culture are thought to be ideas derived from social theory. As a result of this confusion, hypotheses, methodologies, and results are difficult to compare and often inappropriate. Even if these terms were used consistently, research would still suffer from the lack of validity in studying race, ethnicity, and culture as scientific variables (Senior and Bhopal 1994).

An editorial by a physician writing in the *British Medical Journal* (Azuonye 1996) offered the idea that instead of developing a framework for classification of ethnic and cultural groups, it would be more meaningful to use criteria on which people can more validly be compared, such as sex, age, place of residence, environmental conditions, occupation, income, and lifestyle. Azuonye proposed that the validation of the terms "race," "ethnicity," and "culture" encourages the kind of thinking that produces racism, which is endemic in the selection of medical students and in the training, employment, and promotion of doctors in Britain. Furthermore, lifestyle should be included in the list of valid epidemiological variables, not race, culture, and ethnicity. The physician must have an understanding of the patient's background and self-proclaimed ethnicity, but only as it allows for optimal, scientific rendering of diagnoses and treatments of individuals.

The present disparity in health and health care experienced by blacks is attributable in part to the lack of a scientific perspective in the medical profession, along with inconsistencies in medical training, as well as the disparate health delivery system (Byrd and Clayton 1992). In the 1960s, the U.S. government began programs that gave blacks access to effective health care. This was accomplished in part with passage of the Civil Rights Amendment, hospital desegregation rulings, and Medicare/Medicaid legislation. These efforts led to improvements in black health care that lasted ten years. Since then, it seems that blacks have been "assigned" to the second tier of a dual health care system, which led to the "black" health care crisis of the 1990s. This period of neglect and loss of initiative is evident in diminished life expectancy (blacks live 5 to 7 years less than whites) and increased cancer incidence, morbidity, and mortality rates. Diabetes, heart disease, and stroke incidence for blacks are significantly higher than for whites (Byrd and Clayton 1992). Much of this discrepancy in health data is due to minimal health care availability, but differential treatment by the provider may influence accessibility to early and correct diagnosis and treatment. Even more disturbing are the data assessing mortality and morbidity of the different socioeconomic strata of white versus black individuals.

Data from an ongoing longitudinal study of the relationship between socioeconomic status and mortality in the major metropolitan centers of Ohio showed that blacks living in high-income areas did not show comparable health benefits when compared to a similarly situated white population (Stockwell, Goza, and Luse 1997). For whites, there was a direct and inverse relationship between mortality rates and neighborhood economic status. In contrast, the black mortality rate was as high in the high-income area as it was in the very lowest income area. These data suggest that racial differences in health care may be influential and even determining factors, perhaps leading to higher mortality rates. Belonging to a higher socioeconomic group is not sufficient to guarantee to blacks the same access to health care that the equivalent white population enjoys. A partial explanation of this problem may be racially separate and unequal access to health care facilities. The concern is that blacks and whites might not be using the same hospital facilities, which could possibly lead to different and perhaps inferior care (Kahn et al. 1994).

A study that examined hospitals in 126 standard metropolitan areas found substantial racial segregation of Medicare beneficiaries (Smith 1998). Midwestern and northeastern urban areas, where blacks are more concentrated, had higher segregation rates than southern states, reflecting geographic distribution and persistent residential segregation of the black population. The degree of segregation suggests a potential for systematic racial bias in the reporting of health events. Hospitals that are primarily white often do not report race and thus reporting systems cannot be relied on, which in turn can have an impact on market reforms, public policy, and perhaps even medical diagnosis and treatment.

Utilizing records from hospitals that reported race as black or white, Harris, Andrews, and Elixhauser (1997) analyzed 1.7 million discharge records representing 469 hospitals, a 10 percent sample of hospitals in the United States. The sample was stratified on six dimensions: geography, urban/rural location, teaching status, type of control, bed size, and extent of state regulation. Following statistical analyses, they described the influence of race, among other characteristics, on the likelihood of having a major therapeutic or major diagnostic procedure, while controlling for severity of disease, patient age, health insurance, and hospital-level characteristics. The study found that blacks were less likely than whites to receive major therapeutic procedures in 48 percent of the conditions assessed; blacks were also less likely to receive a major diagnostic procedure for 21 percent of the conditions assessed.

Differential care among racial groups could result from poorer access to health care services, regional practices, different care-seeking behavior, or provider discrimination in services. To investigate racial differences in medical treatment among Medicare beneficiaries, Lee et al. (1997) studied the rates of use for selected procedures among two patient groups: the Medicare beneficiaries in eleven geographic regions and a subset of this sample based on local area of residence to eliminate any possible differences in provider access and regional health delivery systems. The major findings from this study were that providers seem to be giving less care to matched sample black Medicare beneficiaries. Residents surveyed in southern states experienced the greatest variability in care. The disparities varied directly with the expense of the procedure, with blacks receiving fewer of the more costly procedures. Whatever the psychological mechanism, providers seemed to be giving less care to matched sample black Medicare beneficiaries and in the southern states. It seems unlikely that these results are due to physiologic differences in incidence, prevalence, and severity of disease. Thus it appears that providers tend to give less intensive treatment to black Medicare beneficiaries, apparently because of the perception of race.

There is growing evidence, then, that black patients are less likely than white patients to receive certain medical procedures and treatments that are necessary to maintain health. To assess whether differences in race-related rates of utilization reflect more use among whites or less use among blacks, Guadagnoli et al. (1995) studied the impact of race on surgical intervention for peripheral vascular disease. Specifically, they assessed whether the number of amputations and leg-sparing procedures for vascular disease of lower extremities differ between black and white patients. The study involved looking retrospectively at 3,000 hospitals and over 19,000 patients who underwent amputation and/or leg-sparing surgery for peripheral vascular disease. Blacks were significantly more likely to undergo amputation of the leg or foot and less likely to undergo lower-extremity arterial revascularization-type surgery. It is possible that unmeasured factors such as the severity of disease upon admission was greater in the black patients, perhaps because they waited too long for treatment or lacked appropriate access to outpatient care. Regardless of whether these findings are the result of racial bias or severity of disease when seen by the physician, the goal should be to intervene and reduce such an outcome. Such differential medical treatment is found in a variety of other diseases and health conditions as well.

Epidemiologic studies have identified differences according to race in the treatment of patients with cardiovascular disease in the United States (Wenneker and Epstein 1989; Peterson, Wright, Daley, and Thibault 1994; Carlisle, Leake, and Shapiro 1997; Blustein and Weitzman 1995). Many of these studies have found that blacks are less likely than whites, following hospital admission for treatment of chest pain or myocardial infarction, to undergo cardiac catheterization or coronary-artery bypass surgery. To what extent are physicians responsible for differential treatment recommendations with respect to race? Schulman et al. (1999) carried out a study in which they developed a computerized survey that assessed the physician's recommendations for managing chest pain, using recorded, videotaped interviews with actors. Following statistical analyses, it was found that blacks, and particularly black women, were significantly less likely to be referred for cardiac catheterization than white men. Previous studies could not assess whether these differences were due to differences in clinical presentation of the patients. By using actors to represent patients with identical histories and controlling for characteristics reflective of their personalities, this study could directly address the effects of general appearance, insurance, occupation, and socioeconomic status. What constituted the nature of the bias seen in this study remains to be explored. Subconscious bias happens when a patient's membership in a target group activates a cultural stereotype in the physician's thinking, despite the level of prejudice that may or may not exist. Nonetheless, it was found that the race of the patients independently influenced the physician's recommendations for the management of their chest pain, making this an example of the influence of the physician's training and experience in decision making that may be an important factor in explaining the differences in the treatment of cardiovascular disease with respect to the perception of race.

It is thus hardly surprising that the rate of mortality from cardiovascular disease is higher in black than in white Americans. The relative risk of mortality is 1.5 for black men and 2.2 for black women when compared with whites. However, it is also true that blacks have a higher prevalence of major cardiovascular risk factors, including smoking, hypertension, and obesity (Rivo et al. 1989; Andersen et al. 1987; Otten et al. 1990). Higher levels of smoking may have more to do with socioeconomic status and education. Increased hypertension in blacks is associated with salt sensitivity, skin color, socioeconomic status, and response to stress.

Another condition that is commonly differentially misdiagnosed is hypercholesterolemia, an important risk factor in cardiovascular disease (Naumburg et al. 1993). Adjusting for the number of office visits, several factors were associated with a reduced likelihood of being screened for hypercholesterolemia. These were female sex, age less than forty-five years, having Medicaid, not having insurance, and being black. Among those whose cholesterol had been determined, blacks were less frequently diagnosed with hypercholesterolemia than whites with comparable cholesterol levels. Patient, physician, and institutional factors may influence whether screening occurs, but once the necessary data are obtained, diagnosis of the disease is the physician's responsibility. In this study, the underdiagnosis of high cholesterol in the black patients suggests a difference in the behavior of health care providers, dependent on perceived racial factors. The proper diagnosis of hypercholesterolemia by the providers are necessary prerequisites for effective treatment. Given that this population may already be at increased cardiovascular risk, underdiagnosis of high cholesterol may contribute to the increased mortality.

The prevalence of hypertension in the U.S. black population is twice that of the white population (Akinkugbe 1985), perhaps resulting in higher rates of morbidity and mortality due to cardiovascular disease and stroke. There is a great deal of heterogeneity among the black population in cardiovascular activity, especially blood pressure levels. Nonetheless, the black–white differences related to hypertension must be interpreted. Although many attribute these differences to underlying genetic predispositions, it is certainly not clear that U.S. black and white populations represent truly distinct genetic populations. Hypothesizing a genetic determinant of a disorder such as hypertension necessitates a look at the genetic composition of the population to be studied. In the U.S. black population as much as 50 percent of genes is derived from Caucasian ancestors. Almost 85 percent of genetic diversity is accounted for by diversity among individuals. Genetic traits of members of the same racial group may not be homogeneous, nor are different racial groups genetically distinct, thus precluding the use of race for the purpose of genetic profiling (Anderson 1989).

The finding that blacks seem to experience far more hypertension than whites may be a physiological phenomenon as a function of income level, education, stress-coping style, socioecological stress, and geographic location (Anderson 1989). The attribution of hypertension differences between blacks and whites to genetic factors has dominated the conventional medical view despite a lack of solid scientific corroboration. But sociocultural factors may influence cardiovascular responsiveness. Amid all of the possi-

ble commonalities, blacks are a diverse group. And in the presence of genetic heterogeneity, social, cultural, and psychological factors must be taken
into consideration when mechanisms that underlie pathologies such as hypertension are investigated. Using an animal model, researchers have
shown that combining chronic stress with a high-sodium diet leads to high
blood pressure (Anderson, Kearns, and Better 1983). Thus the finding that
blacks have a greater degree of hypertension might be the result of sociocultural factors that influence the cardiovascular biology, probably in con-
cert with certain genetic predispositions.

Cooper, Rotimi, and Ward (1999) carried out a series of remarkable
studies in which they looked into the West African and Caribbean populations to study the incidence of hypertension and dietary habits, such as
high-salt diet among these so-called ancestors of U.S. blacks. The three
populations studied were in Nigeria, Jamaica, and Chicago, Illinois. The
American and Jamaican blacks shared 75 percent of their genetic material
with the Nigerians. The rates of hypertension were 7 percent for the rural
Nigerians, 26 percent of the black Jamaicans, and 33 percent of the black
Americans. Body mass index (i.e., weight relative to height) and salt intake
were lowest for Africans and highest for American blacks. Thus up to 50
percent of high blood pressure among American blacks may result from
excess weight, lack of exercise, and poor diet. The authors conjecture that
psychological and social stresses may also account for some of the differences in the groups' hypertension rates.

To look at biochemical factors involved in regulating blood pressure, researchers measured the amount of a compound (angiotensinogen) that is an
important part of the chemical reaction in prompting constriction of blood
vessels (Cooper et al. 1999). The amount of this compound was lowest in
Nigerians and highest in Americans. When they examined the gene for
this compound, the same percentage (80–90 percent) of the population of
Nigerian, Jamaican, and U.S. subjects carried the gene. Carrying the gene
for angiotensinogen sets up the predisposition for hypertension if the necessary environmental factors are present, in this case, diet, obesity and stress.
Only 40 percent of European Americans carry the gene.

To demonstrate the effect of race and its presumed relationship to hypertension, Perneger et al. (1995) conducted a simulation to examine whether
the race of a patient with end-stage renal disease influences the nephrologist's diagnosis of underlying kidney disease. Seven charts were randomly
selected from the dialysis patient population of Johns Hopkins Medical
Center. They were put into half-page vignettes that disclosed each patient's
sex, age, and race and then were randomly assigned. The case studies were
sent to fifty-eight physicians in Maryland; each physician was given three
or four case studies and was asked to diagnose the patient. They were told
that the purpose of the study was to evaluate diagnostic procedures among

nephrologists. The main hypothesis, the impact of a patient's race on diagnosis, was not disclosed.

The most frequent diagnosis underlying the renal disease was hypertension and diabetic end-stage renal disease (ESRD) as primary or causal and secondary or contributing disease. The risk of being labeled as having hypertensive ESRD was far greater for blacks than for whites in six of the seven case histories. This study suggests that the patient's race may influence a nephrologist's diagnosis of underlying renal disease. When the race of the patient was black rather than white, the same case history of renal failure was twice as likely to evoke a diagnosis of hypertensive ESRD. The racial difference in diagnostic patterns provides some useful insights into the largely unexplained racial disparity in the incidence of hypertensive kidney disease. On the individual level, a black patient with a primary renal disease may be misdiagnosed as having hypertensive kidney disease more often than a white patient because race would be considered a diagnostic criterion itself. Consequently, a renal biopsy might not be performed, even though this might facilitate more specific therapy of the underlying disease. Whether this actually occurs in practice remains hypothetical. For the population as a whole, this might be labeled as a racial health problem that could reflect a genetic predisposition, not amenable to prevention.

Similar studies would be quite useful in assessing the differences in the health and well-being in the various cultural entities of our society. Many scientists agree that there is no biological basis to the concept of race (see chap. 1 of this volume), preferring to define the concept in terms of sociocultural characteristics. Medicine still ascribes a biological basis to racial classifications as necessary to the understanding of certain disorders and their prevalence. Scientists are becoming more aware of the need for construct validity of these classifications and categories, which are now used in both clinical and research endeavors. As more reliable studies are conducted on various human populations, progress will be made in understanding differences in morbidity and mortality. However, for progress to be made, the clinician and especially the medical student must be the recipients of such scientific findings.

Evidence for the beginning of this innovative approach can be found in the new medical text, Harrison's *Principles of Internal Medicine* (1998). Although not explicitly defining race, the authors use the term "race/ethnicity" and state that many of the variations in health status across racial/ethnic groups can be explained by lower socioeconomic status and behavioral risk factors. They go on to relate to the clinician that persons with similar ethnic backgrounds share cultural, nutritional, environmental, economic, and social characteristics that influence disease. For the future, they emphasize the importance of recognizing the fact that a large proportion of our population is disadvantaged and has a much shorter life span. Improvements in socioeconomic status and "recognition of the continuing impact of racism on health outcomes are fundamental to achieving that goal" (Fauci et al. 1998).

REFERENCES

Akinkugbe, O. O. 1985. "World Epidemiology of Hypertension in Blacks." In *Hypertension in Blacks: Epidemiology, Pathophysiology, and Treatment,* edited by W. D. Hall, E. Saunders, and N. B. Shulman, 3–16. Chicago: Yearbook.

Anderson, D. E., W. D. Kearns, and W. E. Better. 1983. "Progressive Hypertension in Dogs by Avoidance Conditioning and Saline Infusion." *Hypertension* 53:286–91.

Anderson, J. 1989. "Patient Power in Mental Health." *British Medical Journal* 299, no. 6714: 1477–78.

Anderson, R., M. S. Chen, L. A. Aday, and L. Cornelius. 1987. "Health Status and Medical Care Utilization." *Health Affairs (Millwood)* 6:136–56.

Azuonye, I. O. 1996. "Describing Race, Ethnicity, and Culture in Medical Research: Guidelines Will Encourage the Thinking That Underpins Racism in Medicine." *British Medical Journal* 313, no. 7054:426.

Bates, B. 1991. *A Guide to Physical Examination and History Taking.* 5th ed. Philadelphia: Lippincott.

Bickley, L. S., and R. A. Hoekelman. 1999. *Physical Examination and History Taking.* 7th ed. New York: Lippincott.

Blustein. J., and B. C. Weitzman. 1995. "Access to Hospitals with High-Technology Cardiac Services: How Is Race Important?" *American Journal of Public Health* 85:345–51.

Boas, F. 1938. *The Mind of Primitive Man.* New York: Macmillan.

Byrd, W. M., and L. A. Clayton. 1992. "An American Health Dilemma: A History of Blacks in the Health System." *Journal of the National Medical Association* 842:189–200.

Caldwell, S. H., and R. Popenoe. 1995. "Perceptions and Misperceptions of Skin Color." *Annals of Internal Medicine* 122:614–17.

Carlisle D. M., B. D. Leake, and M. F. Shapiro. 1997. "Racial and Ethnic Disparities in the Use of Cardiovascular Procedures: Associations with Type of Health Insurance." *American Journal of Public Health* 872:263–67.

Cavalli-Sforza, L. L., P. Menozzi, and A. Piazza. 1994. *The History and Geography of Human Genes.* Princeton: Princeton University Press.

Cooper, R. S., C. N. Rotimi, and R. Ward. 1999. "The Puzzle of Hypertension in African-Americans." *Scientific American,* February.

Fauci, A. S., E. Braunwald, K. J. Isselbacher, J. D. Wilson, J. B. Martin, D. L. Kasper, S. L. Hauser, and D. L. Longo. 1998. *Harrison's Principles of Internal Medicine.* 14th ed. Vol. 1. New York: McGraw-Hill.

Gelehrter, T. D., and F. S. Collins. 1990. *Principles of Medical Genetics.* Baltimore: Williams & Wilkins.

240   Priscilla Kehoe

Greenberger, N. J., and D. R. Hinthorn. 1993. *History Taking and Physical Examination: Essentials and Clinical Correlates.* St. Louis, Mo.: Mosby Yearbook.

Guadagnoli E., J. Z. Ayanian, G. Gibbons, B. J. McNeil, and F. W. LoGerfo. 1995. "The Influence of Race on the Use of Surgical Procedures for Treatment of Peripheral Vascular Disease of the Lower Extremities." *Archives of Surgery* 130:381–86.

Harris, D. R., R. Andrews, and A. Elixhauser. 1997. "Racial and Gender Differences in the Use of Procedures for Black and White Hospitalized Adults." *Ethnicity and Disease* 72:91–105.

Kahn K. L., M. L. Pearson, E. R. Harrison, K. A. Desmind, W. H. Rogers, L. V. Rubenstein, R. H. Brook, and E. B. Keeler. 1994. "Health Care for Black and Poor Hospitalized Medicare Patients." *Journal of the American Medical Association* 271, no. 15:1169–74.

King, J. C. 1981. *The Biology of Race.* Berkeley: University of California Press.

King, R. K. 1995. "Race: An Outdated Concept." *American Medical Women's Association Journal* 10:55–58.

Lee, A. J., S. Gehlbach, D. Hosmer, M. Reti, and C. S. Baker. 1997. "Medicare Treatment Differences for Blacks and Whites." *Medical Care* 35, no. 12:1173–89.

McKenzie, K. J., and N. S. Crowcroft. 1994. "Race, Ethnicity, Culture, and Science." *British Medical Journal* 309, no. 6950:286–87.

Naumberg, E. H., P. Franks, B. Bell, M. Gold, and J. Engerman. 1993. "Racial Differentials in the Identification of Hypercholesterolemia." *Journal of Family Practice* 364:425–30.

Otten, M. W., Jr., S. M. Teutsch, D. F. Williamson, and J. S. Marks. 1990. "The Effect of Known Risk Factors on the Excess Mortality of Black Adults in the United States." *Journal of the American Medical Society* 263:845–50.

Perneger, T. V., P. K. Whelton, M. J. Klag, and K. A. Rossiter. 1995. "Diagnosis of Hypertensive End-Stage Renal Disease: Effect of Patient's Race." *American Journal of Epidemiology* 1411:10–15.

Peterson, E. D., S. M. Wright, J. Daley, and G. E. Thibault. 1994. "Racial Variation in Cardiac Procedure Use and Survival Following Acute Myocardial Infarction in the Department of Veterans Affairs." *Journal of the American Medical Association* 271:1175–80.

Rensberger, B. 1990. "Racial Odyssey." In *Anthropology: Contemporary Perspectives,* edited by P. Whitten and D. E. Hunter, 67–71. Boston: Little, Brown.

Rivo, M. L., V. Kofie, E. Schwartz, M. E. Levy, and R. V. Tuckson. 1989. "Comparisons of Black and White Smoking-Attributable Mortality, Morbidity, and Economic Costs in the District of Columbia." *Journal of the National Medical Association* 81:1125–30.

Schulman, K. A., J. A. Berlin, W. Harless, J. F. Kerner, S. Sistrunk, B. J. Gersh, R. Dube, C. K. Taleghani, J. E. Burke, S. Williams, J. M. Eisenberg, and J. J. Escarce. 1999. "The Effect of Race and Sex on Physicians' Recommendations for Cardiac Catheterization." *New England Journal of Medicine* 3408:618–26.

Seidel, H. M., J. W. Ball, J. E. Dains, and G. W. Benedict. 1994. *Mosby's Guide to Physical Examination.* 2d ed. Boston: Mosby Yearbook.

Seidel, H. M., J. W. Ball, J. E. Dains, and G. W. Benedict. 1995. *Mosby's Guide to Physical Examination.* 3d ed. Boston: Mosby.

Seidel, H. M., J. W. Ball, J. E. Dains, and G. W. Benedict. 1999. *Mosby's Guide to Physical Examination.* 4th ed. Boston: Mosby.

Senior, P. A., and R. Bhopal. 1994. "Ethnicity As a Variable in Epidemiological Research." *British Medical Journal* 309:327–30.

Seymour-Smith, C. 1986. *Macmillan Dictionary of Anthropology.* New York: Macmillan.

Sheldon, T. A., and H. Parker. 1992. "Race and Ethnicity in Health Research." *Journal of Public Health Medicine* 14:104–10.

Smith, D. B. 1998. The Racial Segregation of Hospital Care Revisited: Medicare Discharge Patterns and Their Implications. *American Journal of Public Health* 883:461–63.

Stockwell, E. G., F. W. Goza, V. O. Luse. 1997. "Infectious Disease Mortality among Adults by Race and Socioeconomic Status. Metropolitan Ohio, 1989–1991." *Social Biology* 441–42:148–52.

Swartz, M. H. 1994. *Textbook of Physical Diagnosis: History and Examination.* 2d ed. Philadelphia: Saunders.

Swartz, M. H. 1998. *Textbook of Physical Diagnosis: History and Examination.* 3d ed. Philadelphia: Saunders.

Thomas, C. L., ed. 1993. *Taber's Cyclopedic Medical Dictionary.* 17th ed. Philadelphia: Davis.

Thompson, M. W., R. R. McInnes, and H. F. Williard. 1994. *Thompson and Thompson Genetics in Medicine.* 5th ed. Philadelphia: Saunders.

Wenneker, M. B., and A. M. Epstein. 1989. "Racial Inequalities in the Use of Procedures for Patients with Ischemic Heart Disease in Massachusetts." *Journal of the American Medical Association* 261:253–57.

Witzig, R. 1996. The "Medicalization of Race: Scientific Legitimization of a Flawed Social Construct." *Annals of Internal Medicine* 125(8):675–79.

16

The Race for Class

Paul Lauter

When I first read the title of Part IV in which this chapter was to appear, it evoked some childhood memories. For I read it not as "Race or Class: Which *Is* It?" but, perversely perhaps, as "Race or Class: Which Is *It?*" Games of hide and seek generally began with cries of "Not it, not it, not it!" Being It was, of course, something to be avoided—the idea was to stick someone else with that responsibility. But I always felt, perhaps perversely again, that there was a certain hidden power in being It. It was up to you to ferret out all the hiders before any of them could touch home base and "free all," so you were the center of attention, the holder of a certain authority, even. This game and my ambiguous reading of the part title may provide a useful metaphor for this discussion. But this isn't child's play. What is at issue in this debate over race and class, projected nationally, is how to end the cancer of urban poverty.

In recent years, commentators of the left and of the right have tried to claim that when it comes to the Frog Hollows, the Wattses, the Bed-Stuys, and other symbols of urban disaster and the growing inequities of our economy, race can never, ever be It. Neither as cause nor, as in affirmative action programs, cure. From the right has arisen a certain paradoxical analysis: race is said to be declining in significance, even as a racially depicted "underclass" is portrayed as finally responsible for its own catastrophic situation because of its pathological conduct.[1] Guilty of displaying not a "culture of poverty" (that's passé) but "ghetto-specific behavior," such folks had best, like Caliban, be penned up pending sufficient expansion in the American economy to lift even the urban reservations. Meanwhile, the smart money invests in one of America's biggest growth industries, jails. I am, of course, being slightly unfair here, conflating William Julius Wilson and Oscar Lewis, not to say Daniel Patrick Moynihan. But as I want to suggest, the desire to do away with the politics of race, or, as George Lipsitz has called

it, "the possessive investment in whiteness,"² is no substitute for understanding how today's urban poverty grows from the actions of powerful
people such as those who have produced a systematic linkage between race
and the export of jobs from ghettos and have designed specific political
policies to disempower the urban poor.³

From the left, Todd Gitlin has argued that the emphasis on identity politics, modeled particularly by African Americans (and also women) in the
1960s and 1970s, has undermined an earlier commitment to a set of universal ideals. On the basis of such universals, the left could reach out beyond
the particularities of group or class or caste and thus appeal to masses of
people differently situated. But then came identity politics:

> What took place was one of those convulsions in culture that cannot be re-
> duced to the sum of its immediate causes. Certainly, separatism was more than
> an idea, because it was more than strictly intellectual; it was a structure of feel-
> ing, a whole way of experiencing the world. Difference was now felt—
> perhaps had long been felt—more acutely than commonality.⁴

Gitlin argues that even in the best of circumstances and even if free of the
burden of political correctness, identity politics is necessarily the politics of
division and fragmentation. A focus on race or on gender or on sexuality
as organizing principles necessarily flies in the face of the Enlightenment
project of extending both individual agency and a civic collectivity: "the
obsession with difference," he writes, "stands in the way of asking the right
questions."⁵ In an odd way, Gitlin has come to blame those who have been
perceived as black, segregated as black, and victimized as black for taking
themselves for black.

There are many problems with these critiques. I want to emphasize only
one—their fundamentally cultural approach to explaining poverty and the
failure to generate a serious movement to eradicate it. That crucial defect
has again and again been excoriated by critics like Adolph Reed, Stephen
Steinberg, and Micaela di Leonardo. By "cultural" I mean simply this: causality is explained by pointing not to the concrete political and material
factors that overwhelmingly shape the conditions of life but rather to certain attitudes or outlooks or ways of thinking that are offered as decisive for
individual success or failure. Thus it used to be claimed—and still is in some
quarters—that Jews of a century ago succeeded so markedly in America
because, as Milton Gordon put it,

> the Jews arrived in America with middle-class values of thrift, sobriety, ambi-
> tion, desire for education, ability to postpone immediate gratification for the
> sake of long-range goals, and aversion to violence already internalized. . . . It
> is these cultural values which account for the rapid rise of the Jewish group in
> occupational status and economic influence.⁶

But as Steinberg has pointed out,

> to posit cultural values as the fulcrum of success is to engage in an essentially moral interpretation of history. It assumes that a society functions as a kind of moral benefactor parceling out its rewards to the most culturally deserving. . . . To understand the determinants of ethnic success it will be necessary, as a first step, to eschew the self-congratulatory sentimentalism that has impaired objective inquiry, and to address some complex questions. What differences in the background and circumstances of ethnic groups allowed some to advance further than others? What was the institutional context in which ethnic mobility occurred, and did it favor certain groups more than others?[7]

Later, he speaks to the specific issue of Jewish success: "In terms of their eventual adjustment to life in America, what was most significant about the urban background of Eastern European Jews was that they worked in occupations that prepared them for roles in a modern industrial economy."[8]

The obverse of cultural explanations of social and economic success are, obviously, cultural explanations of failure: you fail because you lack the requisite culture for success. Forget a long and persistent history of housing and job discrimination which, in the context of automation, deindustrialization, and plants being moved to whiter or overseas venues, were primarily responsible for producing and reproducing the immiseration of African Americans, Mexican Americans, and other minorities. Or to turn to Gitlin's analogous formulation, forget the daily grind of mistreatment by cops,[9] cab drivers, and mortgage officers; of segregated schools and slums; of overpriced milk and underpaid McJobs. If you experience yourself as black, you will "stand in the way of asking the right questions."

To put it in blunt terms, the racism of the 1990s is the denial of race.

If race refuses to become a declining signifier, class in these polemics undergoes a transformation to something not rich but awfully strange. Class haunts the outer precincts of these analyses, like Marx's *Gespenst*. Gitlin mentions, briefly, how the venue and conditions of labor had once drawn people into a united struggle for progress. But a class analysis, even of the restructuring of the colleges and universities at the center of his concern, his book is not. Of course, the very term "underclass" seems drawn from traditional Marxist categories. But as Reed has pointed out, this notion of "class" is "essentially culturalist," "defining a group by the bundles of attributes its members supposedly possess to help them make it in the market. This view reinforces the notion that people are poor because of characteristics (not money) that they lack."[10] Although the writers I have been discussing race toward some marginal category occasionally masquerading as "class," they never arrive at it.

Well, if race ain't It and class ain't "it," who is It? As they used to say around my neighborhood, it must be the Puerto Ricans.

Fortunately, there are now several studies carefully examining the interactions of race, class, gender, and other factors in the production of poverty.
Among them are Thomas J. Sugrue's *The Origins of the Urban Crisis: Race
and Inequality in Postwar Detroit*, Michael Goldfield's *The Color of Politics:
Race and the Mainsprings of American Politics from Colonial Times to the Present*,
and George Lipsitz's *The Possessive Investment in Whiteness*.[11] Sugrue's book
is important for a number of reasons. First, rather than construct broad and
often inaccurate generalizations about racial and class behaviors, he looks at
a very particular place, Detroit, and a specific time, 1945 to the 1960s and
after. He examines economic changes like deindustrialization, automation,
the redeployment of capital away from existing plants, globalization, reces-
sions, the interaction of such factors with movements of people, white and
black, and the consequent impacts, particularly on jobs, housing, and infra-
structure. What he shows serves a second politically critical function having
to do with the origins of reactionary politics. Industrial jobs in and around
Detroit had begun to decline in the 1950s, even as the black population of
Detroit increased sharply.[12]

At the same time, white working-class people constructed boundaries
around their communities whose primary purpose and certainly whose effect was to exclude blacks. Such exclusionary communities became the
breeding ground for the rightward political shift of working-class whites,
first significantly recognized in the emergence of a large Wallace vote—
George Wallace, that is—in Michigan and elsewhere in 1964.[13] Thus the
second implication of Sugrue's study is to annihilate the basis on which
writers like Jim Sleeper, Mary Edsall and Thomas Edsall, Allan Matusow,[14]
and, in certain ways, Todd Gitlin, base their arguments that the rightward
swing that led to Nixon, Reagan, Gingrich, and company are to be read
as reactions to so-called excesses of the 1960s—racially based policies like
affirmative action, school busing, fair housing laws, and that catch-all vil-
lain, identity politics.

The third implication of his work is explained well by Sugrue himself:

> The last 10 years of research on the so-called urban "underclass" has taken as
> its starting point the pathologies of poverty, that is the individual, familial, and
> cultural attributes of poor people. My starting point is that poverty and resis-
> tance to it are not, by and large, individual choices or outgrowths of "patholo-
> gies" such as dependency, family breakdown, social isolation, the culture of
> poverty, and the declining work ethic. Instead, I offer a structural explanation
> of concentrated, persistent urban poverty. My book is an archaeology of
> power, an attempt to explain, rather than simply assert the ways that race and
> class in the United States have interacted to the profound disadvantage of Afri-
> can Americans.[15]

For me, the theoretical value of Sugrue's book lies precisely in the explanatory power of this paradigm, his effort to portray the particular forms

in which race and class interact in a specific historical moment. For there is, I believe, no single, archetypal theory to account for the relationships between race and class, and also gender. These relationships need to be historicized, for each of these analytic categories is constructed and reconstructed in the changing circumstances in which people engage and generate power.[16]

For example, Goldfield examines trends in the national economy, especially between the post–World War II period and the present, and their impact on racial stratification. He points to the decline in agricultural employment, particularly in the South:

> Although the number of farms in the country as a whole decreased by slightly more than half between 1940 and 1969, those operated by Blacks (and other non-whites) decreased from 723,000 to 104,000, reflecting the almost complete elimination of Black cotton tenancy during this period. John Cogan argues that the decline in the demand for low-skilled agricultural labor had a special impact on Black teenagers, 45% of whom in 1950 were employed in agriculture. By 1970, they had been completely displaced from this venue.[17]

Similarly, Goldfield examines decisions made by manufacturing companies to "move factories and build new ones outside the central cities."[18] Such decisions may not have been overtly racially motivated. Yet, once again, the negative impacts on African Americans were disproportionate, given patterns of housing concentration and discrimination, and severe limits on mass transit. In other words, broad economic trends and private corporate decisions, which on the face of them have little or nothing to do with issues of race, nevertheless combine with historical patterns of work, housing, and education to exacerbate minority impoverishment and dispossession. The details of public and private economic decisions have changed in recent years, but the pattern of discriminatory impact has not.

For example, George Lipsitz points to the methods used by ordinary Americans to acquire and thus pass on assets, or wealth. The primary method of accumulating at least some wealth for most Americans has been through home purchases. Yet the Federal Housing Authority (FHA), the Veterans Administration (VA), and other agencies clearly discriminated against minority applicants, largely restricting their purchases to nonwhite and thus often declining areas within the cities.[19] Such discriminatory practices—at least among government agencies—may have been eliminated, but their legacy lives on. For example, a cut in the capital gains tax, like the one recently enacted, does not equally benefit all, for those whose property has most significantly appreciated are those who had access to suburbs and other desirable housing areas, from which minorities were largely (often by law or compact) excluded. Even if continuing patterns of income distribution, which still favor whites, were reversed to favor minority workers (an unlikely event),[20] the hugely disproportionate distribution of wealth would continue to ensure white economic dominance in virtually every area of American productivity.[21]

The point is simple: although racially exclusionary legislation and Jim Crow public policy are, presumably, things of the past, current laws and decisions, however well intentioned, continue to have racially inflected consequences. Affirmative action programs were efforts to undo the effects of earlier exclusionary practices; as they are eliminated or attenuated, patterns of racial discrimination will continue to operate while policy makers point with pride to the "declining significance or race." Most politicians, bankers, and corporate managers in the United States probably don't talk any more about how to keep "them" out. But that does not for a moment mean that they never think about, or are unaware of, the racially disproportionate consequences of policies they have adopted and continue to implement. In any case, the issue is not intent—which is hard to pin down—but impact, increasingly clarified in the work I have been citing.

I want now to take a further step by attempting (risky proposition) to reinterpret Barbara Fields's account of the origins of racial ideology in the United States. Fields, I am sure most readers know, argues, first, that race is a piece of ideology. As she describes it, "Race is not an idea but an ideology. It came into existence at a discernible historical moment for rationally understandable historical reasons and it is subject to change for similar reasons."[22] Ideology, Fields explains, "is best understood as the descriptive vocabulary of day-to-day existence, through which people make rough sense of the social reality that they live and create from day to day. It is the language of consciousness that suits the particular way in which people deal with their fellows."[23] Racial ideology, she asserts, came into being during the period of the American Revolution in order to provide an explanation for the fact that a nation basing its government on the natural law principle that "all men are created equal" nevertheless was a nation in which slavery was embedded in practice and in fundamental law:

> Racial ideology supplied the means of explaining slavery to people whose terrain was a republic founded on radical doctrines of liberty and natural rights; and, more important, a republic in which those doctrines seemed to represent accurately the world in which all but a minority lived. Only when the denial of liberty became an anomaly apparent even to the least observant and reflective members of Euro-American society did ideology systematically explain the anomaly. But slavery got along for a hundred years after its establishment without race as its ideological rationale. The reason is simple. Race explained why some people could rightly be denied what others took for granted: namely, liberty, supposedly a self-evident gift of nature's God. But there was nothing to explain until most people could, in fact, take liberty for granted.

. . . Euro-Americans resolved the contradiction between slavery and liberty by defining Afro-Americans as a race; Afro-Americans resolved the contradiction more straightforwardly by calling for the abolition of slavery.[24]

This seems powerfully explanatory to me.

But what does it explain? It does not explain quite different uses to which concepts of race have been put: by the British with respect to the Irish, for example, or by the Han Chinese with respect to the Deng Ka people of Kwangtung province; in these instances, color was not a dominant consideration nor chattel slavery nor the social ideals of natural rights democracy. Nor does Fields's paradigm explain the variety of Western European deployments of race with respect to Africans; not only were these different from one European nation to another, but they rationalized not so much slavery as imperialism. Nor can Fields's model serve to explain the academic uses of race in the eighteenth and nineteenth centuries to construct historical accounts of Western civilization rooted in Greece rather than in Egypt or the Middle East, which as Martin Bernal (and during the conference from which this book grew, Dalia Ofer) has convincingly documented,[25] helped lay the groundwork not only for the eugenics movement but for Buchenwald, Treblinka, and Auschwitz. And Fields's model is not terribly useful in understanding the contemporary world. Not that the "contradiction between slavery and liberty" has been erased utterly, but because it just isn't very helpful to view the dynamics of race, class, and gender at the end of the twentieth century through what I can only call a macro ideological lens. In fact, the strength of Fields's argument is in the persuasiveness of her account of the rise of racial ideology in the specific period of the specifically American Revolution. That is, her argument can best be seen not as an account of the invention of race but as a local instance with broad implications of the deployment of race to rationalize and maintain power relationships.

I mean nothing slighting by the term "local." Rather, I use it to denote the formulations of race that seem to me most substantial and useful to understand, in contrast to universalized accounts, either of its supposed evaporation or of its total primacy in human societies. Indeed, I think we need more "local" accounts, like Fields's and Sugrue's, to understand how and for what purposes race has continued to be deployed. That sounds like a characteristic academic move: a call for further study. I do think that's important. And I think race cannot be studied solely as an anachronism, a piece of false consciousness that will go away if we don't mention it, or nothing more than the ground of racism. We also need to understand when and why race, however named, and however ambiguously, has served as one basis of human solidarity. Being It isn't always in all circumstances necessarily a bad thing.

But we would not be here arguing about race and class if only the academic enterprise were at stake. As I said at the beginning, it's not play for children—or for professors. The study of race and class and gender must be directed to the construction not of careers but of movements, not of theories but of political actions. However mistaken Wilson's "underclass" analysis, it has deeply affected the policy goals of the Clinton administration, just as earlier right-wing polemics helped set the agenda for Reaganism. It seems to me that the test of what we do, of an enterprise like this book, will be determined not by prizes, contracts, or even appointments at Harvard, but by the extent to which we arm movements for social justice that are even now, I believe, gathering strength for a new push toward freedom.

NOTES

1. As Michaela di Leonardo has put it, "The new 'underclass' ideology functioned specifically, as had older 'culture of poverty' formulations, to focus attention away from . . . [the] political production of poverty to the 'pathological' behavior of the poor whose characteristics were presumed (in the hard version) to cause or (in the soft version) merely to reproduce poverty." *Exotics at Home: Anthropologists, Others, American Modernity* (Chicago: University of Chicago Press, 1998), p. 114.

2. *The Possessive Investment in Whiteness* (Philadelphia: Temple University Press, 1998).

3. See, for example, Michael Katz, "Conclusion: Framing the Underclass Debate," in *The Underclass Debate: Views from History,* ed. Michael Katz (Princeton: Princeton University Press, 1993), pp. 440–77.

4. *The Twilight of Common Dreams* (New York: Henry Holt, 1995), p. 100.

5. Ibid., p. 236.

6. Milton M. Gordon, *Assimilation in American Life* (New York: Oxford University Press, 1964), p. 185.

7. Stephen Steinberg, *The Ethnic Myth: Race, Ethnicity, and Class in America* (Boston: Beacon, 1989), pp. 86–87.

8. Ibid., p. 95.

9. The current controversies over the shooting of Amadou Diallo in New York and over "racial profiling" in New Jersey have had at least this benefit: they have raised consciousness about some of the ways in which, in daily life, race remains overwhelmingly determinant of how one is treated, especially if one *is* young, male, and minority, and particularly *by* men with guns and badges.

10. Adolph Reed, "The Scholarship of Backlash," *The Nation,* October 30, 1995, p. 508.

11. Thomas J. Sugrue, *The Origins of the Urban Crisis: Race and Inequality in Postwar Detroit* (Princeton: Princeton University Press, 1996). *Labor History* 39, no. 1 (1998): 43–69 has printed a very useful symposium on the book. Michael Goldfield, *The Color of Politics: Race, Class, and the Mainsprings of American Politics* (New

York: New Press, 1997). George Lipsitz, *The Possessive Investment in Whiteness* (Philadelphia: Temple University Press, 1998).

12. Commenting on Sugrue's book, Judith Stein gives the following figures: "Between 1947 and 1977, manufacturing employment in Detroit fell from 338,000 to 153,000, plummeting to 103,000 during the 1982 recession. On the supply side, the African American population rose from 300,000 in 1950 to 759,000 in 1980." "Opening and Closing Doors," *Labor History* 39, no. 1 (1998): 52–53. Or again, "from 1950 to 1960, the number of unskilled and semiskilled jobs fell by 13%, just as Detroit's black population increased from 300,000 to 482,000" (p. 53).

13. See, for example, James N. Gregory, "Southernizing the American Working Class: Post-war Episodes of Regional and Class Transformation," *Labor History* 39, no. 2 (1998): esp. 142–47.

14. Allen Matusow, *The Unraveling of America: A History of Liberalism in the 1960s* (New York: Harper, 1984); Jim Sleeper, *The Closest of Strangers: Liberalism and the Politics of Race in New York* (New York: Norton, 1990); Thomas B. Edsall and Mary D. Edsall, *Chain Reaction: The Impact of Race, Rights, and Taxes on American Politics* (New York: Norton, 1991).

15. Thomas J. Sugrue, "Responsibility to the Past, Engagement with the Present," *Labor History 39*, no. 1 (1998): 61.

16. This is, of course, the approach of Michael Omi and Howard Winant as in *Racial Formation in the United States: From the 1960s to the 1990s* (New York: Routledge, 1994) and Howard Winant, *Racial Conditions: Politics, Theory, Comparisons* (Minneapolis: University of Minnesota Press, 1994).

17. Michael Goldfield, *The Color of Politics: Race, Class, and the Mainsprings of American Politics* (New York: New Press, 1997), p. 329. Cogan's work is to be found in John Cogan, "Decline in Black Teenage Employment, 1950–1970," *American Economic Review* 72 (September 1982): 621–38. Goldfield is also making use of *Historical Statistics of the United States: Colonial Times to 1970* (Washington, D.C.: United States Bureau of the Census, 1972), 1:465.

18. Ibid., p. 331.

19. Lipsitz, *Possessive Investment*, pp. 6–7. For example, Lipsitz writes, "The Federal Housing Administration and the Veterans Administration financed more than $120 billion worth of new housing between 1934 and 1962, but less than 2 percent of this real estate was available to nonwhite families—and most of that small amount was located in segregated areas."

20. The opposite is more likely. As Lipsitz writes, "Forty-six percent of black workers between the ages of twenty and twenty-four held blue collar jobs in 1976, but only 20 percent by 1984. Earnings by young black families that had reached 60 percent of white families' income in 1973, fell to 46 percent by 1986. Younger African American families experienced a 50 percent drop in real earnings between 1973 and 1986, with the decline in black male wages particularly steep." *Possessive Investment,* pp. 18–19. Among other sources, Lipsitz is using Noel J. Kent, "A Stacked Deck: Racial Minorities and the New American Political Economy," *Explorations in Ethnic Studies* 14 (January 1991): 11.

21. Melvin Oliver and Tom Shapiro, "Wealth of a Nation: A Reassessment of Asset Inequality in America Shows at Least One-Third of Households Are Asset Poor," *Journal of Economics and Sociology* 49 (April 1990).

22. Barbara Jeanne Fields, "Slavery, Race, and Ideology in the United States of America," *New Left Review* 181 (1990): 101.

23. Ibid., p. 110.

24. Ibid., p. 114.

25. Martin Bernal, *Black Athena: The Afroasiatic Roots of Classical Civilization,* vol. 1, *The Fabrication of Ancient Greece, 1785–1985* (New Brunswick, N.J.: Rutgers University Press, 1987), esp. chaps. 6–9.

Index

Page references followed by *t* or *f* indicate tables or figures, respectively.

253

256 *Index*

Deep Sightings and Rescue Missions (Bambara), 157–58, 160
deferring behavior, 196
de Gobineau, Joseph Arthur, 63
Delphi, 104, 106
democracies, Western liberal, ix
Deng Ka, 249
Detroit, Michigan, 201, 246, 251n12
Devil's Night, 201
Diallo, Amadou, 250n9
dietary habits, 237–38
difference(s): background, 190; medieval notions of, 79–97; racial, 233–35, 238
disability: interaction, 197; "problem" of disabled persons, 71
discrimination: in labor market, 190–92; racial, 189–90; tastes for, 195
discriminatory preferences, 210n16
disequilibrium model, 212n42
distancing, racial, xiii
doctrine of fixity of species, 29–30
Dominican Republic, 150
Douglass, Frederick, 21n25
Drake, Clair, 126
DuBois, W. E. B., 45–46
Dumond, Dwight, 117
Dunham, Katherine, 123, 126–28

Earls of Kildare, 87
earnings: black weekly wages, 208f; black-to-white ratio, 190, 191t; black-white income gap, 192, 193f, 213n65, 222, 251n20
Earth: age of, 37–38
East Indians, 9
école des otages (the hostages' school), 179
economics, 189–214
Eden, 28
education: black-white gap, 192, 193f, 196, 209n7, 220–21; Chicago public schools, 195; French colonial school, xiii, 177–86; Mississippi school data, 192, 193t; success, 225n18
Egyptians, 15, 25n79, 105, 249

eighteenth-century racial science, 27–43
Ellison, Ralph, 155
employment: agricultural, 247; black-white gap, 251n20; job status for employed adults, 190, 190t; labor markets, 189–97; McJobs, 245; non-white occupational positions, 190, 191t; occupational positions of non-white workers, 190, 191t; plantation slavery, 111–22
England, 249; British medicine, 232; Cromwellian era, 97n60; degeneracy in Ireland, 86–87; occupation of Ireland, 85–90; segregation index, 210n26
enslavement. *See* slavery
Eskimo. *See* Inuit
Ethiopian (category), 229
Ethiopians, 99, 145
ethnic groups, 6, 22n28, 54, 230
ethnicity, 54–55, 100, 231–32, 238; in China, 174n3; in Taiwan, 174n3
ethnicity theory, 216
ethnic variations, 231
ethnographers: marginalized, 123–37; native, 133
eugenics, 64, 66, 71–72, 249
eunuch slaves, 101
Euro-Americans, 249
"European" (category), 26n94, 28
European Jews, 84, 124, 148
Europeans: classification of, 21n26, 25n75; expansion of, 94n28; eyelid and orbital structure, 11; hair color and type, 12; nose form, 11; physical features, 12–13; skin pigmentation, 9; slaves, 147
euthanasia, 66, 72
Eve, 81, 83
"The Evening of the Life of Uncle Gan'geng" (Huang), 166
evolution: Darwin's theory of, 29, 38; multiregional, 13
eyelid and orbital structure, 10–11

Federal Housing Authority (FHA), 247, 251n19

About the Contributors

Dina L. Anselmi is associate professor of psychology at Trinity College, with special interests in language development, gender development, and family influences. She is the coauthor (with Anne Law) of *Questions of Gender: Perspectives and Paradoxes* and the author of the forthcoming *The Developmental Context of the Family*.

Janet Bauer is associate professor of international studies and educational studies at Trinity College, and assistant director of the Center for Collaborative Teaching and Research. She has written about migrant and refugee women, women in anthropological history, and religious fundamentalism for numerous journals and in two anthologies: *Mixed Blessings: Gender and Religious Fundamentalism Cross-Culturally and Iranian Refugees and Exiles since Khomeini*.

Daniel G. Blackburn is professor of biology and director of the electron microscopy facilities at Trinity College. He has published about forty papers and one edited volume in the fields of vertebrate zoology and evolutionary biology. Among his current interests are the history of evolutionary ideas and their sociopolitical use and misuse.

Jack Chatfield, associate professor of history at Trinity College, has written on the Connecticut Federalist party during the Jeffersonian era and on Connecticut politics and society during the War of 1812. In addition to the early Republic, his interests include Jacksonian and antebellum America, the Civil War era, and the twentieth-century South.

Andrew J. Gold, associate professor of economics at Trinity College, has also served there as director of the Urban and Environmental Studies Program and the Public Policy Program. His recent publications include "In the Aftermath of Sheff—Considerations for a Remedy" and "The Trinity Initiative in Economic Perspective," both appearing in the *Connecticut Law Review*.

Priscilla Kehoe, professor of psychology and director of the neuroscience program at Trinity College, has worked mainly in the area of developmental neuroscience. Her recent publications include "Infant Stress Leads to Vulnerability to Drug Abuse" and "Infant Stress and Neuroplasticity."

265

Berel Lang is professor of humanities at Trinity College. His books include *Act and Idea in the Nazi Genocide, Writing and the Moral Self, Mind's Bodies,* and *The Future of the Holocaust.*

Paul Lauter is Allan K. and Gwendolyn Miles Smith Professor of Literature at Trinity College. He has served as president of the American Studies Association and is general editor of the *Heath Anthology of American Literature;* his most recent book is *American Studies as Done by Paul Lauter.*

Sonia M. Lee, professor of French and African literature at Trinity College, authored *Camera Laye* and edited the anthology *Les Romancieres du Continent Noir.*

James Muldoon is professor of history (emeritus) at Rutgers University and Research Scholar at the John Carter Brown Library. A specialist in medieval and early modern legal history, he is the author of, among other books, *The Americas in the Spanish World Order: The Justification for Conquest in the Seventeenth Century.*

Colbert Nepaulsingh is professor of Latin American and Caribbean Studies at the State University of New York at Albany, where he has also served as associate vice president for academic affairs. His books include *Toward a History of Literary: Composition in Medieval Spain* and *Apples of Gold in Filigrees of Silver: Jewish Writing in the Eye of the Spanish Inquisition.*

Dalia Ofer is the Max and Rita Haber Professor of Holocaust Studies at the Hebrew University of Jerusalem. Among other books, she is the author of *Escaping the Holocaust: Illegal Immigration to the Land of Israel, 1939–1942,* and is the coeditor of *Women in the Holocaust.*

Margo V. Perkins is assistant professor of English and American studies at Trinity College. Her book, *Autobiography as Activism: African American Women Writing Resistance,* is due for publication in spring 2000.

Gary Reger, associate professor of history at Trinity College, is the author of *Regionalism and Change in the Economy of Independent Delos* as well as numerous articles on aspects of the history of the Hellenistic world. His current projects include a monograph on the history of Mylasa in southwestern Asia Minor.

King-fai Tam, associate professor of modern languages at Trinity College, specializes in the study of modern Chinese literature. His book on autobiography and the genre of the essay, *A Garden of One's Own,* will be published by the University of California Press.

Maurice L. Wade, professor of philosophy at Trinity College, is also director of public policy studies and chair of the Philosophy Department. His areas of interest include political philosophy and issues of race and racism; he is currently working on a study of the role of sympathy in Hume's theory of the self.

Johnny E. Williams is assistant professor of sociology at Trinity College. His principal interests lie in the sociology of religion and political sociology; his forthcoming book is titled *African-American Religion and Activism: Politicized Religious Beliefs and the Civil Rights Movement in Arkansas.*